For
my
Sweetheart
I Love You.

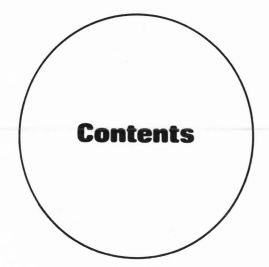

**Contents**

List

of

Illustrations

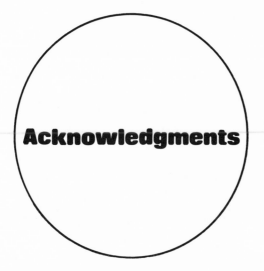

# Acknowledgments

First thanks must go to the more than 150 pitchers who shared with me their feelings and observations about relieving. Many of the men expressed satisfaction that someone would want to tell their story, or rather the story of their dangerous and often unappreciated trade. I hope this book serves to gain for relief pitchers the greater recognition they deserve.

Thanks go as well to:

The National Baseball Hall of Fame and Museum, for making available its excellent research facilities, and particularly librarian Jack Redding, who graciously assisted me.

The public relations directors of the major-league clubs that provided me with photos and information concerning their past and present relievers.

Martha Millard and Richard Curtis, my agents, who exhibited considerable patience and goodwill in soothing the anxieties of a fretful writer.

Marian Skedgell, my editor, who skillfully guided the manuscript to publication.

Peter Hughes, who typed the manuscript with professional aplomb despite my frequently unreasonable demands.

Andy and Robin Fisher, great friends who showed faith in me.

My two-year-old son, Jed, who would sternly tell me, "Go write a book," whenever I had the temerity to emerge from my study during daylight hours.

And saving the greatest debt for last, heartfelt thanks to my wife, Sharon, who put aside her own writing to permit me to do mine.

**Foreword**

**by**

**Rollie Fingers**

The multimillion dollar men can never know what it's like, but sometimes baseball is just a job. Don't take that wrong, but you have to understand that the fame and the glory haven't yet found their way to the ranks of the relievers. Even if that never happened in a big way, reading John Thorn's book gave me a thrill. We've been recognized. And when I say "we" I don't just mean Lyle, McGraw, Gossage and the current batch of often used and well known firemen, I mean Marberry, Wilhelm, Murphy, Face: old timers who won games, saved games and often barely gained acceptance by fans and broadcasters. After all, shouldn't the starter who pitched seven smoking innings before fading get the glory? A save isn't a win, said the doubters. But maybe that's changing.

I guess it was just about ten years ago that managers and owners began to realize that since many games are won—or lost—very far down the nine inning road it would be smart to have a level headed guy with good stuff ready to step in. I'm personally glad they came to that realization, sure. But I'm also glad for baseball, and baseball fans.

Back in the early sixties when I was honing my own awareness of the game and its glories, I remember watching Ron Perranoski. I was truly impressed! I marveled at the way he could calmly take the mound in the midst of an incredible late inning clutch situation and bring off a win for the Dodgers. Nerves? It didn't seem like it. Perranoski didn't have a million dollar contract, aftershave ads or a lot of press attention, and it didn't much matter. He did the job with style.

And Ryne Duren! He's always been a favorite of mine, but the stories in this book really gave me a new appreciation. I've never seen much written about him, but his records, his style, were amazing.

Roots is a popular theme these days, right? And a feeling of roots is what I got from John Thorn's effort. He's done his homework, and it was great reading about some of the men who paved the way, established some precedents and set some records long before media hype picked up on the financial end of the game.

I understand that Thorn enjoys juggling figures, analyzing the past, predicting what's coming. It's obvious that statistics are seductive to him. It's a good thing, since baseball's notoriously full of facts. The result is a most enjoyable look at the history of the species—my species!—just the thing for pre-season reading as I prepare for my 11th season in the pros.

I don't need to have what I do glamorized. I don't require ego stroking and I don't think most players do. (There are a few exceptions, of course, but I'll resist temptation here . . .) But as I said in the beginning, it's a job, and there sure is a lot of pleasure and satisfaction in getting some recognition for a job you try to do well.

I hope you readers say, as I believe John Thorn has, "Hey, now that I read these stories and relive those games, I see what a valuable contribution those relievers make." That would be great.

1

# Baseball's New Hero

When the final pitch of the 1978 World Series was thrown, it was thrown by a relief pitcher. The final out of each League Championship Series, too, was recorded by a fireman. And so was the last out of the one-game play-off in the American League East. When the critical contests were on the line, when the entire season would end for the losing team, the starting pitchers stepped aside. As Yankee manager Bob Lemon once said, "Every time an important game or series is played these days, a bullpen will probably win it." Or, in the more memorable phrasing of Yogi Berra, "If you ain't got a bullpen, you ain't got nothin'."

Even the best starter, baseball professionals recognize, hopes to take credit for at most 25 to 30 winning games in a season (his own wins plus team wins in which he departs with the score tied or in his favor). A great reliever, by winning the game himself or by saving the win for the starter, can play a vital role in 45 to 50 wins per year. Today's fans also appreciate that role, and to them the Yanks' Rich Gossage or the Padres' Rollie Fingers is no less a hero than a 20-game winner, a .300 hitter, or a home-run slugger.

Relief pitchers have not always been so prized. Indeed, when major-league baseball was in its infancy there was no bullpen, and a relief pitcher was merely a fielder who exchanged positions with the starting pitcher. Although Firpo Marberry and Wilcy Moore were snuffing out rallies in the 1920s, the general view of relievers was that they were part-timers who, because of inexperience, infirmity, or ineptitude, couldn't be trusted to start a game. That perception prevailed until thirty-odd years ago, when Joe Page and Jim Konstanty showed that a first-rate fireman was indispensable. This book, besides describing the slow but steady ascent of relief pitching, profiles the ten best who ever plied the trade.

The reliever's rise to prominence in recent years represents the most profound tactical change in baseball since the introduction of the lively ball reshaped offensive strategy. An ever-diminishing percentage of games are completed by starting pitchers and in an ever-increasing percentage of games a fireman registers a save. The table below * breaks down the complete-game and save ratios into the six eras that displayed distinct changes in the way relievers were regarded and employed.

| | COMPLETE-GAME PERCENTAGE | SAVE PERCENTAGE |
|---|---|---|
| 1876–1904 | 90.5 | 1.3 |
| 1905–1923 | 63.3 | 5.4 |
| 1924–1946 | 45.9 | 8.7 |
| 1947–1958 | 35.1 | 12.7 |
| 1959–1973 | 25.8 | 18.7 |
| 1974–1978 | 25.6 | 17.6 |

The leveling-off of the complete-game percentage in recent years is largely due to the advent of the designated hitter in the American League: The presence of the d.h. removes the necessity of pinch-hitting for a starter who is hurling effectively. Figures for the National League alone over this period show a continued decline in complete-game percentage (to 20.9 percent).

What accounts for this growing reliance on relievers? Many old-timers will tell you that the answer is simple—today's pitcher is inferior. They can point to a pitcher like Jack Taylor of the Cubs and Cards who, from 1898 to 1906, started 273 games and completed all but three. Joe Oeschger, who in 1920 pitched all 26 innings of a 1–1 tie, says: "If you were unable to pitch nine innings in my day, you had better look for some other occupation." Pete Donohue, who starred for the Reds of the 1920s, observes: "We pitched nine innings when I pitched. We didn't go five or six innings and get credit for a win. They got more relief pitchers now on clubs than our whole pitching staff."

* A summary of the comprehensive table to be found in the appendix.

If a man has the ability to go nine, these men imply, he does not need to be relieved. The simplicity of that view is appealing and the logic seems unassailable, but the fault lies in the word *ability*. If the ability to go nine is found less frequently than it once was, this may be because modern managers have placed less value on it. Today's very best starters know how to coast in spots to make sure they have something left for the last three innings; a Tom Seaver or a Jim Palmer will strive for a complete game as a matter of professional pride. But on a team blessed with a strong bullpen crew, a manager is quite content to get seven good innings from his starter (Gaylord Perry, winner of the 1978 Cy Young Award in the National League, completed only five of his 37 starts). Accordingly, most of today's starters scorn pace and go as hard as they can as long as they can.

In the first two decades of the century, when a team's pitching staff numbered five or six, starters had no choice but to complete most of their games, even some of those in which they were being clobbered. Today, with most staffs comprised of ten men, five of them bullpenners, a manager doesn't have to subject a starter to a continued thrashing just to preserve his staff.

Many observers, myself included, would say that—great as the stars of yesterday were—the current level of pitching is *on the whole* superior to that of, say, 1920, the first year of the lively ball. Despite the expansion of franchises and rosters, today's batters have a tougher time of it than their forebears. In 1930, when starters were completing nearly 45 percent of all games, 35 men in the American League and 31 in the National batted .300 or better. Thirty years later, when starters were completing one game in four, each league could boast only five .300 hitters. Were they playing today, Cobb and Hornsby might each bat over .400 for three seasons,[*] Ruth might still hit 60 homers, Wilson might drive in 190 runs— but we would not see an entire league bat .303, as the National League did in 1930, or a team bat .349, as the Philadelphia Phillies did in 1894.

Since 1930, batting averages have dropped off 45 points in the National League and 27 points in the American. A prime reason for this decline, though by no means the only one, is the greater use of relief pitchers. A fireman offers a fresh arm in place of a tired one, of course, but he may also be a lefty succeeding a right-handed starter; he may be a power pitcher following a curveballer; or he may present an eccentric pitching motion on the heels of a conventional delivery. (Dave Baldwin, a reliever for the Senators in

---

[*] Pete Rose, however, has said, "With all the good relief pitchers there are now, Ty Cobb would hit maybe .315 and that's all."

the sixties, gives this as the source of his success: "An unorthodox delivery, more than anything else. My style contrasted sharply with any pitcher I would replace.") In short, the entrance of a new pitcher represents a change in rhythm, a change to which the batter must adjust within a few pitches. As offense is the establishment of rhythm, defense consists of its disruption. This is true in any sport—in basketball, a defender waves a hand in the face of a shooter to make him alter the arc of his shot; in football, a cornerback bumps a receiver at the line to throw off the timing of his pass route; in hockey, a winger forechecks to prevent a puck-carrier from gathering momentum.

In baseball, says Boston catcher Carlton Fisk, "the biggest thing a pitcher has to do is break down a hitter's concentration and rhythm." A hurler does this by mixing pitches, changing speeds, pitching to spots, and occasionally chucking a "wild" heave at a batter's chin. Some pitchers rely almost exclusively on their fastball, yet they will "show" the breaking ball: not trying to throw it for a strike, but only to keep the batter "on his toes," to prevent him from "digging in."

As a game progresses, a pitcher's powers of deception may wane, and the hitters who were mystified their first three trips to the plate may be terrors on their fourth. Thus, modern managers will pull a starter at the first sign of late-inning trouble, rather than let him pitch his way out of it, and they will not hesitate to yank one reliever for another if they feel a change will give them even the slightest edge. That edge, or "percentage," often consists of the proven statistical advantage that same-side pitchers enjoy over same-side batters, particularly lefty versus lefty. In slavish adherence to "the book," some managers "run pitchers in and out of there like rabbits," complained Jimmy Dykes, 22 years a player and 21 years a manager. It slows the game, he acknowledged, but "it's that much rougher on the batters."

And that's why relievers are called in when the game hinges on a single pitch—because today's managers know that in the late innings, in the big games, a reliever is rougher on the batters than a starter would have been. For example, from 1903 to 1971, only one World Series failed to produce a complete-game performance. Yet in 1972, 1973, and 1974, no pitcher on either side was able (or allowed) to go nine. Come World Series time, said Alvin Dark, manager of the 1974 World Champion Oakland Athletics, "you don't think in terms of a pitcher holding a lead. You think in terms of a *staff* holding it."

In recent years, some managers—notably Dark, Sparky Anderson, Dick Williams, and Danny Ozark—have constructed their pitching staffs around their bullpens, feeling that if the other ingredients were there, it was possible to win without top-flight starters. The 1970 Cincinnati Reds, under "Captain Hook" Anderson, took the N.L. flag despite only 32 complete games from their starters, the lowest total ever recorded by a pennant winner to that time. The record has since been surpassed—by the Reds of 1972 (25 complete games) and the Reds of 1975 (22). The Oakland A's won the World Series three straight years without registering a complete game. They had three excellent starters in Jim Hunter, Vida Blue, and Ken Holtzman, yet it was the bullpen that secured their victories. Phils' manager Danny Ozark, blessed with four first-rate firemen, said, "It used to be in baseball that we called on our bullpen to give our starters a rest. Now, during the regular season, we hope for complete games by starters in order to rest our bullpen."

Recent salaries give further testimony to the new importance of the reliever. Of the four top firemen who were able to test their worth on the free-agent mart of 1976 and 1977, Bill Campbell signed a five-year pact with the Red Sox for $1 million; Rollie Fingers with the Padres, five years for $1.6 million; Rawly Eastwick with the Yankees, five years for $1.1 million; and Rich Gossage, also with the Yankees, six years for a staggering $2.7 million. Many other relievers—among them Mike Marshall, Sparky Lyle, Terry Forster, Dave LaRoche, and Gary Lavelle—have earned in excess of $100,000 per year. "Seems that pay for good relief is not now the problem it once was," observes Allie Reynolds, a great reliever and starter for the Indians and Yanks.

Forty to fifty years ago, when firemen were seen as part-timers, they were accorded part-time pay. In 1935, Yankee skipper Joe McCarthy approached Johnny Murphy, who had gone 11-8 for him as a spot starter the year before, and asked him to try his hand at short relief exclusively. Murphy said he would do whatever McCarthy asked—it was that or a one-way ticket to Newark, he knew—but he couldn't be expected to accept a demotion cheerfully. McCarthy assured him that the move was lateral—that it would not only benefit the team, but also aid Murphy, whose great curveball would be an invaluable asset in late-inning jams when a grounder was needed for a twin killing. But, countered Murphy, what about his diminished earnings as pitching's equivalent of a benchwarmer? McCarthy assured him that he would be paid like a regular, for that was how he thought of him. Murphy went on to become the premier rescue artist of his era, and perhaps the only one to earn "starter's scale."

By 1935, Murphy's first full year in the pen, rescue work

had long since been elevated to the state of art by the scribes. Dan Daniel had lavished praise on Marberry of the Senators and Moore of the Yanks, and Damon Runyon had hung the moniker "Doc" on the Giants' Otis Crandall because he restored sick ball games to health. Yet despite the ink given some members of the firemen's fraternity, the bullpen retained its image as a rest home for aging starters and an audition studio for green kids. If being sent to the minors was, for faltering starters, the descent into hell, then the bullpen was purgatory.

Among pitchers, to be a professional reliever was to be of a lesser order. Starters who also did some relief work (as so many of them did until the 1950s) were not actually *relieving* but "filling in between starts." To be called a reliever was the same thing as being called a second-rater. I asked Rip Sewell, famous for his lobbed "eephus" pitch in the 1940s, whether he preferred relieving or starting. Sewell, who trudged in from the bullpen 147 times in his 13-year career, replied, "I did not know what it was like to be a relief pitcher," and castigated me soundly for implying that he did.

Much of the stigma attached to relief work was that if you were handed a lead, you could not get a win unless you blew the lead *and* were still around to be bailed out by your batsmen; if you came on the scene trailing, no matter how well you pitched the decision was not in your hands. Firpo Marberry said 50 years ago, "If the relief pitcher holds the opposing club in check, he gets no credit. The pitcher who preceded him and couldn't stand the pace wins the game." There was no "saves" statistic in baseball until 1960 when, at the initiative of Jerry Holtzman of the Chicago *Sun-Times, The Sporting News* adopted saves as a more accurate index of a reliever's performance than won-lost percentage or earned-run average.

*The Sporting News* credited a fireman with a save if he finished another pitcher's win in which he faced the potential tying run. Saves did not become an official baseball statistic until 1969, when it was proclaimed that a reliever could earn a save by protecting any lead, even one of 20–6 (the Mets' Ron Taylor picked up a save in 1971 for pitching the ninth inning of that wipeout of Atlanta). Rules governing saves were tightened in 1973 and liberalized in 1975. Today a reliever may gain a save by (a) finishing a team win and protecting a lead of three runs or less for one inning or more, or (b) facing the potential tying run on base, at bat, or on deck, or (c) pitching effectively for three innings regardless of the team's lead.

Modern relievers are grateful for the saves column. As any

one of them will tell you, it is possible to post a mediocre won-lost record, say 8–9, and a mediocre ERA (for firemen, that is; they enjoy an advantage in this category), say 3.00, and have had one hell of a year. Ask Rollie Fingers—that was his record in 1977, when he was *The Sporting News* Fireman of the Year in the National League, thanks to the 35 saves he coupled with his eight wins. In the days before the press recorded saves, "you either won or lost the game," says Johnny Gorsica, a reliever for Detroit in the forties, "and there was no credit except experience in no-decision games. I know, because when contract time rolled around the only record that mattered was how many games a pitcher won or lost."

Like all players—like all people—relief pitchers crave recognition for their work, and they wish to be paid fairly for it. Until L.A.'s Larry Sherry electrified baseball with his relief exploits in the 1959 World Series, and *The Sporting News* followed one year later with its Fireman-of-the-Year competition, most denizens of the pen labored in relative anonymity and penury.

In the course of preparing this book, I asked more than 150 major-league pitchers who enjoyed success in relief work whether they preferred relieving or starting. Burleigh Grimes, the great spitballer who was a star 60 years ago, told me he preferred starting "because you got credit" if you pitched well. Al "Boots" Hollingsworth, who hurled for the Reds and the Browns in the thirties and forties, similarly preferred starting because he had a "better chance to win. No 'save' column in my day." Joe Beggs, whose exceptional relief work in 1940 helped the Reds to the World's Championship, would rather have been a starter because "at that time relievers did not get a starter's salary." Russ Kemmerer, who started and relieved for four clubs between 1954 and 1963, observed, "During this period the starters were the only ones able to make any money. Relief pitchers with few exceptions were considered as subs. Today the situation has changed."

Yes, the situation certainly has changed. Some firemen have become instant millionaires in the reentry draft, or have been given lucrative long-term contracts to keep them out of the free-agent market. But what about the relievers who toil honorably for second-division clubs, or those who cashed in their chips just before the wheel of fortune hit their number? Do they resent the riches showered on the likes of Gossage and Fingers?

Dave Heaverlo of the A's, who with Bob Lacey and Elias Sosa formed one of the game's better bullpens in 1978, says that "Marshall, Fingers, Lavelle, and Gossage have done a lot to improve the salary structure for all relievers." He recognizes that this higher pay scale reflects the higher esteem in which relievers are held today, and that makes him "feel honored to be a major-league relief pitcher."

Bob Lacey is a young left-hander whose nickname "Spacey" was earned by such stunts as, in his major-league debut, taunting Reggie Jackson, then proceeding to fan him twice. Lacey feels "Fingers and Lyle belong in the Hall of Fame, not only because of their success, but because they have brought a new respectability to the art of relief." Lacey defends his colleagues against the old charge that relievers are simply extra pitchers not good enough to start: "Most big-league relievers are not (contrary to popular belief) usually pitchers who have lost the ability to go nine, but rather, pitchers who have exceptionally strong arms. They are found to be able to throw effectively every day and then are made relievers." Turning around the proposition that relievers do not make good starters, Lacey goes on to say that very few starters "have the arm, the control, or the psychological makeup to be effective as a reliever."

Dave Giusti, longtime rescue ace of the Pirates, perhaps best encapsulated the attitude of the modern reliever toward his special domain. An effective starter for the weak Houston Astros in their early years, Giusti came to prefer relieving, "because I felt more valuable to the club."

The sentiments expressed by Heaverlo, Lacey, and Giusti, the self-esteem and the pride in their trade, were echoed by virtually all of the active relievers whom I surveyed—and by very few of the relievers whose careers ended before 1960. Today's firemen enjoy the challenge of coming in with the game on the line. They take satisfaction in the roles they fulfill for their teams. Recognition? They're getting it now as never before. The adulation of the fans, the salaries, the All-Star selections, the Rookie-of-the-Year Award, the Cy Young Award.

What laurels remain to be won? Another Most Valuable Player Award would be nice—it's been quite a while now since Jim Konstanty became the first reliever to cop one. Another *Sporting News* Pitcher of the Year Award would be fine too—only Konstanty and Marshall have won one from the bullpen. And the Hall of Fame. The electors of Cooperstown have to date spurned the candidacy of Hoyt Wilhelm, the game's greatest fireman. Induction into the Hall of Fame would really be appreciated, not only by Wilhelm but by all his colleagues who labored in the shadows before him, and by those who perform in the limelight today.

**2**

**The Relievers Speak**

*"What made you a good reliever?"* I posed that question to more than 150 major leaguers who pitched notably in relief from 1912 to the present day. Some men stressed their physical attributes: Tom Ferrick, an American League fireman of the forties and fifties, cited "good control of at least two pitches, and the ability to loosen up your arm quickly." Others emphasized their qualities of temperament: Bill Lee, now with the Expos, said the feature that makes a good reliever is the "same thing that makes a good Kamikaze pilot. Don't worry about tomorrow." A broader analysis of relief success was offered by Jim Brosnan, author of two of baseball's best books—*The Long Season* and *Pennant Race*—and not incidentally a fine pitcher in the fifties and sixties. He recalled Yankee pitching coach Jim Turner's evaluation of him: " 'Brosnan has good stuff, one exceptional pitch [the slider], throws strikes, and challenges the hitters.' Invariably," Brosnan continued, "those qualities are found in all successful relievers."

Many firemen chose to add two other qualities: an arm that would withstand the work load, and a mind that would withstand the pressure. Less frequently mentioned requisites were strikeout capability, good fielding, and top conditioning.

Clearly, most of these traits could be said to characterize successful starters as well; what makes a difference is the heightened immediacy demanded of a reliever's performance. Because of the game situation—the closeness of the score, the lateness of the inning, the number of men on base—every pitch is crucial.

Take the case of control. A starter who issues only two passes in each game—at whatever point—is a "control artist," while a reliever who walks two men per outing is soon carrying a lunch pail. Only that legendary wild man Ryne Duren flourished in relief despite subpar control. (Or, in his case, *because* of it. Asked to explain his success, Duren gave equal credit to his fastball and his "wild reputation." As Dave Baldwin notes, "Many good relievers have stopped rallies before they have thrown a pitch.")

With Duren as the lone exception, the ability to throw strikes is essential for a fireman because he so often enters the game with the tying or winning run on base. In this predicament, control means more than merely avoiding a base on balls. A relief pitcher must "get ahead of the hitter," cautions Mace Brown, the National League's top reliever of the 1930s. "Don't get behind the batters," echoes Gary Serum, the Twins' young reliever; "go right at them." With men on base you can't nibble at the plate or waste one pitch to set up another (unless the count is 0–2 or 1–2). You have to make the batter swing at the ball, and the only way to force the issue is to put him in the hole.

Just as the need for control is more immediate for a reliever than it is for a starter, so is the necessity of retiring the batter. A starter opens a game with a clean slate. He experiments with his repertoire of pitches, speeds, and deliveries, letting the batters tell him which ones are working best that day. If in the process he permits a base hit or two, or allows a couple of early runs, he may still go on to pick up a win. A fireman does not enjoy that margin for error. He "must be at his best from the first pitch onward," says Lindy McDaniel, a relief ace in three decades. "He must throw strikes with good stuff on the ball. He has no time for fine adjustments. It's more like: 'Here's my best pitch, hit it if you can!'"

While there have been successful relievers who threw a variety of pitches and changed speeds, like Detroit's John Hiller, most top firemen have relied on a single "out" pitch, a pitch they would almost invariably go to in a jam. For Hoyt Wilhelm it was the knuckler; Ron Perranoski, the curve; Sparky Lyle, the slider; Dick Radatz, the fastball. Roy Face had the forkball; Dave Giusti, the palmball; Tug McGraw, the screwball; Ken Sanders, the sinker. All these top firemen employed other pitches, too, but when facing a batter who could beat them with a base hit, they would go with their best, and hope for the best.

Until Duren burst on the scene in the late fifties as the bullpen's first strikeout artist, managers hungered for hurlers who could "throw those grounders," as Casey Stengel used to say. A ground ball might produce a double play, or hold a runner at third with less than two out, or at worst skitter through the infield for a hit. A ball lofted in the air might land in the loges. (Stengel and John McGraw were particularly enamored of sinkerballers because both Yankee Stadium and the Polo Grounds were short down one or both lines and transformed many an anemic fly ball into a "Chinese" home run.)

If your fireman had a good pitch, you wanted him to throw it; if he was going to be beaten, you didn't want it to be with his second- or third-best pitch. Johnny Gorsica had a good curveball that he displayed to good advantage as a starter, but when he was called in from the pen, "it was always in a critical situation with men on base and I had to get them out with my sinker." Similarly, Rosy Ryan, relief star of the 1923 World Series, at that time complained, "Every time I look to the bench for a sign, it's a curve. All I pitch are curves, curves, nothing but curves until my arm is warped."

Relievers who rely on the single outstanding pitch may become less effective if left in long enough for the batters to get a second shot at it. Ralph Houk once said of Sparky Lyle that, using his slider 90 percent of the time, he was great for short relief, but if you needed four or five innings from your fireman, he preferred a guy who could mix it up, like John Hiller. Accordingly, in 1973–1974, when both were outstanding, Hiller appeared in only seven more games than Lyle, yet pitched in 275 innings to Lyle's 196.

How much can a rescue man pitch? Today we think that Mike Marshall reached—or exceeded—the limit when he relieved in 106 games and 208 innings in 1974. Tom Seaver has said about Marshall: "One year he pitched in 106 games and three years later he was out of a job." Yet 61 years before Marshall's epic feat, observers thought that Otis Crandall was testing the bounds of endurance by becoming the first man to relieve in 30 or more games. As Dave Danforth passed the 40 mark, Firpo Marberry 50, and Clint Brown 60, baseball brahmins each time proclaimed that forces of nature were being tampered with, that arms could not bear up under the strain. The same remarks accompanied the successive fractures of the 70, 80, and 90 relief game "barriers" by, respectively, Jim Konstanty, John Wyatt, and Wayne Granger.

Is there no physical limit? Can a man pitch an inning or two virtually *every* day? If you believe Marshall and his first big-league pitching mentor, Johnny Sain, yes—provided the muscles of the arm are conditioned correctly. Marshall and Sain believe that the way to strengthen arm muscles is to use them, working with weights and doing plenty of throwing on the sidelines. They go against the conventional baseball wisdom that pitching is an "unnatural" activity for the arm, which has only so many pitches in it before giving out. (Seaver on Sain's theories: "I wouldn't let him near me.")

Seldom does a reliever complain of overwork, or express fear that he might be "burned out" early in his career. Rather, it is inactivity that worries firemen and threatens their livelihoods. When relievers have had too much rest between appearances, they are "too strong": The ball comes in faster but breaks less. Many sinkerballers vow that they are more effective when tired, that their ball tails and dips more when they aren't muscling it up to the plate. Bob Humphreys, who relieved for five clubs from 1962 to 1970, said that part of being a reliever is "to get over the mental 'hangup' that you don't have good stuff because your arm is stiff" from overuse.

Periodic inactivity is an occupational hazard for the reliever that he must accept. A run of complete games from the starters or, more plausibly these days, a string of arson jobs by the fireman himself, may shelve him for weeks. Get blasted in short relief and it almost invariably means a loss for the team—barring a miracle rally, the game is simply too far advanced for the batters to square accounts. Managers like steady employment, and cannot allow a stopper to work his way out of a slump in clutch situations, possibly at the team's expense. The errant fireman will be told to "work on a few things" in the pen, or will be allowed to pitch mopup, or, as the Mets did with Tug McGraw, will be given a start. That tactic underscores the value of the modern reliever: Where yesterday a struggling starter would be sent to the bullpen and a wavering reliever would be sent to Chattanooga, today the struggling reliever may be steered toward the mound to open the game.

When the inning is late, the score tight, the starter shaky, and the bullpen phone is ringing for someone else, that may mean the end of the reliever's season—if not his career. With a good team, mopup opportunities are few until the dog days of August, when bats warm up and doubleheaders pile up and there's more than enough work to go around. But a reliever who has been idle for the better part of June and July is not apt to shine in August. The longer the reliever is out of action, the poorer his control and the flatter his stuff when he returns. The scenario is familiar: three or four bad outings by a fireman, followed by two weeks without game action, followed by a manager's hunch or desperation call with the game on the line, resulting in yet another pasting, and at last a trade or waiver deal.

A starter who is idle because of injury or ineffectiveness may, upon his return to the box, allow a few early runs, but will be permitted to stay on and regain his rhythm and control. Not so the fireman. As Lindy McDaniel said, "Nothing compared to my good years in relief, as each day I could look forward to possibly getting into the game. . . . However, during the poor years when I wasn't used frequently, it was the worst job in baseball. Managers tend to get down on relievers quicker than starters, and due to infrequent work it is very hard to come out of a slump."

This goes a long way to explain why so many relievers have exhibited the syndrome of good year/bad year/good year. Walter Alston's theory is that successful relievers, because of their success, are overworked, which leads to adhesions forming in the arm. These harden further in the off-season. Next spring, the reliever conditions himself as usual but does not completely break down the adhesions. He has a rough time of it in April and May, the manager loses confidence in him, and he gets buried in the bullpen or in Triple-A for the rest of the campaign. Traded in the off-season, he often as not rewards his new team with a performance equal to his previous standards. (Examples: Ted Abernathy, Phil Regan, Al Hrabosky, Hoyt Wilhelm, Lindy McDaniel—the list goes on and on.)

Two qualities that are desirable yet not indispensable for a reliever are good fielding and a strikeout capability. A manager would like his reliever to be a "fifth infielder" handling bunts, covering the bag on a grounder to first, backing up the bases on relay throws from the outfield. But if the pitcher can get the batter out, all else is forgiven, even an inability to hold runners close. Some of the best relievers to play the game, including not a few of those active today, make an adventure of routine plays and a farce of difficult ones.

Strange as it sounds, the strikeout is a fairly new addition to the reliever's arsenal. In the early years, when most hitters concentrated on making contact rather than on activating the scoreboard fireworks, a pitcher who could whiz the ball by the batters was rare, and was prized as a starter. A reliever who could dig down deep for something extra and notch a K at a critical point of the game has always been appreciated, but the star firemen before 1950 seldom brought it off. Crandall, Murphy, Marberry, Moore, Brown, Adams, Casey—all struck out fewer than four men per nine innings over their careers. The first prominent departure from that pattern was the Yankees' Joe Page, who fanned nearly six per nine innings.

More recently, three relievers—Dick Radatz, Ryne Duren, and Bruce Sutter—have struck out batters at the rate of more than one per inning over their careers. Today, with artificial turf replacing natural grass in so many ball parks, the premium is increasingly being placed on the K-men like Sutter, Gossage, Hrabosky, and Kern. On the synthetic surface, the sinkerballer can come in and induce the ground ball, only to see it scoot past or through an infielder who would have made the play easily on sod.

Those are the physical qualities that, in varying degrees, mark successful firemen. But many relief pitchers insist that qualities of character—an "aggressive personality on the field, and an even temperament," as former Oriole and Phillie Eddie Watt puts it— are equally important, if not more so. As a reliever you can't "be afraid to challenge the hitter with your best stuff, throwing to his power," says Al Aber, Tiger reliever in the fifties. Don Nottebart, pitcher for five clubs in the sixties, adds, "Only two things can happen in relief. Either you do or you don't. Challenge hitters from the word go. Have some guts!"

Staring in at the batter, a reliever has to feel as Barney Schultz did when he starred for the World Champion Cardinals of 1964: "I was the boss. I had the ball." In the same vein, Sparky Lyle once said, "I don't worry about who's up. No matter who it is, I know I'm going to throw inside to the right-handers and outside to the left-handers. So I just concentrate on psyching myself up to attack them, to put them on the defensive."

The danger in "psyching up" is that a reliever might fire his combativeness to such a white heat that either his judgment, or his nerve, or his control suffers. Some relievers, like Lyle, Hrabosky, and McGraw, are intense personalities who thrive on tension, are energized by it, and are able to direct that nervous energy toward the task at hand. Most relievers, however, go about their jobs with all the visible emotion of a plumber stopping a leak. They are inured to the pressures of their trade, because that is the only way they can handle the steady diet of near-impossible situations. Don Elston, former Cub reliever, says, "The most important asset of a reliever is his temperament. I wasn't too crazy about the term 'ice water in his veins,' but that is a good description."

What makes that ice water flow through the veins? Walt Masterson, who pitched for the Senators, Red Sox, and Tigers for 14 years, cited "self-confidence," which enables a pitcher to "relax and concentrate under pressure." Jack Aker, American League

Fireman of the Year in 1966, says, "At least 90 percent of a successful relief pitcher's successes are a product of confidence and
concentration." Stan Williams credited his prosperity as a reliever
with the Dodgers, Indians, and Twins to "a personal belief in my
ability to succeed . . . elimination of negative thoughts and stressing
the positive."

Williams's philosophy was sorely put to the test after the
deciding game of the 1962 National League play-off between the
Dodgers and Giants. The Dodgers were leading 4–3 in the ninth
inning, with the bases loaded and one out. One Giant had already
crossed the plate in the inning when Williams replaced a tiring
Ed Roebuck. "Orlando Cepeda was the hitter," Williams recalls.
"Cepeda popped to short right, Mays scoring from third to tie
the game." After a pitch in the dirt enabled the runner on first to
move up to second, "Alston demanded we intentionally walk the
lefty hitter Ed Bailey to reload the bases. At that point I 'uninten-
tionally' walked Jim Davenport to go behind and lose the pennant.
(P.S.—No one remembers that I was the winning pitcher the day
before.) I think I'm the only pitcher in history to have won two
league play-off games in the old one-division leagues [Williams
won the deciding game of the 1959 play-off against the Braves].
Still, I'll always be remembered for my goat's role.

"Losing the Giant play-off game could have had a terrible
effect on me, except I knew that I had done the best I could that
day, and it wasn't good enough. Had I let up, to get the ball over,
and Davenport had got a base hit, I'd have had a hard time
accepting that. As it was, my wife and I played 'putt-putt' golf
on the way home that day."

Once the game is over, leaving it at the ball park is a necessity
for all players: Brooding over failure occasions few constructive
thoughts. In this regard, relievers enjoy an advantage over "regular"
pitchers, who must wait four or five days to redeem themselves
after a bad outing. In fact, many relievers declared that one of
the main attractions of their job was, in the words of the Reds'
Dave Tomlin, "going to the park knowing that I might pitch
that day." Jack Aker preferred bullpen duty because, "simply, I
felt like a regular player."

As mentioned earlier, most of the active relievers I questioned
enjoy their roles and would not, given the choice, be starting
pitchers. Most of the retired relievers, given that choice, opted for
starting—including such surprises as Ryne Duren, who very seldom
started in the majors. "Scheduled work keeps you in better condition and leads to a longer life [career]," he said. Another veteran
relief pitcher said: "It's a lot easier on the mind knowing in ad-

vance you will be out there; certainly easier on the arm. Many short relievers have had only one or two years of heavy use in a row with success."

Contrast this relief pitcher's feelings with those of Hal Woodeschick, a top fireman for Houston and St. Louis in the mid-sixties: "I preferred relieving because when I started I would get too up-tight and think too much [in advance] about the game and the hitters. In relief I didn't know when I was going to pitch." Rollie Fingers suffered the same anxieties when he was placed in the starting rotation at the start of the 1971 campaign.

Before relief pitching became the specialty it is today, most starters would do some relieving between starts, especially in the heat of a pennant race. Joe Genewich of the 1920s Braves and Giants says: "Only at the end of the season did Mr. McGraw tell his four first-string pitchers that they were expected to hold up the team." Thus the men who had hurled primarily in relief before September—the superannuated starters who got by on savvy, the kids shuttling back and forth from the farm—would be shelved when wins became imperative. The comment of Bill Bayne of the 1920s Browns is typical of those early relievers: "All pitchers want to be starters and so did I—but you do what the manager tells you." Waite Hoyt, the Hall of Famer who closed out his career by doing much fireman duty for the Pirates and Dodgers, says: "Every pitcher in the development stages of his career wants to become a starter." Not until recently were youngsters actually groomed as relievers in the minors; Bruce Sutter, for example, has started only two games at any level of pro ball.

While it's pretty well agreed that few top relievers could be equally effective as starters (Hoyt Wilhelm proved he could, Rich Gossage showed he couldn't), there is no consensus about the converse. Here are some representative observations:

Stanley Coveleski, Hall of Famer who began in the majors in 1912: "In my day, relievers and starters were all the same; relief pitching was the harder job."

Jack Aker: "Not very many great starters would have made equally great relievers, mostly because of the importance of warming up quickly and producing instantly. It's like comparing a dash man to a miler."

Stan Williams: "Some yes—some no. Not all pitchers can work two or more days in a row with the same effectiveness. Sandy Koufax and Luis Tiant were two of the greatest starters I ever saw, lefty and righty, but I don't believe either could have been a good reliever—Don Drysdale probably would have been as good either way."

Tom House of the Seattle Mariners: "Yes—the *physical* requirements can be learned and if the ability exists to be a great starter then it most certainly will be there as a reliever."

Mike Caldwell of the Milwaukee Brewers: "Some would but most would not. Reason—starters usually have a variety of pitches that they can use and they don't always throw strikes. A relief pitcher usually has one outstanding pitch that will overpower hitters for two or three innings."

George Uhle, top starter and spot reliever for the Indians, Tigers, and Yankees, 1919–1936: "Most good starters, you have to get to them early since they get tougher as the game progresses, as was my case; therefore I don't believe they would also be able to relieve."

Jim Brosnan: "I don't know. No reason, physically, why they wouldn't have been just as effective out of the bullpen. But relieving is a specialty; a reliever has to love pressure situations, be able to psyche himself up for them. Starters tend to be 'in-the-groove' pitchers who are more comfortable when they pace themselves."

Paul LaPalme, knuckleballer for four clubs in the fifties: "Yes, if that's what they want to do. The late Ellis Kinder is a great example of that [Kinder was 23–6 as a starter in 1949; two years later he led the A.L. in relief wins and saves]."

Bob Savage, Philadelphia A's, 1940s: "Maybe, but what a waste. Bob Feller in short relief—inconceivable."

Sam McDowell, strikeout king of the A.L. in the sixties who ended his career as a reliever with the Pirates: "No. [In past years] a starter who couldn't cut it usually was made into a reliever. Today they are specialists. They are just as good if not better than the starters. They just don't have the overall stamina."

McDowell's words pretty well expressed this writer's convictions. A Rich Gossage or a Bruce Sutter is not a *poorer* pitcher than a Nolan Ryan or a Don Sutton, but only a different sort. Of course, Gossage and Sutter are "limited"—they rely heavily on a single pitch, and their effectiveness would certainly diminish if they were asked to go nine. But by that token, Ryan and Sutton are also "limited"—they cannot heat up fast, their first innings on the mound are often their weakest and, in the case of Ryan, his erratic control would be a liability were he called in to get a big out with men on base.

The roles of starter and reliever are not interchangeable, and it is an arguable point which is today the more valuable. Mike Marshall, after losing out to Tom Seaver in the Cy Young balloting of 1973, said: "Seaver won 19 games and I won 14 and saved 31 more. . . . Who do you feel is more valuable to your club, Seaver or me? You have a good starter, he wins a game. What does he do for the next four? He sits around and watches. . . . But here is a relief pitcher who can pitch his nine innings in three or four of these games and can help you win three or four."

No reflection on Seaver in the least, but I must take sides with Marshall. With a century-old trend of completions decreasing and saves increasing, I'll place my bet on the firemen as the more valuable in the future.

**3**

**The Pre-Relief Era: 1876-1904**

While the future of the relief pitcher is assuredly "ahead of him," in that immortal baseball tautology, his past lies farther behind him than one might imagine. It goes back beyond Page and Konstanty, beyond Murphy and Marberry, beyond even Otis Crandall, often identified as the game's first reliever. In fact, the story of relief pitching begins with the man to whom so much of major-league baseball traces its roots, Harry Wright.

"The Father of the Game," as Wright was called during his lifetime, was personally involved in the early development of our national pastime, from cricket's "poor relation," to the amateur game of gentlemen, to the early professionals, to the major leagues. Harry's father was a professional cricket player in England, where Harry was born in 1835. He came to New York in infancy, and as a young athlete he followed in his father's path, becoming the star cricketeer of the St. George, Staten Island club. In 1858 he joined the fabled New York Knickerbockers, baseball's first organized team, but cricket continued to be his favored game. Harry's brother George, twelve years his junior and native-born, passed cricket by, starting his illustrious baseball career with the N.Y. Gothams in 1864.

In the summer of 1865, the Union Cricket Club of Cincinnati hired Harry Wright as a player-coach. Following his practice in

New York, Wright affiliated himself simultaneously with the local baseball nine. In 1867, the touring Washington Nationals, ostensibly an amateur nine comprised of government employees, defeated Cincinnati's Red Stockings by the score of 53–10 (Washington's shortstop was Harry's brother George). This massacre so wounded the Queen City's civic pride that the baseball club's directors hired Harry Wright away from the cricket club. Instructed to put together the best team money could buy (George Steinbrenner didn't invent the practice), Harry Wright disbursed $9,300 in salaries and formed baseball's first avowedly professional team.

The 1869 Red Stockings immediately demonstrated the worth of that investment. Touring the country from Maine to California, the Reds played 66 games without defeat. The team's shortstop and star (.629 batting average!) was Harry's brother George. Harry himself was the manager, center fielder, reporter—and relief pitcher, or "change pitcher," as the fireman was called back then.

The rules of the day stated that a player could not be replaced "unless for reason of illness or injury," or if the opposing team consented. If the starting pitcher was taking a pasting, he could not look to the bullpen for relief; there was no bullpen. He had to exchange positions with a fielder, who had warmed up before the game in preparation for just such an eventuality. A change pitcher was customarily a strong-armed outfielder who could whip the ball in as fast or faster than the starter, but this was not always the case—Wright, for example, was not possessed of an outstanding arm.

Yet "change pitcher" was a particularly apt term for him because, in his amateur days in New York, he was the first to throw the change of pace, or "dew drop," as it was known then. Wright noticed that even the fastest pitchers, like Jim Creighton of the Brooklyn Excelsiors, would sometimes get shelled in the later innings as the batsmen were able to time the uninterrupted succession of fastballs. (Although the pitching rules of the day required a straight-armed, underhand delivery—like that of a cricket bowler, which Wright on occasion had been—men like Creighton were able to generate considerable speed by adding an illegal, though scarcely perceptible, wrist snap to the release.)

On June 14, 1870, in the most publicized game to that time, the Reds finally met defeat as the Brooklyn Atlantics scored three runs in the bottom of the eleventh inning to win 8–7. Their in-

Harry Wright, father of relief pitching. (*Courtesy The Baseball Hall of Fame*)

vincibility punctured, the Reds went on to lose a few more games after that; as their 1870 tour progressed, they played to more and more empty seats. In the off-season the club directors publicly decried the "enormous" payroll and announced that an 1871 tour would be impossible. This stance was only intended to drive down the players' salary demands, but instead it drove the players out of Cincinnati to other cities where the fever for professional baseball had taken hold. Five Reds starters went to Washington, while the Wright brothers, first baseman Charlie Gould, and right fielder Cal McVey went to Boston.

In their first year with Harry Wright at the helm, the Boston Red Stockings finished third in the pennant race of the newly formed National Association. Al Spalding, whom Wright spirited from the Forest Citys of Rockford, Illinois, was the team's starter in each game that year, and only twice was he dispatched to center field to trade places with Harry Wright. In 1872, the first of four straight Boston championships, Wright again relieved Spalding twice. In 1873, Wright, now thirty-eight years old, tried his hand at pitching for the last time, making three appearances.

In three years, seven relief performances—that's two weeks' work for the fireman of today, but more appearances than any other rescue man of his day. The substitution rule that prevailed in Wright's day inhibited the use of relievers and shaped attitudes toward the relief pitcher to such an extent that even after free substitution was permitted in 1891, managers were still loath to pull a starter.

The year of Wright's final turn in the box also marked the debut of an individual who, under Wright's guidance, would later become major-league baseball's first bona fide relief pitcher. His name was Jack Manning.

A native of Braintree, Massachusetts, Manning had attracted Wright's attention while playing with the Boston Juniors, an amateur nine that served as an informal farm club for the Red Stockings. Boston first-baseman Gould, who had come over from Cincinnati in 1871, retired to go into the sporting goods business. The nineteen-year-old Manning was elevated from the Juniors to replace him (salary: $800 a year). However, he hit only .260 and was compelled to share the position with another first-year Red Stocking, Orator Jim O'Rourke. At the end of the season, Manning called it quits.

Wright convinced him to return by promising him playing time with the Lord Baltimores, to whom he "lent" Manning for one season only, as he had lent Cal McVey to them the previous season. This seeming generosity was negated as Wright then raided

Jack Manning, major-league baseball's first outstanding relief pitcher. (*Courtesy The Baseball Hall of Fame*)

Baltimore of its best hitter, George Hall—Harry Wright exacted stiff payment for his loans. Thus weakened on balance, Baltimore won only nine of its 47 games and dropped out of the National Association before the end of the year.* Manning, however, got plenty of action at three infield positions—not first base, which was now reoccupied by Charlie Gould—and as a pitcher.

Wright could not have asked for a finer finishing school for his raw recruit. He knew his own pitching days were over, and

---

* Wright's use of Baltimore as a farm club is reminiscent of the Yankees' relationship with Kansas City in the fifties.

that he needed a change pitcher he could rely on. In 1874, while Manning was learning his trade with Baltimore, Al Spalding pitched every inning of every game Boston played, going 52–18. Wright felt Spalding would need some help in 1875, and he was counting on the strong-armed Manning.

On Boston's opening day of 1875, Manning was the right fielder, as he was through most of the season; he also took to the box 17 times, most of these as a starter. With Boston roaring to the flag with a 71–8 record, 15 games in front, Wright saw little need for relief.

Eighteen seventy-six was another matter. The National Association disbanded in a shambles, with only seven of its 13 teams able to complete the 1875 schedule. From its ashes emerged the eight-team National League. Harry Wright's Boston team, renamed the Red Caps, lost its battery of Al Spalding and Deacon White, plus its league-leading hitter, Ross Barnes, to Chicago, which swept to the pennant while Boston fell to fourth. While Spalding was toying with the league's batsmen, Wright scrambled to assemble a pitching staff from an unlikely bunch of candidates. Joe Borden, alias Joe Josephs, threw the first two no-hitters on record, yet before the season was over he was made the stadium grounds keeper; Foghorn Bradley lasted through season's end, but was not invited back for 1877; brief trials were allotted to former N.A. star Dick McBride (0–4 in four starts) and the inappropriately named Tricky Nichols, who in 1875 had logged a record of 4–28. Clearly, this was a crew in need of relief.

And Manning supplied it. Fourteen times he trudged in from the outfield as the "saver," as the press dubbed him; on one occasion he alternated every two innings with starter Joe Borden.* If this total sounds puny, note that Boston played only 70 games; relieving in one fifth of a team's games in the post-1900 era would mean 31 or 32 games, a total not attained by any reliever until 1913. Manning posted four relief wins and five saves (applying today's standards to yesterday's box scores). In 40 innings of relief, Manning compiled an earned-run average of 0.68 and did not suffer a loss. His five saves were not surpassed for 29 years, and his relief-point total held as the unofficial record until 1908.

Manning's accomplishments are remarkable because, achieved in the pre-relief era, they stood for more than a decade after

---

* On June 17, 1876, Boston's Borden and Cincinnati's Cherokee Fisher became the major leagues' first relief pitchers. Borden replaced starter Jack Manning after two frames of a 12–8 loss to St. Louis. Borden moved from right field to the box, trading positions with Manning. Fisher replaced Reds' starter Amos Booth, also in the third inning and also in a losing cause, against Philadelphia. Booth replaced Fisher at shortstop.

the restrictive substitution rule was abolished. As another measure of Manning's accomplishment, consider that the saves total for the entire National League in 1878 was *one*.

Manning also started 20 games in 1876, compiling an overall record of 18–5 with an ERA of 2.14. It was a magnificent year, yet by August a Beantown newspaper, commenting on Wright's continuing search for pitching help, observed that Manning "was still around with Boston but no longer considered a potential pitcher." In 1877, he wasn't even around with Boston. Despite being in the second year of a three-year contract, Manning was once again lent out to a franchise in trouble—the Cincinnati Reds, who under the leadership of (yes, again) Charlie Gould had finished dead last in 1876 with a record of 9–56.

Manning was the opening-day shortstop of the Porkopolitans, as they were named by the press and their few admirers. By season's end, Manning had played five positions, including ten games in the box. He notched only one save for the last-place Reds, and was smacked around resoundingly, allowing 83 hits in only 44 innings of work. Whatever magic Harry Wright had worked on Manning in 1876 was lost forever. As Lindy McDaniel was to say a century later, a fireman cannot be successful without "a manager who understands relief pitching."

As his contract stipulated, Manning returned to Boston in 1878 and opened the season in right field. He later was given a start and won it, and he relieved twice. His ERA of 14.29 told Manning his pitching days were over, but he did continue in the big leagues as an outfielder through 1886, with three minor-league sabbaticals along the way. He reunited with Harry Wright at Philadelphia in 1884.

Wright and Manning combined to give relief pitchers a place in baseball strategy long before they had their own place in the ball park. The bullpen is a development of the early 1900s. (Prior to 1891, a reliever came in from a position on the field.) The term *bullpen* is persistently and mistakenly said to derive from the Bull Durham tobacco signs ("Hit this sign and win $50") that adorned outfield fences in the days before World War I. Relief pitchers would warm up beneath these signs and behind the section of the outfield roped off for standing-room-only overflow patrons—thus, goes the argument, the name bullpen. If the sign had promoted Camel cigarettes or Murads or Lady Fatimas, would the term *bullpen* still have been used?

Yes. As baseball historian Lee Allen pointed out, the Bull Durham sign was not in evidence at major-league parks until 1909, while the term *bullpen,* signifying the foul areas in back of first and third bases, was in use as early as 1877. On May 4 of that year, the Cincinnati *Enquirer* frowned on the practice some clubs followed of admitting latecomers to the park for less than the league's standard admission of fifty cents—"for ten cents or three for a quarter, herding them in like bulls within a rope area in foul territory, adjoining the outfield." This simile no doubt has its basis in two earlier usages of the word *bullpen*—as a prison enclosure, primarily an open-air improvised demarcation; and as a "schoolboys' ball game, played by two groups, one group outlining the sides of a square enclosure, called the *bullpen*, within which are the opposing players" (*The Oxford English Dictionary*). The ball game, popular on the Ohio-Indiana-Kentucky frontier of the 1850s, is first mentioned in print in Edward Eggleston's homespun classic *The Hoosier Schoolmaster* (1871): "He could not throw well enough to make his mark in that famous Western game of bull-pen." Both senses of the word—the prison enclosure and the ball game—imply enforced occupancy in the bullpen, which reflects the status of the substitute pitcher in the pre-relief era.

As Appendix D details, from 1876 through 1904, starters completed over 90 percent of their games and saves were registered in only 1.3 percent of all games played. Relief pitchers were used so seldom that in 1902 the *Reach Guide,* in a statistical review of the past season, offered a category *Pitching Knock-Outs of 1901,* and identified three Milwaukee Brewers who set the pace with six dismissals from the box.

But the figures for the years preceding 1891 are even more astounding by the standards of today, when starters finish barely one game in five. From 1885 to 1888, big-league starters completed 97.8 percent of all games, and the number of saves totaled by the two major leagues in that period is 48, only 10 more than Detroit's John Hiller collected in 1973. In eight different years, the league leader(s) in saves had a total of one; three times an entire *league* produced one save.

In the days before free substitution, two names besides Manning's stick out: John Montgomery Ward and Tony Mullane. Ward was a superb athlete who, in his 17-year career, played numerous games at every position except catcher and first base. In separate seasons, he batted .369, stole 111 bases, won 47 games, and pitched a perfect game. Added to those accomplishments, which earned him a plaque in Cooperstown, he twice led the N.L. in saves and three times in relief wins, and in 1879–1880 he allowed only four earned runs in 65 innings of relief duty.

Tony Mullane was a formidable hurler indeed, and the most prolific reliever of his day. In 13 years in the big leagues, he won 285 games, copping 30 or more in five straight seasons. He topped

Monte Ward, the man who could do everything

his circuit in relief wins three times and saves five, in the process becoming the first man to appear in 50 relief games over his career. His five saves in 1889 equaled Jack Manning's mark. Like Ward, Mullane was an excellent athlete, playing every position except catcher.

Mullane was nicknamed "Count" and "The Apollo of the Box" because of his dandified appearance and legion of female admirers. Management noticed that an extraordinary number of women were in attendance on the days Mullane was scheduled to pitch, and in response created the venerable institution of Ladies' Day.

Born in Cork, Ireland, the Count was the only ambidextrous pitcher in baseball history. In 1881, as a rookie with the Detroit Wolverines in the National League, the Count entered a pregame field meet. Although he won the throwing contest with a heave of 416 feet, 7¾ inches, he was left with a limp, useless right arm. Not wanting to miss a turn in the box, Mullane switched to the port side for the remainder of the season. He hurled without particular distinction, but he did complete every game he started as a lefty. His right arm recovered for the 1882 campaign, but he continued to offer left-handed serves to some lefty batters in succeeding years. No manager had to play the percentages with Tony. Also, his ambidexterity gave him a devastating pick-off move (most of his career took place before pitchers used a fielder's glove).

In addition, Mullane had an itch to travel. He played for five teams in his first five years and was slapped with a one-year suspension for signing too many contracts for the same season. While with Toledo in 1884—then a major-league franchise—he formed a battery with Fleet Walker, the first black big leaguer (Jackie Robinson was the fourth).

As mentioned earlier, the change pitcher was legislated into limbo in 1891, when rulesmakers formalized the practice of free substitution that had been creeping into the game by gentlemen's agreement for at least two years. It was not until 1892, however, that someone realized that the new policy permitted the use of pinch hitters, whose employment means work for relief pitchers.

The year 1891 was highlighted by the relief performances of three outstanding pitchers: Bill Hutchison, Kid Nichols, and Clark Griffith. "Wild Bill" Hutchison was not a rip-snortin' hell raiser out of the West but a graduate of the Norwich Free Academy and Yale University, Class of 1880. Pitching for Cap Anson's Chicagoans, the 5-feet-9 right-hander appeared in relief eight times,

Tony Mullane, "The Apollo of the Box" and the game's only ambidextrous hurler. (*Courtesy The Baseball Hall of Fame*)

Kid Nichols in uniform for Omaha, his last minor-league stop before coming to Boston in 1890. (*Courtesy The Baseball Hall of Fame*)

and eight times he got the job done. He won seven, a new high, and saved one to go with a 36–19 log as a starter.

Wild Bill led the White Stockings to a second-place finish behind Boston, which was paced by the sensational twenty-one-year-old Kid Nichols. Besides winning 30 games for the first of what proved to be seven straight years, the 145-pound Nichols had the most saves in the N.L., a feat he repeated three more times. The Hall of Famer used one pitch, the fastball, and one motion, straight overhand, to win 360 games. (In 1884, the rulesmakers had finally abandoned the stricture against over-the-waist throwing, which had not been enforced for some time.) The keys to Nichols's success were two: He was the first to throw a fastball that jumped, and he changed speeds constantly, without altering his delivery.

Making his big-league debut in 1891, Clark Griffith also notched seven wins in relief. He led in relief wins two more times, the last in 1905, when he was manager of the American League entry in New York, the Highlanders. As managers, Griffith and his crosstown nemesis, John McGraw, were the two men who lifted relief pitching to a prominence in baseball strategy. But more on that in the next chapter.

Griffith was called "The Old Fox" before his thirtieth birthday; the sobriquet was a tribute to his cunning on the mound. As Cy Young said of him in later years, Griffith "was what I call a dinky-dinky pitcher. He didn't have anything, but he had a lot of nothing, if you know what I mean." That "nothing" produced a record of 242–131. Griffith relied on a fast-revolving sinker or "slip pitch," as it would be called today, learned from Hoss Radbourn; a screw-ball, which Griffith said he invented; the "quick pitch," another of his innovations; "shadowing" the ball, or hiding it in the plane of his body until the last instant, as Luis Tiant does today; and cutting the ball with his spikes to provide greater friction and thus a more explosive drop to his sinker. (Oddly, when trick deliveries such as the spitball, emery ball, shine ball, and so forth were banned in 1920, Griffith was at the head of the legislative crusade.)

At the turn of the century, two all-time great hurlers renowned for their endurance as starters put their talents to relief work as well. Iron Man Joe McGinnity led *both* leagues in games pitched seven times in eight years (1900–1907, excluding 1902). He came by his nickname because he had been a foundry worker, though it came to express perfectly his indomitability on the mound. Stocky Joe led his league in relief wins four times and saves three times. His most outstanding year was 1904, when in seven relief appearances he saved five and won two, while amassing an overall record of 35-8.

McGinnity was an underhand pitcher, or submariner, whose knuckles would almost scrape the ground as he delivered his specialty, the raise curve. As he once said, the raise curve or upshoot "is the heritage of the old days of pitching—when no curves were known—combined with the outcurve of the present day." He credited invention of the pitch to Billy Rhines of Cincinnati, but others have cited Bobby Mathews, who starred in the National Associa-

Clark Griffith. Himself a successful reliever, The Old Fox was the first manager to make full use of his bullpen.

tion. McGinnity's raise ball created an optical illusion, he explained; the batter "finds it almost out of the question to estimate its speed, and generally hits under it, lifting the ball into the air for an easy out." Most firemen have been sinkerballers whose aim was to get a ground ball, but there have been several other submariners who pitched well in relief, most recently Ted Abernathy.

Denton True "Cy" Young earned his nickname as a youngster for his cyclonic speed. As Honus Wagner said of him, "Johnson and Rusie were one as fast as the other, but Young was faster than both of them." He also had two great curveballs, Wagner added, one of the wide-breaking sort and the other the late-breaking "nickel curve," today known as the slider. But Young's greatest asset over the long haul—22 years, 511 victories—may have been his control, for he allowed less than 1.5 walks per nine innings.

Like McGinnity, Young never suffered from a sore arm and needed only a dozen pitches to get warm, for a start or for a turn out of the pen. He won seven games in relief in 1895, leading the N.L. and falling one short of the record set by his teammate Nig Cuppy two years earlier. He also led in saves in 1896, and in 1905 repeated as the relief-win champ. But it was a relief win in 1904 that stood at the center of one of the greatest pitching feats of all time.

On April 25 of that year, in Philadelphia, the thirty-seven-year-old Young and his Red Sox lost to Rube Waddell of the A's, 2–0; he permitted no hits in the last three innings after a leadoff double in the sixth. On April 30, Young relieved starter George Winter in the third, with none out and two on; he hurled seven hitless relief innings for the 4–1 win. On May 5, in a rematch with Waddell, the Cyclone threw a perfect game, bringing his hitless streak to 18 innings. Finally, on May 11, he breezed through the first six innings against Detroit before allowing a hit after one man had gone down in the seventh. He had pitched 25⅓ consecutive innings without allowing a hit, a record that still stands, three quarters of a century later.

We ought not to leave the pre-relief era without calling off a few of that period's fabulous names—relief pitchers of differing degrees of distinction whose mellifluous cognomens are so evocative of the times in which they played: Oyster Burns, Phenomenal Smith, Bones Ely, Adonis Terry, Pop Corkhill, Patsy Flaherty, Pink Hawley, Stump Weidman, Silver King. Except for the wonderful name Vida Blue, they just don't make them like that anymore.

# 4

# The Early Firemen: 1905-1923

By the first decade of the twentieth century the rules had been refined, most of the strategies had been devised, and except for the equipment, the game very much resembled the one played today. While relief pitching was not widely regarded as a specialty, the challenge was still there for the man sauntering in from the bullpen in a tight spot. A starter would generally be allowed to work his way out of a jam he had created, but a few managers, blessed with a top-flighter who was a real workhorse, would not hesitate to use him to bail out one of the lesser starters. Bringing in a McGinnity, a Young, an Ed Walsh, or a Three-Finger Brown to protect a late-inning lead was an irresistible temptation. But this was also the era which produced the first relief specialists.

Since 1891, the complete-game ratio had settled at the 85 percent level. Nothing portended more activity for the bullpen. Indeed, in 1904 complete-game percentages in the leagues were 89 and 90 percent, up from the norm that had seemed to be established. What happened in 1905 to account for the sudden drop of ten points in the American League and seven in the National? Two managers—Clark Griffith and John McGraw—and one entirely obscure relief pitcher, Claude Elliott.

As the century opened, Griffith was the dean of the Chicago Cubs' pitching staff, and his best years were behind him. When

Charles Comiskey offered him the pilot's post of the American League's new Chicago franchise, Griffith became the first N.L. star to jump to the junior circuit.

In 1903, when the American League shifted its anemic Baltimore club to New York, league president Ban Johnson asked Griffith to leave Chicago, where he had won a pennant, and become field boss of the Highlanders. The Old Fox agreed. He continued to take his turn on the hill, too, winning 14 games. But the next year, Griff appeared in only 16 games as Jack Chesbro (41 wins) and Jack Powell (23) carried the team to within one celebrated wild pitch of the pennant.

However, in 1905 Chesbro and Powell felt the effects of the 845 innings they had put in the previous year. Neither had the stamina to go nine as frequently as he had before, and Griffith was forced to go to the bullpen as no manager had ever done. His 1904 staff had completed 123 games; in 1905 its total was 88. Griffith himself was the team's best reliever, also topping the American League in relief games, wins, and ERA.

Griffith's strategy born of desperation could not keep the Highlanders from falling to the second division, but it paid off in 1906. Once again, in his use of the hook Griffith "seemed to be the most energetic in the American League," reported the *Reach Annual.* "He removed 65 pitchers, and benched himself on one occasion." The Highlanders regained their second-place perch, finishing three games back of the White Sox.

The Old Fox left New York in 1908, capping a long feud with the owners, but his experience there left him with a lasting appreciation of the bullpen. After three fairly dismal years at the helm in Cincinnati, in 1912 Griffith came to Washington to stay. Calvin Griffith recalled his uncle's earliest days there, before The Old Fox retired from the field to the front office in 1920: "It was always Mr. Griffith's idea to have men in the bullpen who didn't start regularly." Thus The Old Fox and his appointed managers went on to develop such outstanding early firemen as Allan Russell, Fred Marberry, Garland Braxton, and Jack Russell. To highlight the tactical revolution that Griffith wrought, his Highlanders of 1904 had the fewest complete games in the majors with 123; only four years later, that total would have topped all others.

When Griffith died in 1955, his obituary in *The New York Times* stated that he had had "two pet dislikes in his lifetime. One was John McGraw and the other was the New York Yankees." Griff neither forgot nor forgave the meddling and backbiting of Highlanders owners Frank Farrell and Bill Devery when he was manager. Nor did he forget the day in 1894 when, tiring rapidly on the hill in the ninth, he had been driven to near exhaustion by Baltimore Oriole John McGraw. The Little Napoleon, in the last year in which a foul tip was not counted a strike, deliberately fouled off pitch after pitch for five minutes. Griffith somehow held on to win the game, but the memory of his tormentor stayed with him.

As manager of the Giants, McGraw further irritated Griffith in 1903 by denigrating the quality of the Highlanders and the American League—after having stripped the Highlanders of their best players. In 1902, it was McGraw who had been Ban Johnson's designate to bring American League baseball to the Big Apple. But McGraw grew impatient with Johnson's procrastination and made a deal with the Giants whereby he would pack off his Baltimore stars to the Polo Grounds and assume the helm there himself.

John McGraw learned his attacking, aggressive style of play as the third baseman of the Baltimore Orioles, that scourge of the baseball world in the 1890s. McGraw was good enough at the hot corner and with the stick to have made the Hall of Fame had he never managed a day; his batting average over 16 years was .334, with a high of .391.

Oriole pilot Ned Hanlon's academy of baseballology produced five managers who among them won 22 pennants—Hughie Jennings, Wilbert Robinson, Kid Gleason, Fielder Jones (a product of Hanlon's Brooklyn years), and McGraw, the greatest manager of them all. Joseph Shaner wrote in the Baltimore *Home News:* "Foxy Ned was baseball's catalyst, refining the game and sending forth disciples to preach his gospel across the land." Part of that gospel was a willingness to go to the bullpen, as demonstrated by Hanlon's championship Brooklyn nines of 1899–1900; contrary to the trend that only faltering teams gave steady employment to relief pitchers, Hanlon's Superbas led the National League in saves each year while registering the fewest complete games.

McGraw followed that lead when he took the helm of the New York Giants in 1902. His pitching staff led the N.L. in saves in each of the next seven years, at first relying on starters Joe McGinnity, Christy Mathewson, and Hooks Wiltse, later breaking in relief specialists Claude Elliott, Cecil Ferguson, and Otis Crandall. (McGraw's Giants also led the league in saves seven of the eight years 1917–1924.)

Claude Elliott came to the majors with the Reds in 1904, winning three of four decisions, one of them a shutout. Despite his creditable record, he was passed on to New York, where he pitched only three games, losing two. Five of his twelve appearances in the season were in relief, yet he did not register a win or a save.

Claude Elliott, baseball's first relief specialist. (*Courtesy The Baseball Hall of Fame*)

The 6-feet-1, 190-pound right-hander had a major-league cup of coffee in 1904, and in truth little more than that in 1905, when he unobtrusively surpassed the mark for saves that Jack Manning had set before Elliott was born.

Claude pitched only ten games for Mr. McGraw in 1905, of which two were route-going starts. The other eight outings were as rescue pitcher—the preferred appellation at the time—and Elliott proved up to the task. Though he neither won nor lost, he saved six games and, in 25 innings of relief work, notched a respectable ERA of 2.88. Yet when 1906 rolled around, Elliott was gone, never to pitch in the big time again. Like the man whose record he surpassed, Claude Elliott was a comet, shining brightly but briefly.

The next year, McGraw's casting call brought forth another

relief hopeful, Cecil Ferguson. Again he obtained excellent results: In 21 relief chores, the most in the league, the nineteen-year-old rookie won one, lost none, and, like Elliott, saved six. What's more, his only start yielded a shutout. Yet McGraw called on Ferguson less frequently in 1907, and traded him to the Braves before the 1908 season. McGraw was looking for a young pitcher with nerve and a rubber arm whom he could make into a full-time fireman, and he would soon find his man.

In 1906, the big news in baseball was that the "second city," Chicago, produced two first-place teams while New York had to content itself with two bridesmaids. Frank Chance's Cubs stormed to the flag with a record of 116–36, which remains the best ever, and Fielder Jones's White Sox copped the A.L. flag despite batting .230 and collecting only six home runs. The World Series produced perhaps the greatest upset in baseball history, as the "hitless wonders" beat the powerful Cubs in six games. In Game Five, palmball artist Doc White registered the first postseason save with two and two-third innings of one-hit ball, then came back next day to wrap up the conquest with a complete-game win.

The victorious starter in Game One, Nick Altrock, had led the A.L. with seven relief wins—one of them earned without throwing a single pitch! Summoned to the mound in the top of the ninth with the Sox trailing by one, the bases loaded, and two out, Altrock's first and only heave picked the runner off first base and turned back the threat. When Chicago rallied for two runs in its final turn at bat, Altrock emerged with one of the queerest wins in baseball history.

In the next few seasons, the windy city continued to supply much of the story in relief pitching. Three-Finger Brown of the Cubs, a great starter, was high in the N.L. in saves four straight years (1908–1911), while Ed Walsh of the White Sox topped the A.L. in saves four of five years (1908, 1910–1912).

Mordecai Peter Centennial Brown's nickname derived from a boyhood run-in with a feed chopper that left him without an index finger on his right hand and with a middle finger bent at right angles at the first joint. This handicap proved a blessing when he became a pitcher, for it imparted a peculiar rotation to his ball that caused it to break sharper and sink more abruptly than any curve seen to that time. From contemporary descriptions of it, Brown's "hook curve" seems to have acted much like today's popular forkball.

Brown and Christy Mathewson were the two top N.L. pitchers in the first decade of the century. In no year from 1907 through 1910 did either pitcher permit so much as two earned runs per

Three-Finger Brown, a great starter whose 18 relief points in 1911 remained the National League high for two decades. (*George Brace Photo*)

game nor win fewer than 20 games. In head-to-head competition, Brown at one point took nine straight, but the final count stood at only 13–11 in his favor. Never did the Indiana miner gain a more important decision over his rival than in the final game of the 1908 season, on which the pennant rode. This game was a replay of the famous "Merkle boner" game of two weeks earlier, in which the young Giant, in the custom of the day, neglected to run from first base all the way to second after the "winning" run had scored from third on a single. As the Giant fans swarmed across the Polo Grounds field in jubilation, Cub second-baseman Johnny Evers retrieved the ball, or *a* ball, and stepped on second for a force-out. None in the throng paid him any mind, except the umpire, Hank O'Day. He ruled that the game was still tied, but because of the flood of humanity, could not be resumed. The league declared the game no contest; Cub followers had hoped for a 9–0 forfeit. When the clubs ended the season deadlocked for first, baseball's first play-off was scheduled, as a one-game affair rather than a three-of-five at the request of the injury-racked Giants.

The play-off, or replay, rematched the original starters— Mathewson for the Giants, Jack "The Giant Killer" Pfiester for the Cubs. But in the first inning, Pfiester belied his nickname, retiring only one of the first five batters (another was caught stealing). Three-Finger Brown, who had appeared in 14 of the previous 19 games, was summoned from the bullpen. He got out of the inning without further scoring and breezed the rest of the way as the Cubs solved Matty's fadeaway for four third-inning runs. It was Brown's fourth relief win among 29 that season, his personal high.

"Big Six," as Matty was called after the famous nineteenth-century fire engine, had an even better year, though he came up short at the end. He led the National League in wins (37), ERA (1.43), games, starts, completions, innings, strikeouts, shutouts (12), and saves (a tie with Brown). The hardest earned of these saves came in a game against, naturally, the Cubs. The N.Y. starter, twenty-year-old rookie Otis Crandall (not yet transformed into a fireman), entered the ninth with a four-run margin. Mathewson had warmed up earlier when Crandall was on the ropes, but now felt certain of the outcome and headed for the showers. Then the Cubs began to pound Crandall anew. Although he was able to retire two men, that last out was beyond him. With two runs in and a man on base, McGraw signaled for Matty. When word reached McGraw that Mathewson was trying to retrieve the far-flung elements of his uniform, the skipper instructed the infield to stall for time. At last the umpire would brook no further delay,

Ed Walsh. The workhorse spitballer became the first to pitch 100 contests in relief. (*George Brace Photo*)

and McGraw was forced to bring in Joe McGinnity, who had just got up in the bullpen. His first pitch was smacked for a run-scoring hit, and the potential winning run was coming to the plate. At this point a disheveled Mathewson appeared at the clubhouse gate in center field and was urgently waved onto the field. Three fadeaways later, Cub batter Del Howard was fanned out and the Giants and Crandall had their win.

On the south side of Chicago, Three-Finger Brown's opposite number was handsome Ed Walsh of the White Sox. Like Brown, Walsh had played semipro ball at off moments from his occupation as a miner. And like Brown and Matty, in the period 1907–1910 his ERA never ascended to the 2.00 mark, and he too enjoyed his finest year in 1908. He led the American League in wins (39), strikeouts (269), shutouts (12), games, starts, completions, and saves. His 11 relief points—seven saves, four wins—broke Jack Manning's 32-year-old record (and was in turn shattered in 1911 by Brown, with 18).

Walsh was primarily a spitballer, whose lifetime ERA of 1.82 may never be equaled. His bread-and-butter pitch was unusual because it didn't float to the plate as other spitters did; it revolved five or six times. With his sidearm-underhand motion, by turning his fingers up and his thumb down at the moment of release, he could make the ball jump, which no other spitballer could do.

The principle behind the wet one, as described by one of its top exponents, Jack Chesbro, is that by keeping the moistened side of the ball out, toward the batter, "the air piles up denser . . . than against a dry surface, and the spitball gains its effectiveness that way." Invention of the pitch is generally attributed to Elmer Stricklett, who broke into the majors with Walsh on the 1904 White Sox. But baseball historian Francis Richter, writing in 1920, credited Bobby Mathews with throwing a spitter as far back as 1868.

Walsh's fabulous record before his arm went bad in 1913 was as much a tribute to his prodigious strength and endurance as it was to his baffling spitter. From 1907 to 1912, he led the A.L. in games five times, starts three times, and saves four times. Midway through the 1912 season, he became the first to pitch 100 games in relief over his career.

Two weeks after Walsh hit the 100 mark, so did Otis "Doc" Crandall of the Giants. McGraw had drafted the Indiana farm boy from Cedar Rapids of the Three-I League in 1907—not for his record, which was an unimpressive 6–7, but out of sheer sentiment. The Little Napoleon had played in Cedar Rapids himself in 1891, and was always grateful to its management for his midseason sale to the majors. Built along the lines of Mike Marshall at 5 feet 10 and 180 pounds, Crandall made the Giant squad in 1908 as a starter, splitting 24 decisions. McGraw liked the laconic youngster's composure in pressure situations and his ability to produce ground balls with his "outcurve." The next year, Crandall was converted to primarily relief work.

After two disappointments with Elliott and Ferguson, McGraw had found his man. The young right-hander made 22 trips from

Otis Crandall, the doctor of sick ball games. (*Courtesy The Baseball Hall of Fame*)

the bullpen in 1909, tops in the N.L., going 5–1 with four saves. His work over the next four years made him a star and earned him the nickname "Doc." "Crandall is the Giants' ambulance corps," Damon Runyon rhapsodized in the New York *American*. "He is first aid to the injured. He is the physician of the pitching emergency . . . without an equal as an extinguisher of batting rallies and run riots. . . . He is the greatest relief pitcher in baseball."

It was Crandall's heroics in 1910 that inspired Runyon to such figurative flights. He won seven games in relief against only one loss and added four saves (overall record: 17–4). The press also made much of the fact that he surpassed Al Spalding's 1875 record as "All-American Pitcher." This competition, which has since sunk into oblivion, was based on an amalgam of pitching, fielding, and batting percentages that signified little about a pitcher's ability. (To wit: Spadling's won-lost percentage was .919, fielding .859, batting .318—thus 2,096 "All-American" points; Crandall's figures were .810 on the mound, .984 in the field, .342 at the plate—total 2,126 points.) All-American or not, the good doctor was certainly an outstanding hitter for a pitcher. His lifetime batting average was .285, and he frequently was used as a pinch hitter.

Crandall was even better in 1911 with seven won, none lost, and five saves. In Game Five of the World Series that year, Crandall entered in the eighth inning with the Giants trailing 3–1. He hit a ninth-inning double to drive in a run, then scored the game-tying run, and pitched scoreless ball until the Giants could win it for him in the tenth. His star began to dim a bit in 1912, but still he topped the N.L. in relief wins for the third straight year.

The next season marked the fourth consecutive time he led in rescue calls, but it also marked his departure from New York—twice. As the *Reach Guide* reported, Doc was "transferred to the St. Louis [Cardinals] as part consideration for catcher McLean, but the deal caused so much dissatisfaction in New York that the New York club quickly repurchased him," after only two appearances in a Cardinal uniform. However, when 1914 rolled around, Crandall was on the west bank of the Mississippi again, this time with the St. Louis entry in the newly formed Federal League. His glory days over, he continued to pitch in the Pacific Coast League until 1929.

In 1913, when Crandall was asked to put out the fire 32 times to establish a new high, relief pitching was advancing on other fronts too. Charley Hall (born Carlos Clolo) also crossed the 30 barrier for the Red Sox; Larry Cheney took the torch from departed Cub teammate Three-Finger Brown and notched a league-high 11 saves; and Connie Mack made firemen of his two best starters, Eddie Plank and Chief Bender. Because of the season-long illness of Jack Coombs, who had won 79 games for him in the previous three years, Mack had no choice but to lean on young hurlers Joe Bush, Bob Shawkey, Byron Houck, and Boardwalk Brown—up to a point. He left them on the mound until the seventh or eighth inning, when he would send in one of the veterans to safeguard or gain the victory. Despite preseason predictions that without Coombs the Mackmen would be hard-pressed to match their third-place finish of 1912, the A's swept to the World Championship—with fewer complete games and more saves than any other team.

Mack, looking back on more than 60 years in major-league baseball, considered Bender "the greatest one-game pitcher, the greatest money pitcher baseball has ever known." In 1913, the curveballing Minnesota Chippewa pitched 26 games in relief against only 22 starts, winning six as a fireman and saving 12 more, equaling Brown's record for relief points.

In 1914, twenty-two-year-old Hub "Dutch" Leonard enjoyed a remarkable season. He won 18, lost 5, and posted an ERA of 1.01, the lowest ever recorded by a starter. The Boston lefty also tied for the American League saves lead with four, but it was a relief victory he notched that year that deserves mention. On July 20, Fritz Coumbe started for the Sox against Detroit, and carried a 2–0 lead into the ninth. However, he was smacked for the tying runs before he could retire a batter, and Leonard was called in to stem the tide. He did, and the game wore on into extra innings. By the time the Sox pushed a run over for the win, Leonard had hurled eight frames of relief, without allowing a hit.

The 1915 season was marked by two great relief performances, both in the National League. For Tom Hughes, a former Highlander rescued from the minor-league scrap pile by the Boston Braves, the entire season was covered with glory. He appeared in 50 games, winning 20. His 25 starts produced a mediocre 10 wins against 14 losses, but as a fireman Hughes was 10–0, a new record, with an ERA of 1.34. The next year he "fell off" to a relief log of 9–2, and soon fell out of the big leagues for good.

George "Zip" Zabel's flirtation with fame was even briefer. Although he pitched effectively in his two full seasons with the Cubs, he is remembered today, if at all, for what he did on June 17, 1915. In the first inning at West Side Park (the Chicago Whales of the Federal League were using the park that was later to be known as Wrigley Field), Cub starter Bert Humphries was struck on the pitching hand by a liner off the bat of Dodger Zack Wheat. Unable to continue, Humphries turned the ball over to Zabel with two men

Ernie Shore. He relieved roommate Babe Ruth and hurled a perfect game. (*Courtesy The Baseball Hall of Fame*)

down and one run in. Eighteen and one-third innings later, the winning pitcher was—Zip Zabel. In the longest relief stint ever, Zip's "sweeping curve" and "corking fastball," a contemporary account states, held the Dodgers to two unearned runs and only nine hits. Like so many of the relievers before and after him, Zabel had the career of a mayfly: Next year, he was gone.

In 1917 we come to what must rank as *the* greatest single-game relief performance of all time. On June 23 at Boston's Fenway Park, in the first game of a twin bill with the Washington Senators, Red Sox starter Babe Ruth walked lead-off batter Ray Morgan. The Bambino took exception to umpire Brick Owen's call of ball four and charged off the mound. Catcher Pinch Thomas tried to head Ruth off at the pass, but Ruth shoved him to one side and slugged the umpire. Thomas was ejected along with the Babe, according to the custom of the day. A new battery was brought in: catching, Sam Agnew, and pitching, Ruth's roommate, Ernie Shore.

Shore was not a reliever by trade—this was to be one of only two bullpen calls that year. Perhaps he developed a distaste for bullpen duty after his major-league debut with McGraw's Giants in 1912. In that late-season tryout, the twenty-one-year-old Shore was allowed to pitch the ninth inning of what was shaping up as a lopsided Giant win. Shore did protect the huge lead, but only just: He allowed eight hits, one walk, and ten runs (only three were earned). This outing earned Shore a ticket to the International League, whence he emerged again two years later. Owner Jack Dunn of the Baltimore Orioles sold his two top pitchers, Shore and Ruth, to the Red Sox on the same day.

While Shore was pitching to the second Washington batter, Morgan broke for second. Agnew's throw cut him down. The next 26 batters went down in order. In a statistical oddity, reliever Shore pitched a complete game, and the ultimate one at that. Shore's perfect game is one of only 11 ever pitched in the majors.

In that same year, Cincinnati's Hod Eller closed out a relief win over the Giants with a flourish—he fanned the side on nine pitches. Also in 1917, "Dauntless Dave" Danforth, inventor of the shine ball, became the first to relieve 40 times in a single season, helping the Sox to a World Championship. His fine work as a fireman led manager Pants Rowland to pencil him in for more starts in 1918, with a horrifying result: no wins and ten losses in 13 starts. Danforth's slide from favor gave fuel to the argument that even the best reliever is simply a pitcher not good enough to take a place in the rotation.

The early twenties witnessed the first great long-relief performances in World Series competition. The 1921 classic matched the Giants and the Yankees in their first postseason appearance. (This was not, however, the first "Subway Series," for the Yanks were at this time the Giants' tenants at the Polo Grounds.) Some of the luster of the confrontation rubbed off when an injured Babe Ruth was forced to the bench for the last three games, all Giant wins. But this Series belonged to the pitchers anyway. The Yanks' Waite Hoyt pitched three complete games without permitting an earned run, virtually duplicating Christy Mathewson's heroics in the 1905 World Series, when he threw three straight shutouts. And the Giants' Jesse Barnes won Games Three and Six in long relief.

Barnes, the Giants' fourth starter during the regular season, was called in to replace starter Fred Toney in the third inning after the Yanks had rattled him for four runs without a man being retired. Barnes went the rest of the way, fanning seven and allowing only four hits. In Game Six, Toney didn't make it out of the first frame, getting blasted for three scores. Barnes again took him off the hook, fanning ten and once more permitting only four safeties. Jesse Barnes became the first reliever to win two games in a World Series, and one of only five ever to accomplish the feat.

The 1923 World Series again brought together the Yanks and Giants, this time in the "house that Ruth built," Yankee Stadium. John McGraw's surprise choice for the opening game start was Mule Watson, a midseason pickup from the Braves who had gone 8–5 for New York. His serves afforded no surprise to the Yanks, however, and he was yanked for a pinch hitter in the top of the third as the Giants rallied for four tying runs.

Rosy Ryan, who had won Game One of the 1922 World Series in relief, was called upon to repeat himself. And he did, allotting only one run the rest of the way and emerging victorious on Casey Stengel's ninth-inning, inside-the-park home run.

Ryan had been no slouch during the regular season, forming one half of a redoubtable bullpen duo with Claude Jonnard. In both 1922 and 1923, Ryan topped the N.L. in relief wins while Jonnard was high in saves. Unlike Ryan, who started 35 games over that span, Jonnard was a true specialist, relieving in all but one of 78 contests.

Over in the American League, Clark Griffith's Washington Senators were developing their first full-time fireman, veteran spitballer Allan Russell. Like the one-eyed Jonnard, Russell had had to overcome a severe physical handicap. In 1920 he suffered a blood clot in the brain, the result of an earlier beaning, which left his right side paralyzed for five weeks. But he recovered completely and resumed pitching for the Red Sox the following year.

The rawboned right-hander had relied on the spitball from the time he broke in with the 1915 Yankees. Thus when the rulesmakers banned the wet one in 1920, Russell was one of 17 men permitted to use the pitch the rest of their careers. (Interestingly, Rosy Ryan was also a pre-1920 spitballer, but John McGraw failed to designate him as such—no doubt deliberately—leaving Ryan no choice but to develop a curve, which proved the making of his career.) A poor 1922 season prompted the Red Sox to outright Russell to his native Baltimore, where Jack Dunn turned a tidy profit by selling

Allan Russell. The most active reliever before Marberry, he was the first to relieve 200 times.

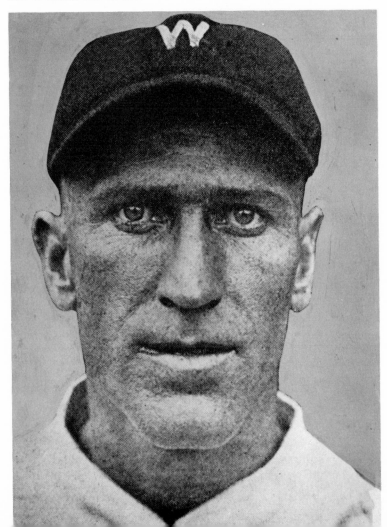

that last-second hop on the ball would produce pop-up after pop-up.

Though Marberry was strictly a power pitcher in his early years, his strikeout ratio does not compare with that of today's firemen. This is more a reflection of how batting styles have changed than of Marberry's speed. Bucky Harris said Marberry's ball was so "heavy" that it would "knock the bats out of their hands." Just as Ryne Duren would later throw his first warm-up pitch on the fly to the screen behind home plate to intimidate the hitters, Marberry and Muddy Ruel had their warm-up ritual. Ruel would allow each pitch to strike his glove square in the pocket, producing a pop that could be heard throughout the stadium, and he would stagger back a bit with each impact, exaggerating the power of a pitch that was plenty fast without embellishment.

Marberry saved a record 15 games in 1924, three of them coming on successive days in Cleveland when he threw a combined total of five pitches. It was not always this simple, however. In a game against the Yankees, said Marberry, "I warmed up in every one of the first eight innings. Trouble was always brewing, and I had to be ready. In the eighth inning I was called upon to go in and finish the game. I might just as well have pitched the whole game. I was doing it in the bullpen, anyway."

The 1924 Senators took the A.L. pennant by two games over the Yankees, who had won it the previous three years. Washington's Walter Johnson was the league's top starter and won the Most Valuable Player Award, yet St. Louis Browns' star George Sisler insisted that Marberry was the team's MVP, and he was not alone in that view. Marberry was, after all, the only notable addition to a 1923 squad that had finished under .500.

In the World Series that year, Griffith's men were pitted against the New York Giants, still led by his old enemy, John McGraw. The Giants were making their fourth straight appearance in post-season play and were substantial favorites.

New York broke on top by smacking Walter Johnson for 14 hits in the opener, but the Senators squared accounts in Game Two. Washington's Tom Zachary took a 3–1 lead into the ninth, but allowed the New Yorkers to tie the score before Marberry came in to get the final out of the inning. When Roger Peckinpaugh drove in the winning run in the bottom of the frame, the official scorer awarded the victory to Zachary; Marberry had to wait 45 years to be credited with a save.

Firpo started and lost Game Three, lasting only three rocky innings. In Game Four he pitched the final one and two-thirds to save the win for George Mogridge, but sat idly as Walter Johnson absorbed another pounding in Game Five. Zachary equalized the Series with a complete-game victory in Game Six, and the season came down to one game, in which Marberry would figure large.

Despite having lost two games in as many tries, Walter Johnson was the sentimental choice to start the final game. Perhaps the greatest pitcher the game has ever seen, "Old Barney" had labored 18 years for the Senators before getting into a World Series, and this might be his last chance for a postseason win. Clark Griffith and Bucky Harris wanted to give Johnson one more outing, but they had devised a master plan to outwit John McGraw, a plan in which no Washington starter could possibly pick up the win.

The Giant batter whom Griffith and Harris least wanted to face in the late innings was Bill Terry, the young first baseman who had hit .500 through the first six games. McGraw had platooned Terry with Irish Meusel, sitting Terry down in Games Two, Four, and Six when lefties Zachary and Mogridge started for Washington. Meusel would go to the outfield and George Kelly would move from the outfield to first. Zachary had gone all the way in Game Six and could not be tapped for Game Seven. Mogridge could not be relied upon to go nine; if he was given the start and had to be pulled in the late innings, Terry would undoubtedly be called upon to hit when the game was on the line—Washington had no lefty in the bullpen.

The "surprise" choice to start Game Seven was right-hander Curly Ogden, who had not pitched at all in the first six games of the Series. As Harris had hoped, Terry was installed in the starting lineup. Ogden faced two batters, walking one and striking out the other. He was then excused for the day, and Mogridge took the mound. He pitched scoreless ball through the fifth inning, as the Senators took a 1–0 lead. Twice he faced Terry, and twice he sent him back to the bench.

In the sixth, however, the Giants broke through for three runs. In the midst of the rally, McGraw yanked Terry for pinch-hitter Irish Meusel. With Terry out of the way, Harris called on the right-handed Marberry to hold the fort. Firpo permitted one unearned run as he recorded all three outs in that sixth inning, but threw goose eggs in the seventh and eighth to keep his team within striking distance. And strike they did, with the aid of Dame Fortune. In the bottom of the eighth, with two men on, Harris hit a routine grounder to third, which struck a pebble and bounced over Fred Lindstrom's head for a hit. The tying runs crossed the plate.

Marberry had been replaced by a pinch hitter in that rally, and now Harris could give Walter Johnson a chance to win. Old Barney struggled through four frames of constant trouble before a pair of improbable events brought the Senators their first, and only, championship. Leading off in the bottom of the twelfth, Muddy Ruel lifted a foul pop behind home plate. Giant catcher Hank Gowdy tripped over his mask and watched the ball drop to earth. Thus reprieved, Ruel responded with a two-bagger. Johnson was retired without advancing Ruel to third, but Earl McNeely followed with a grounder to third that *again* found a pebble, or *the* pebble, and bounded into left field to end the Series. John McGraw had been beaten in what turned out to be his last World Series.

Washington breezed in to repeat as A.L. champs in 1925 while the Yanks nose-dived to seventh place. And Marberry was even better than he had been in 1924. His games total increased from 50 to 55, but what is more significant is that those 55 appearances all came in relief, whereas in 1924 he had made 15 starts. He again recorded 15 saves, but lifted his relief wins to eight, and finished 39 contests to set a new high-water mark.

Yet in the World Series against the Pirates, Firpo saw action in only two contests, saving Game Three with two shutout innings and pitching one third of an inning in Game Five. Bucky Harris took a lot of heat for underutilizing his relief ace, particularly in the memorably soggy Game Seven. Walter Johnson, who had pitched brilliantly to win Games One and Four, was left in all the way, dissipating leads of 4–0, 5–3, and 7–6, ultimately losing 9–7. Pittsburgh, which allowed only seven hits to the Senators, used four pitchers while Harris let Johnson take a 15-hit pounding. Asked by league president Ban Johnson why he stuck with Walter so long, Harris replied, "I went down with my best."

In 1926, as if to make up for sticking his head in the sand in the 1925 Series, Harris called on Marberry 64 times, all but five appearances coming in relief. Firpo responded with the best season of his career, posting 22 saves and 9 relief wins. His 31 relief points would not be surpassed until Joe Page blew past him with 40 in 1949.

In his first three full years with Washington, Marberry had worked in 169 games, throwing smoke all the way. Fearful of Firpo's collapse, Clark Griffith fortified his bullpen with left-handed screwballer Garland Braxton, a Yankee discard. In 1927, Braxton and Marberry combined to make 102 trips from the bullpen, yet together accounted for only the same number of saves logged by Marberry alone the previous year. Firpo's so-so 1928 was highlighted by a 6–4 record in 11 starts. He was beginning to develop a curveball and a change of pace, weapons necessary to the continued survival of a pitcher nearing his thirtieth birthday.

When Bucky Harris was fired in 1929, new manager Walter Johnson couldn't make up his mind whether to use Marberry in relief or in the rotation. "A regular pitcher is always an important man on your club," Johnson said. "But I still think the most important one can be a relief pitcher. That's specially so with a relief pitcher as good as Marberry." So Old Barney gave Firpo 26 starts, in which he won 16 and lost 8, and called him for late-inning help 23 times, in which he won 3 and compiled a league-leading 11 saves. All in all, Firpo worked 250 innings; his ERA of 3.06 was second behind that of Lefty Grove, and compared quite favorably with the league average of 4.24.

After that kind of year, Marberry decided that he preferred starting. "Relief pitching is a job for a young pitcher," he said. "His arm can stand the wear and tear of uncertain work. . . . In my own case, I feel that I have earned the right to a change. I've certainly had my share of relief work. I do it now, when called upon. But I have deliberately changed into a regular." He continued to rely on his fastball, though it had slowed down a bit, but he learned how to use off-speed pitches to set up his out pitch. The result in 1930 was a record as a starter of 15–2, followed by a 13–3 record as a regular the next season.

In 1932, Firpo had one last fling as a fireman, answering the call to the bullpen 39 times and once again leading the A.L. in saves. It was also his last full year with Washington. Walter Johnson was let go as manager, and Marberry was traded to Detroit, where Bucky Harris awaited him. Detroit was a young team on the edge of greatness, and already had Chief Hogsett in the bullpen. Harris used Marberry as a starter, and he responded by going 16–11.

The next season, Detroit went to the head of the class in the American League, but Bucky Harris was not around to take part in the festivities, having been dumped with two games to go in the previous campaign. For new manager Mickey Cochrane, Marberry split his time between the rotation and the pen, putting together another fine mark of 15–5. However, he got lit up for four runs in two thirds of an inning's work in the Series opener.

Firpo pitched five games for the 1935 Tigers before a bad arm led to his release. He was offered a chance to become an American League umpire without a minor-league training period—the requirements were an easygoing nature and impressive physical stature, and Firpo fit the bill on both scores. He leaped at the chance to don the blue. He had had a good life in baseball, and he wasn't quite ready to return to his six-hundred-acre spread back in Texas. Being an umpire, he thought, would keep him involved with the game he loved and with the men who played it.

But the lot of the arbiter is not a happy one, he soon discovered —he quit after only a few games, saying, "It's too lonely for me. I like to be around the players and have companionship." That need to be one of the guys explains, as much as anything else, his attempt to come back as a pitcher in 1936. He was invited to spring training by Bill Terry, manager of the N.Y. Giants, around whom had swirled the managerial derring-do of the 1924 World Series. "Marberry talked with me in Chicago," said Terry, "and asked me to give him a chance. He said his arm was OK again and he was sure he could help me." Marberry's arm was indeed OK, but simply past its prime. He went north with the club in April, but was released after pitching in only one National League game.

He hooked on with Dallas, where he showed a spark of his old flame. He asked Clark Griffith for a job. Griffith had brought Bucky Harris back to manage in 1935, and Harris had an enduring respect for Marberry's temperament and ability. When the thirty-seven-year-old veteran signed on with the Senators, he said, "Mr. Griffith will never have to fire me. The moment I think I'm through as a pitcher I'll walk up to him and tell him." After five games, one of them a start, Marberry handed in his uniform. He went home to Texas.

From 1937 through 1941, he continued to pitch for and manage the Dallas and Forth Worth teams, as well as putting in some time with Toledo. He also managed one year after he hung up his glove for good.

Nineteen forty-two was Marberry's last year in professional baseball. After that he went into business in Mexia, Texas, where he had played his first pro ball in 1921, and where he was to pass away in 1976.

6

# The
# Ten Best:
# Murphy

One other reliever of pre-World War II days takes a spot on the
ten-man honor roll: Johnny Murphy of the Yankees. As dominant a
figure as Fred Marberry was in the 1920s, Murphy was no less
paramount a relief pitcher in the late thirties and early forties.
Though not the classic workhorse type of fireman—he never appeared in more than 40 games—he topped the American League
in relief wins six times and in saves four times. In each of the seven
years 1937–1943, he led his league in saves or wins or both—an unparalleled record of consistency among relief pitchers. And pitching
for the Bronx Bombers, he had many opportunities to shine in postseason play. Murphy pitched in six World Series, and in each one
registered either a win or a save, sustaining no losses.

New York born and bred, Johnny Murphy was the object of
Yankee attentions from the time he was a shoolboy star at Fordham Prep. Like Marberry, he was a big lad, 6 feet 2 and 190
pounds, but unlike him relied on the curveball. The Yanks had to
bide their time, for Johnny enrolled at Fordham University, and
stayed on to get his Bachelor of Arts in 1929 at the age of twenty-
one. He did not want to sign with the Yanks and cut short his eligibility to pitch for Fordham, but on the morning before his final
start for the Rams, against arch-rival New York University, he
inked a contract put before him by superscout Paul Krichell. Then
he went on to beat the Violets. Were N.Y.U. inclined to protest

the outcome of that game, played 50 years ago, it would be upheld.

Actually, Murphy had jeopardized his collegiate athletic career the summer before when, under the name of "McNamara," he had pitched professionally for Scottdale in the Mid-Atlantic League. But this kind of under-the-table summer payout had been a tradition with college boys for decades. Eddie Collins, Christy Mathewson, Lou Gehrig, Jim Thorpe—all had played for pay under assumed names while in college; only Thorpe had been penalized (the International Olympics Committee stripped him of the medals he won at the Stockholm Games of 1912).

Johnny Murphy. Grandma was a curveballer and dominated his profession for a decade.

After graduation, Murphy joined Albany in the Eastern League, where he was impressive enough to warrant promotion the following year to St. Paul in the American Association. There he gave up 246 hits in only 195 innings and compiled a stratospheric ERA of 5.68; only the fact that he won more games than he lost kept him from demotion. He was not cuffed about so severely in 1931, but he still permitted more hits than innings pitched, a bad sign in any league.

It is often the case that curveball and off-speed pitchers are less a mystery to inferior hitters than they would be in the majors, where everyone is a "fastball hitter." Besides, the Yankees were impatient to see whether their investment would pan out; Murphy was old to be working his way up through the minors. He was promoted to New York's top farm club, the Newark Bears, for 1932. Although his record there was only 6–7, he did allow fewer hits than innings pitched.

At the end of the year, Murphy was summoned to New York for his major-league initiation. And it was quite a hazing he got, being rapped for seven hits and seven runs in only three innings' work. Back to Newark for 1933.

There and then he became a relief pitcher—and a winner. At the start of the season, Murphy failed to complete his first three starts. Manager Al Mamaux moved him to the bullpen, where he found a home. In one string of 20 relief appearances, he allowed not a single score. In one week during that skein, he shut the door on the opposition six times.

"How did I become a relief pitcher?" Murphy said to an interviewer in later years. "Well, it all came through a sore arm. When I was with Newark I caught cold swimming in the South [spring training]. Al Mamaux refused to wait until I really was ready. In that way I got the relief pitching habit. I am as strong physically as anyone else. I think I have enough stuff to go nine innings. But I will admit there is a circumstance which perhaps has a lot to do with my being more suited to relief than starting. I pitch so many curves. It seems that if you keep curving they finally get to you in the late innings."

In 1934, Murphy went south with the big club, ticketed for Joe McCarthy's bullpen. Wilcy Moore, the Yanks' busiest fireman in 1933, had retired and new blood was needed if the boys from the Bronx were to improve on their second-place finish of the previous year. The word from Mamaux was that Murphy was good for seven innings, tops. Yet when the season opened and young starters Johnny Allen and Russ Van Atta were forced to the sidelines with injuries, Murphy stepped in to start 20 contests and complete half of them. His rookie season was an outstanding one as he went 14–10 with an ERA of 3.13, third in the American League.

He also added four saves, one of them decidedly weird. On September 7, in the bottom of the ninth inning at Chicago, the White Sox drove starter Red Ruffing to the showers. He had given out three straight singles, producing one tally and leaving Jimmy Dykes, the tying run, on second, and Marty Hopkins, the winning run, on first. Murphy was called in to pitch to Charley Uhlir, a local semipro just signed on by the last-place Sox. Hitting for the pitcher, Uhlir was appointed to bunt the tying run to third and the winning run to second. He offered at Murphy's first pitch and missed, and Yankee catcher Art Jorgens picked Dykes off second. Three pitches later, Uhlir struck out and Hopkins was doubled up trying to steal second. The inning and the game were over, and Murphy had recorded three outs while throwing only four balls to one batter.

Although he threw an average fastball and could change speeds a bit, Murphy relied very heavily on his out pitch, and only a few great ones got by that way for long. He had fared well enough for one season, but McCarthy suspected that Murphy's success as a starter would be short-lived. Equally important, with Murphy thrown into the starting rotation in 1934, that had left no one to pick up the slack caused by Moore's departure. Although the Yanks had managed another second-place finish, more of the burden had fallen on the team's top starters, Ruffing and Lefty Gomez. McCarthy knew he had to lighten their load in 1935.

In the spring of that year, McCarthy asked Murphy how he'd feel about being a full-time fireman. It was a difficult question. Murphy knew that it didn't really matter how he felt, if McCarthy was convinced that the bullpen was where he belonged. But all the rewards—the glamour and the money—accrued to the starters. Despite the feats Marberry and Moore had performed while leading their teams to pennants, few teams had come around to the idea that a top-flighter in the bullpen was worth as much to the team as an ace starter. But McCarthy *was* a subscriber to that idea and convinced Murphy that he would come to enjoy the bullpen.

Several years later, after Murphy had become the top reliever in baseball, he was asked whether he was content to remain in the bullpen. "Yes, I am," he responded, "but I don't know how I'd feel about it if I had to go to another club. On the Yankees they appreciate the necessity, the value of relief pitching. McCarthy repeatedly has told me that he rates me on a par with any of his starting hurlers. I am paid the starters' scale. I am happy."

His performance in 1935, when he led the league in relief wins, made the Yankees happy. Although they again ended up one rung from the top of the ladder, they had found the man who would secure their bullpen for the glory years to come, in which they would take the pennant seven of eight years, and capture the World Series six times.

Nineteen thirty-six was the only year between 1935 and 1943 in which Murphy did not lead the A.L. in either wins or saves. However, it was the year of his first World Series appearance, the game that Murphy would always call his biggest. Through the first five games of the Series with Bill Terry's Giants, Murphy had sunned himself in the bullpen. On the two occasions when Yankee starters required relief, the call went out to Pat Malone, who had been the number-one fireman all year. But in Game Six, when Lefty Gomez blew up in the seventh inning, it was Murphy who was ordered to clean up the mess.

"El Goofo" had been sailing along with the 5–2 lead his teammates had given him in the fourth. He gave back a run in the fifth, but retired the Giants without further ado in the sixth. Nine outs stood between the Yankees and the World Championship, their first without Babe Ruth, and their first with Joe DiMaggio. But Gomez ran out of gas. Dick Bartell greeted him with a double, then scored on Terry's single. DiMag bobbled the ball in center, and Terry advanced to second. Hank Leiber, in a mysterious bit of strategy, sacrificed Terry to third. N.L. home-run king Mel Ott was the next batter, and he represented the tying run. Playing percentage, McCarthy left Gomez in to face the left-handed slugger. But when Ott went to first on a free pass, Marse Joe walked out to the mound and waved for Murphy.

"Grandma," as Murphy had come to be called by his teammates for his fussy, fastidious manner, took the ball from his manager and began manicuring the mound, as was his habit. Once all the rough spots were made smooth and the smooth spots made rough, Grandma set to work. He induced Sam Leslie, pinch-hitting for catcher Gus Mancuso, to hit a foul pop, which pinned Terry to third base. He then walked Jimmy Ripple, hitting for second-basemen Burgess Whitehead, to load the sacks. The lead run was now in scoring position. From his perch on third base, Bill Terry then reached into his managerial bag of tricks for a third pinch hitter, one-time Yankee shortstop Mark Koenig. Batting for Travis

Jackson, Koenig fanned, and the crisis was past. The Yanks scored seven runs in the top of the ninth, and took the Series in style.

In 1937, Fireman Johnny won 12 games in relief and saved ten more as the Yanks blasted past all opposition for their second straight pennant. Several of his ten saves came in rescue of Lefty Gomez, who credited his success to "clean living, a fast outfield, and Johnny Murphy." Another Gomez tribute to his rescuer came in response to a reporter who inquired about his health: "How I feel isn't important. The important thing is how Murphy feels." The two-headed pitcher named Gomez-Murphy had an offspring 25 years later in the tandem of Whitey Ford and Luis Arroyo.

The next year, Murphy was high among relievers in *both* wins and saves for the first time in his career. In 1939, he hit a personal high of 19 saves. Success followed upon success, both for Murphy and the Bronx Bombers. What is remarkable about Murphy's wins and saves during this great period is that he was pitching an average of only 35 games a year—not once in his 13 years in the big leagues did he ever lead the fireman's fraternity in appearances. McCarthy, who termed Murphy his "pennant insurance," hardly ever called for Murphy unless the Yanks were within one run of the lead. Look at the record for 1941: Murphy's 35 appearances yielded 15 saves, eight wins, and three losses; in only nine games did he not affect the outcome.

That 1941 campaign may have been Grandma's finest. In addition to the accomplishments given above, he recorded his best ERA, 1.98, and pitched two hitless innings to win the key game of the World Series against Brooklyn. That was the famous fourth game when Dodger catcher Mickey Owen dropped the third strike that, had it been held, would have evened up the Series. Instead, the Yanks scored four runs with two outs and the dispirited Dodgers began their long lament of "wait till next year." Murphy added to his laurels by pitching four scoreless innings in Game Two, which the Dodgers won.

The only thing that put a halt to Murphy's dominance of American League relief pitching was World War II. He had had a fine 1943 season, winning 12, losing only four, and notching eight saves. In 68 innings, the thirty-five-year-old hurler permitted a scant 44 hits; he gave no evidence of giving in to Father Time. Yet in 1944 he voluntarily retired from the game to do defense work, and baseball bade farewell to the greatest fireman of his day.

The farewell proved premature. Once the war was over, the now thirty-seven-year-old Murphy began to get the itch again and asked the Yankees to restore him to the active list. He pitched well for them in 1946, though not to his previous standard; he was released the following April. He had won 73 games in relief for New York, still an A.L. record for one team, and had become the second man to log 100 lifetime saves. The Red Sox took him on for one last tour of duty in 1947, and he gave them 32 turns in relief, with no won-lost record and three saves. He was not hit hard—a 2.80 ERA and only 41 hits in 55 innings—but he lost his ability to get the ball over the plate. He walked 28 men while fanning only nine, and as Joe McCarthy said in the last of his *Ten Commandments of Baseball*: "A pitcher who hasn't control hasn't anything." It was time to hang 'em up for good.

The Red Sox organization hired Murphy as its director of minor-league operations, a post he held until 1961, when he was swept out by a new front-office broom. He hooked on with the embryonic New York Mets in that same year, becoming chief scout for a team that had yet to play a game. In 1964, the Mets elevated him to vice-president, and in 1967 to general manager.

Thus, 20 years after his retirement from active duty, Johnny Murphy was to take on a rescue job that made his work on the mound seem like a piece of cake—the transformation of a team that was a bad joke into Champions of the World two years later. His astute trades and patient shepherding of the youngsters whose signing he had engineered earned him the honor of Major League Executive of the Year.

Regrettably, Johnny Murphy did not have long to savor his accomplishment. On December 30, 1969, he suffered a heart attack in his Bronxville home, and two weeks later he fell victim to a second coronary while in hospital recuperating from the first.

Murphy's death notice in *The New York Times* termed him "the game's first fully glamorized relief pitcher." If glamour attached itself to Murphy, it was not for a flamboyant manner; he was a quiet, subdued man off the field and was content to let his pitching speak for him on the field. Publicity surrounded his achievements more than it had Firpo Marberry's because Murphy excelled in the media capital, and because his team was in the national eye almost every October.

Was he a better relief pitcher than Marberry? Even at his very best, he probably should be rated a notch below the Marberry of 1924–1926. But Murphy was the best there was for nearly a decade, while Marberry shuttled between the bullpen and the starting rotation throughout his career. Marberry the more brilliant, Murphy the more consistent—it's a toss-up which one was "better." What's certain is that neither can be denied a spot on the relief pitchers' honor roll.

# 7
# The
# Advance Slows:
# 1924-1946

Marberry and Murphy, both relief pitchers almost from the start of their careers, were the exception during this extended period of transition. Earlier, most successful relief pitchers were starters doing extra duty as gamesavers; the full-time denizens of the pen were second-raters doing mopup chores. After Marberry blazed a trail in 1924, other teams followed by appointing their own relief specialists. But these men were, as a rule, (1) veteran starters of suspect stamina; or (2) experienced starters down on their luck; or (3) youngsters fresh from the farm, looking for a chance to show their stuff. In short, the bullpen was manned by rejects and, in the lingering practice of an earlier day, starters working overtime.

Of course there were exceptions like Murphy and Mace Brown, and many a reject from the rotation found, to his surprise, that he was more valuable as a rescuer than he could have hoped to be as a starter. The remarkable performances of these rejects and retreads set the stage for relief pitching to boom in the years after World War II, when every contending team called on its fireman 50 to 60 times a year, and found him absolutely indispensable in World Series play.

From 1924 to 1946 the use of relievers reached a plateau after the dramatic increase in the preceding era. A dry spell in the mid-1930s carried over into World War II, when few teams could muster enough able bodies to put a top pitcher in the pen. As Dan Daniel wrote in 1942, "Relief pitching [is] . . . one of the departments of major-league baseball which is not moving ahead. Not so long ago the two circuits boasted a flock of emergency specialists. [Today] about 90 percent of our relievers are slingers with no particular aptitudes for that type of work." Complete-game percentages, which had dipped from the 90 percent level of 1904 to 50 percent in 1923, declined only to 45 percent by 1937, and were virtually unchanged over the next ten years. The percentage of games in which a save was recorded also varied little from 1937 to 1946.

Yet when the stars came back from the armed forces, the firemen resumed their advance. Complete games fell off steeply, and saves rose in the same fashion. By 1948, major-league starters were completing only 36.5 percent of their games. Nearly 13 percent of all games were highlighted by a save, twice as many as in 1923.

Nineteen twenty-four was dominated by the record-shattering performance of Fred Marberry, as were the next two years. While Firpo was piling up annual saves totals of 15, 15, and 22, the leaders over in the N.L. notched six, five, and six—the kind of figures that had topped the league two decades earlier. The senior circuit's failure to develop a crop of relief specialists until the late thirties may bear upon the National League's decline during these years. The Nationals continued to be viewed as the inferior league through the 1950s, much as the American League suffers in comparison today.

In 1925, the St. Louis Browns' Elam Vangilder became the first American Leaguer to gain 10 or more relief wins in a season. A typical fireman of this period, Vangilder was a starter fallen on hard times. He had won 35 games for the Browns in 1922–1923, in the latter year posting the third best ERA in the American League. But his ERA ballooned to nearly 6.00 in 1924, and he was cast aside to the bullpen, where he was handed a mop and bucket. In 1925, used as a gamesaver, Vangilder protected a lead six times in addition to his 11 wins.

Vangilder's relief-win total was matched two seasons later by thirty-six-year-old Hooks Dauss, converted to relief for his fifteenth and final season with the Tigers. Dauss represents the second type of pitcher used as a fireman in the era.

The third type, the minor leaguer trying to make it, was well illustrated in 1925 by Joe Pate. After six seasons with the Fort Worth Panthers of the Texas League, during which time he had won an impressive 159 games, Pate won a place in the bullpen of the Philadelphia A's. Though the rookie went 9–0 with six saves, Mr. Mack did not install him in the rotation in 1926. The bullpen comet fizzled and was back in the bushes in 1927.

The fourth type of fireman, the starter doing double duty, was the vestige of a custom that dated back to 1891, when the free-substitution rule was enacted. Guy Bush of the Cubs, Pirates, and Braves was used in this way throughout his long career. He led the National League in relief wins or saves in four separate years (1925, 1926, 1929, 1935), and in none of these years did he start fewer than 15 games. In his 17 years in the N.L., he started over 300 games and relieved in more than 200; the secret to his ability to fulfill the demands of relief pitching, he says, was that while "some pitchers take 15 or more minutes to warm up," he "could warm up on about ten pitches and do a good job." And it was quite a job The Mississippi Mudcat did, winning 43 and losing only 20 in relief, giving him the second-best won-lost ratio of all rescue men.

Nineteen twenty-six was highlighted for the National League by a starter's dramatic relief performance in Game Seven of the World Series. For the $4,000 waiver price, Grover Cleveland Alexander had come over to the St. Louis Cardinals from the Chicago Cubs in midseason, following a difference of opinion with Cubs' manager Joe McCarthy on the subject of discipline. The thirty-nine-year-old Alexander helped the Cards win a hotly contested pennant race and was brilliant in the World Series.

In Game Two, "Old Pete" evened the Series by utterly stifling the Yankees: He allowed only four hits, fanned ten, and retired the last 21 men in succession. In Game Six, he again squared accounts with a complete-game win. Alex began Game Seven snoozing in the bullpen—sleeping off a hangover, some have said—while Jess Haines took the hill for the Cards. The Redbirds scored three unearned runs in the fourth, providing Haines with a two-run cushion that he nursed into the sixth, when the Yankees halved the deficit.

But it was in the next inning that Haines and the Cards truly teetered on the brink. A blister that had been forming on the middle finger of Haines's pitching hand throughout the game was giving him ever more trouble. He walked Earle Combs, the first batter of the inning. Mark Koenig laid down a sacrifice bunt. Next came Babe Ruth, who had already hit four home runs in the Series. Haines issued him an intentional pass. The Cards won a momentary reprieve as Bob Meusel forced Ruth at second, leaving runners at first and third for Lou Gehrig. Haines gave Gehrig a highly unintentional pass, and the sacks were full for

Tony Lazzeri, the rookie second baseman who had sent 114 runs across the plate in the regular season.

Manager Rogers Hornsby walked to the mound from his second-base position to check on Haines's condition. He saw right away that the blister had opened and was bleeding. The call went to the bullpen, where Flint Rhem and Art Reinhart had been throwing. But the figure who sauntered to the mound was neither of these—it was Alexander the Great, who had pitched nine innings just the day before.

His first toss to Lazzeri was off the mark; the next one caught the outside corner. Alex's third pitch bisected the plate, and

Grover Alexander. His relief role in the deciding game of the 1926 World Series is an all-time high point of the fall classic.

Lazzeri ripped a line drive into the left-field stands—foul by a yard. Now ahead on the count, Methuselah could toy with the rookie, and he did. A low, outside curve tantalized the over-anxious Tony, who swung and missed. The climax past, the Yankees went down without a hit in their remaining two tries at Alexander, and the Cardinals were World Champions.

One year later, the "Murderers' Row" Yankees swept to the flag by a whopping 19 games and won the World Series in four

Wilcy Moore. His baffling sinker produced one of the finest years any reliever has ever enjoyed—his rookie season, 1927.

straight. The team was virtually the same one that had barely clawed its way to the top of the A.L. in 1926, except for the addition of a thirty-year-old rookie fireman named Wilcy Moore. A dirt farmer from Hollis, Oklahoma, Moore had been kicking around the low minors since 1921, when he broke in with Paris of the Texas-Oklahoma League. Other stops along the way to the majors were Fort Worth, Ardmore, Okmulgee, and Greenville. It was in 1925 with Greenville, South Carolina, that Moore's pitching arm was fractured by a batted ball. When he returned to the hill later in that season, his wrist still hurt each time he released the ball. In an attempt to relieve the strain, Wilcy dropped down to a sidearm delivery which, to his surprise, gave him a natural sinker that he hadn't possessed before.

Back with Greenville in 1926, he lost his first start, then won his next 17. Relying exclusively on his sinking fastball, he went on to post a mark of 30–4, which attracted the attention of the Yankee front office. Although no New York scout had ever seen him pitch, the Yanks bought his contract on the assumption that any man who goes 30–4, even in the South Atlantic League, must have something to offer.

Did he ever! The elderly freshman took A.L. relief honors with 13 wins and an equal number of saves, against only three losses. All in all, in 38 rescue jobs and 12 starts, Wilcy was 19–8, with an ERA of 2.28. Capping off that remarkable debut season, he saved Game One and started, completed, and won Game Four of the World Series, completing the sweep of the Pirates.

His effectiveness dropped off considerably after that, although he enjoyed sporadic success through the 1933 campaign. In later years Moore was to claim that overwork in 1927 had put a practical end to his career. Indeed, as the Yankees squared off against the Cards in the 1928 rematch of their World Series thriller of two years back, Moore was not with the team. The arm miseries that had hampered him throughout the season finally forced him to the sidelines in late September, when his name was withdrawn from the roster of players eligible for postseason play.

The Yankees did not blast past their A.L. opposition in 1928 as they had in 1927. The Philadelphia A's, in second place in both years, narrowed the gap from 19 games back to only two and a half. Unable to rely on Moore to put out the late-inning fires, manager Miller Huggins turned to his starter Waite Hoyt—only twenty-eight years old, yet in his eleventh year in the big time— to bail him out. "As the A's were close behind us in September," Hoyt recalls, "I was asked to relieve and work in regular turn also. Which I did"—to the tune of a league-high eight saves as well as two wins in his 11 trips from the bullpen, most of them in the final month. Overall, he finished 23–7. "I thought I had an outside chance at MVP," Hoyt says, "but the nominators chose Mickey Cochrane one month before the season closed."

Hoyt's record as a starter tailed badly after that grueling regimen of 1928. He played with five teams in three years before being converted to a fireman by the Pirates in 1933, with outstanding results. "When I signed with Pittsburgh," he remarks, "it was on a trial basis and as I was getting older the Pittsburgh management followed the tendency of the day to consider older pitchers best for relief work, based on their years of pitching experience." Hoyt led N.L. firemen in relief wins in 1934 and 1935.

In 1929, Connie Mack's A's demonstrated that turnabout is fair play, as they raced to the flag by 18 games over the second-place Yanks. In the Series against Chicago, Mack held his top starter, Lefty Grove, out of the starting rotation, ostensibly because he feared the Cubs' right-handed power.

After winning the opener, the A's moved out to an early 6–0 lead in Game Two. But when George Earnshaw yielded three scores in the fifth inning, speedballer Grove was called in to put out the fire. He got the final out of the inning and hurled scoreless ball the rest of the way, fanning six. Under the rules of the day, the official scorer was permitted to, and did, give Earnshaw the win despite his not having completed five frames. In the famous fourth game of the Series, the A's rallied from 8–0 to tally ten runs in the seventh. Grove then came in to nail the lid on the coffin with two innings of hitless flamethrowing, fanning four batters. A fireballing fireman if ever there was one, Grove altogether fanned ten Cubs in his six and two-thirds shutout innings.

Two other hurlers with those 1929 A's also made their mark on relief-pitching history—Eddie Rommel and Jack Quinn. Rommel had been used as both starter and reliever from the time he broke in with the A's in 1920. He relied almost exclusively on the finger-tip knuckleball he had learned in 1917, for fear that his spitter would be banned before he could reach the majors. His mentor was the man who claimed to have invented the pitch, his teammate in the Blue Ridge League, Charles Druery. Druery's knuckler was thrown in the same fashion as today's pitchers throw the butterfly ball. (The earlier variety of knuckleball—for which the top joints of the middle three fingers gripped the ball—was first thrown with success by Detroit's Ed Summers in 1908–1912.)

Rommel had won as many as 27 games for the A's (1922); he had led the A.L. in relief wins three times; and his won-lost ~~rcentage~~ in relief is third best of all time. But in the history of relief pitching, Rommel is assured immortality because of an outing on July 10, 1932.

On that day, a Sunday, the A's arrived in Cleveland to play a single game with the Indians; Sunday ball was still taboo in Philly. To cut down on expenses for these one-game trips, Mack would bring only enough players to take the field, plus a few subs. On this occasion he took only two pitchers: Lew Krausse and Rommel.

Eddie had pitched three innings on Saturday and two on Friday, so he didn't figure to see action at all this Sunday. He threw batting practice, then sat down for what he thought would be the rest of the afternoon. But Krausse got ripped for four hits and three runs in the first frame, and Mack sent a surprised Rommel in to open up the second. Seventeen innings later, in a score at once close and grotesque, the exhausted veteran went to the clubhouse with an 18–17 victory. It was to be the last big-league game he would ever win.

Rommel allowed 29 hits, 9 walks, and 14 runs. Cleveland's shortstop Johnny Burnett got 9 of those hits, setting a record. Of the 14 scores Rommel permitted, 12 came during regulation play—once he got into extra innings, he was all right.

Lusty as the Indian bats were, the A's had nothing to be ashamed about for their day's work at the plate. To Cleveland's 33 hits they added 25 of their own (three by Rommel), and Jimmy Foxx connected for a trio of home runs.

One month later, on August 14, 1932, John Picus Quinn, born John Quinn Picus, won a game in relief for the Brooklyn Dodgers. What made this event remarkable was that he had just celebrated his forty-eighth birthday, thus becoming the oldest man to win a major-league game. In his forty-eighth year, the spitballing Pennsylvania coal miner led the N.L. in saves, as he had the previous year. Asked why he was still pitching at his age, Quinn laconically replied, "A wife and six kids."

Jack Quinn pitched his last major-league game for the Reds in 1933, just after he turned forty-nine, but he continued to play minor-league ball into the 1935 season—his thirty-fourth as a pro. This was the man who in 1912, after four years with the New York Highlanders, had been returned to the minors as "too old"!

The 1933 World Series rematched the Giants and the Senators, the protagonists of the 1924 epic. The casts were different. John McGraw had handed over the reins to Bill Terry midway through the prior year. Bucky Harris had been deposed after the 1928 season, and Clark Griffith had just given the heave-ho to Walter Johnson in favor of another boy manager, his shortstop and son-in-law, Joe Cronin. Each team was a surprise pennant winner, and each had its league's top fireman in the bullpen: for the Giants, the veteran of 18 big-league seasons, Dolf Luque; for the Senators, the retreaded starter Jack Russell.

"Lucky" Luque, the "Pride of Havana," had topped the National League with 27 wins a decade earlier. Now, at age forty-three and in his second year as the Giants' stopper, the diminutive Cuban had been the N.L.'s leader in relief wins. Bullpen mate Hi Bell led in saves, to duplicate the tandem accomplishment of Giants Rosy Ryan and Claude Jonnard ten years back.

Jack Russell had come to Washington before the 1933 season, just as Fred Marberry was packing his bags for Detroit and creating

Jack Quinn. He was still a major-league fireman at age forty-nine—for "a wife and six kids." (*George Brace Photo*)

a void in the bullpen. He'd had a miserable record as a starter: Over the previous four years with the Red Sox and Indians, he was 31–70, with an ERA of 4.92. Griffith converted Russell to relief, and the failed starter became the majors' best fireman in 1933, with an overall record of 12–6 and a 2.69 ERA.

While Russell saw action in Games One and Four, and was flawless in those lost causes, Luque did not leave the bullpen until the sixth inning of the fifth game. Fred Schulte had just hit a three-run homer to chase the Giants' starter Hal Schumacher and deadlock matters. Russell had entered the game in the top of the sixth, quelling a Giant rally that had produced their third counter. The two master firemen hurled goose eggs at each other through the seventh, eighth, and ninth innings. But in the top of the tenth, Mel Ott hit a drive to deepest center field that Schulte got a glove on as he tumbled into the stands. There he lost possession. Umpire Charles Pfirman directed Ott to second base with a ground-rule double, then, on protest from the Giants, reversed himself and called the hit a homer. Luque set the Senators down again in the bottom of the tenth, and the Senators concluded their last appearance in a World Series.

In 1934, both Luque and Russell fell off from their peak performances. Nonetheless, Russell was named to the American League All-Star squad, becoming the first fireman so honored. He did not see action, as Cleveland's Mel Harder shone in relief to get the win.

The first fireman to pitch in an All-Star game was Pittsburgh's Mace Brown, who was named to the N.L. team in the midst of a spectacular 1938, which he finished with a record 15 wins in relief. In the midsummer classic at Cincinnati, the tall right-hander saved his side's win by pitching the final three innings and, in the pinch, fanning Rudy York with the bases loaded.

The University of Iowa grad joined the Bucs in 1935 as a reliever and stayed that way, with the exception of spot-start duty in 1939 and 1940. His 1938 season was unhappily punctuated by an 0–2 pitch that Gabby Hartnett hit for the "homer in the gloaming" at Wrigley Field to knock the Pirates out of the pennant race.

Brown relied on "a good overhand curve that produced ground balls," he recalls today, and that made him as effective against left-handed batters as he was against the righties. After he was traded to the Dodgers, and the Dodgers sent him down to the Pacific Coast League in 1941, Mace developed a slider and bounced back to the big time with the Boston Red Sox, for whom he pitched three fine seasons. In later years he served as the Red Sox pitching

Mace Brown, winner of 15 games in relief in 1938, but victim of Gabby Hartnett's famous "homer in the gloaming" at season's end.

coach, and as a scout he was responsible for signing current slugger Jim Rice.

Pitchers love to brag about their hitting ability, even relief pitchers, who seldom get a chance to wave a bat in their own defense. On August 28, 1937, Chicago Cubs' reliever Clay Bryant had plenty to crow about. In the tenth inning of the second half of a twin bill with the Braves, Bryant won his own game with a grand-slam homer off Frank Gabler. For the big fastballing right-hander, this had to be the sweetest of his seven relief wins against no losses that year. (Over in the American League, on September 15, 1946, Washington's Early Wynn pinch-hit a grand slam off

Detroit's Johnny Gorsica, then pitched the rest of the way for his only relief win of the year.)

Nineteen thirty-nine featured a bold strategic innovation by freshman Cardinal manager Ray Blades that foreshadowed today's pattern of employing relief pitchers. In 1938. the once-proud Cards had sunk to seventh place, costing Frankie Frisch his job as pilot. Blades decided that it would be his bullpen that would lead the Redbirds back to respectability. Leaning on firemen Clyde Shoun and Bob Bowman and double-hitching starter Curt Davis, Blades's pitchers completed only 45 games—no first-division team would have fewer until 1953—and notched a major-league record of 32 saves. The left-handed Shoun and the right-handed Bowman tied for the league lead in saves, and each worked in more than 50 games, while Davis added seven saves to his 22 wins. The Cards shot up from seventh to second, and Blades was hailed in some corners as a genius.

However, next season Shoun was needed as a starter 19 times, Bowman was a bust, and Davis was shipped to the Dodgers. The Cardinals' complete games rose to 71, and their saves sank to 14. Shorn of the bullpen that had won him such surprising success in 1939, Blades's men finished a distant third. Accused by many of having burned out his staff in 1939, the genius overnight became a dummy and was given his walking papers.

Over in the American League in 1939, while the Yanks' Johnny Murphy was registering a league-high 19 saves, Clint Brown of the White Sox was even better. To his 18 saves the right-hander added 11 relief wins, while appearing in a record 61 games as a fireman. The thirty-six-year-old junkballer, contrary to the practice of most of today's bullpen aces, tailored his pitches to the batter. Not only did he possess a curve and a sinker, on both of which he changed speeds, but he also had three deliveries—underhand, side-arm, and three-quarters.

Like so many firemen of the day, Brown had been a starter, for the Indians from 1930 through 1933, then lived in the Cleveland doghouse the next two years, making a total of 40 ineffectual appearances. White Sox manager Jimmy Dykes acquired Brown in a waiver deal in 1936, and immediately made him his stopper. He became a star in 1937, saving 18 games, but had to sit out almost all of 1938 with an elbow injury. Then he amazed observers by coming back, at age thirty-six, better than ever.

In 1940, another of the Brown boys—following Mordecai, Mace, and Clint—wrote his name in relief annals. Walter "Jumbo" Brown, who tied for the N.L. lead in saves that year, came by his name fairly. His height was 6 feet 3½, and his playing weight varied between 245 and 295 pounds. The latter tonnage was more common during his last years in the majors. No big-league player ever tipped the scales over as far as Jumbo Brown did.

In his early years with the Yanks, 1932–1933, Jumbo was a big disappointment, a fastballer whose fastball lost its hop after four innings. When the Yanks tried him in relief, the results were not much better, and big Walter spent the 1934 season down on the farm with the Newark Bears. Although he bounced back into the big time the following year, he really didn't produce until he linked up with the Giants in 1938. From then until his exit after the 1941 season, Brown was a solid gamesaver, and perhaps the only fastballing full-time fireman between Marberry and Joe Page.

Jumbo's co-leaders in saves for 1940 were Mace Brown and Joe Beggs of Cincinnati. Beggs had come up to the Yankees as a starter in 1938, and failed to stick. In 1940, he led the Reds into the World Series against the Yanks. Beggs, a breaking-ball pitcher with a good sinker, was 12–3 as a fireman, with seven saves and an outstanding relief ERA of 1.58; his one start of the year was a shelling that lifted his overall ERA to 2.00.

The finest performance of his career, Beggs says, occurred that year in Brooklyn in the early part of the season, before the Reds blew past the Bums to take the flag by 12 games. "The Dodgers under Larry MacPhail purchased Joe Medwick and Curt Davis, and the N.Y. papers said they bought the pennant," Beggs recalls. "We came in for a doubleheader. In the first game, a fight started in the seventh inning around second base. Junior Thompson, our pitcher, was spiked in the fight. I took over with the score tied, two men on base, and no outs. I got out of it, and we went to the fourteenth inning to win 4–3. I pitched the last seven innings of shutout ball."

Another game that stood out in Beggs's memory took place in 1941. "I relieved John Van Der Meer in a game with St. Louis. The situation was bases loaded, no one out, and three left-handed hitters coming up. The count was three balls and no strikes on Enos Slaughter; I struck him out. Stan Musial was next; he popped up. Then Johnny Mize struck out. P.S.—All three men will be in the Hall of Fame."

Beggs faded in 1941, but other noteworthy firemen appeared. Howie Krist of the Cards won six coming out of the bullpen on his way to a 10–0 season; in 1942 he bagged eight wins in relief. And Hugh Casey became Brooklyn's late-inning rescuer as the Dodgers captured their first flag since 1920. Casey took the league's

Hugh Casey. Like Wilcy Moore, he became a better pitcher after an arm injury. (*George Brace Photo*)

relief-win honors in 1941; he would go on to become the N.L.'s top fireman of the decade and, had it not been for World War II, a probable choice for the all-time top ten.

A native of Atlanta, Casey was discovered by old Oriole and former Dodger manager Wilbert Robinson, who signed the burly right-hander with the Atlanta Crackers of the Southern Association. The year was 1932, and Casey was only nineteen; like most young pitchers, he relied heavily on his fastball. In 1935, the Crackers sold his contract to the first-place Chicago Cubs, who gave him a 13-game trial and passed. Casey was demoted to Birmingham.

There he hurt his arm, and made his career. No longer possessed of a major-league-quality fastball, Casey was forced to develop another pitch or find another line of work. Over the next two years, he developed the sinker—or spitter, as teammate Gene Mauch recalls—that brought him a second shot at the big leagues.

After the 1938 season, Larry MacPhail purchased his contract from Memphis for $7,500. Casey paid the Dodgers immediate returns in 1939, winning 15 games, mostly as a starter. The next year he saw more action out of the bullpen, and by late 1941 the die was cast. In 27 relief turns, Casey was 8–4, with seven saves and an ERA of 2.29; in his 18 starts, he went 6–7, with an ERA of 4.81. On balance it was a fine year, but it ended on a sour note.

In Game Three of the fall classic, with the first two contests split, Fred Fitzsimmons took a 1–0 lead into the seventh. With two out, Yankee pitcher Marius Russo drove a liner off the forty-year-old starter's knee. Marius was retired, but so was Freddie. Called on to nurse the slim lead in the eighth, Casey instead was lit up for four hits and two runs in one third of an inning, and lost the game.

The next day was the real heartbreaker. Casey was called in to get the final out of the Yankee half of the fifth inning, when the Dodgers were trailing 3–2. He did, and stood to win the game as the Bums rallied for two in the bottom of the fifth. Casey mowed the Yankees down through the next three innings and seemed to have the win under his belt when, with two outs in the ninth, Tommy Henrich swung and missed for strike three. But the ball got by catcher Mickey Owen, who could not retrieve it before Henrich raced to first. Then the barrage started.

DiMaggio singled. Charley Keller doubled to the wall, sending in the tying and lead runs. The shell-shocked Casey then walked Bill Dickey, who scampered home with Keller on Joe Gordon's two-base hit. Johnny Murphy set the dazed Dodgers down 1–2–3 in the bottom of the ninth, and the Series was for all practical purposes over.

After the game, Casey told reporters, "I guess I've lost 'em about every way now. Everything happens to me. I've lost one when a balk was called against me, and just about every funny way you can think of. But I never lost one by striking out a guy. I had Henrich 3–2 on the count so I figured I'd rear back and give him the curve. It broke too much." Because it broke so sharply, many who witnessed the game contended that the pitch was not a curve but a spitter. Dan Daniel wrote in mid-1942, "Casey's abilities as a relief pitcher trace to a rubber arm. And a tireless physique. Hugh hasn't a good curve, he isn't especially fast, he tosses nothing freakish." In those days, however, writers were reluctant to imply in print that a pitcher occasionally loaded one up.

Casey recovered from his disastrous October to repeat in 1942 as the National League's top fireman, with 13 saves and six wins. He helped the Dodgers win 104 games, four games more than they had copped in 1941, but two games short of the total attained by the Cardinals.

The next three years were spent in military service. When Casey came back, he picked up where he had left off, posting a 1.99 ERA and topping all firemen with 11 wins. Again the Dodgers were nipped for the flag by the Cards, who defeated them in a play-off. One of Casey's better performances that year, though one for which he received no credit, occurred on September 11. After starter Hal Gregg had pitched ten shutout innings against the Reds to no avail, Casey was called on to match serves with starter John Van Der Meer. Five innings later, with the score still 0–0, both Casey and Van Der Meer called it a day. Art Herring and Hank Behrman continued the shutout string for the Dodgers over the next four innings, while Harry Gumbert slung zeroes for the Reds. After 19 scoreless innings, the game was called on account of darkness.*

Nineteen forty-seven was the height of Hugh Casey's career. He set new league records with his 18 saves and 28 relief points, and led in relief wins as well. Brooklyn beat out St. Louis and readied for a Series rematch with the Bronx Bombers, who had a star reliever of their own in lefty Joe Page.

Page and Casey put on quite a show as the teams battled through seven games. Of Brooklyn's three wins, Casey took two and saved the other, and finished all six games for which he was called. Page appeared in four games, winning one, losing one, and saving another. Both men gained dramatic victories. Casey entered Game Four in the top of the ninth, with the bases full and only one out. He threw one pitch to Tommy Henrich, his nemesis of 1941, who hit into a twin killing. Casey got the win when Cookie Lavagetto's double with two out in the ninth ended Bill Bevens's no-hitter and the ball game. Page took the deciding game of the Series with five scoreless innings in relief of Bevens.

In 1947 Casey had reached his peak, and then all of a sudden he was past it. He absorbed a fearful pounding with the Dodgers in 1948, and again with the Pirates and Yanks in 1949. In 1950, he returned to his hometown, Atlanta, where he pitched for the Crackers once more. Then his personal life started to come apart.

---

* In a strange coincidence, another extra-inning tie game that same day also produced a remarkable relief performance. The Cubs' Hank Borowy and Emil Kush came out of the bullpen to combine for 12⅓ innings of one-hit ball in a 17-inning 3–3 tie with the Braves, also called on account of darkness.

A restaurant he had started in Brooklyn during his glory years folded, and he lost a paternity suit brought against him by a Brooklyn woman. On July 3, 1951, living in an Atlanta hotel, he placed a midnight call to his estranged wife, telling her that he intended to kill himself. Mrs. Casey pleaded with Hugh to calm down, but he replied, "I feel just like I was walking out to the pitcher's box. I was never any more calm than I am right now." Minutes later, he put a shotgun to his neck and killed himself.

During the war years 1942–1945, when Casey and so many other stars were serving their country, the quality of play was not what it had been in 1941. Many fading veterans magically found their powers restored by inferior competition; many newcomers of arguable abilities wore big-league uniforms they could never have filled before the war, and were not permitted to fill after the war. Nonetheless, there were several relief pitchers whose performances during this period bear recognition.

In 1943, the Chicago White Sox bullpen greeted a thirty-year-old rookie with the improbable name of Gordon Maltzberger. Maltzy surprised everyone by leading the American League in relief points and saves in both 1943 and 1944. Actually, in 1944 he shared honors with a thirty-nine-year-old rookie, Joe Berry of the A's, and a thirty-seven-year-old veteran, George Caster of the Browns.

Berry's 10 relief wins and 12 saves in 1944 matched Maltzberger's totals exactly. And in 1945 the graybeard came back to lead the A.L. in relief wins and games pitched. When the boys came marching home again, however, Jittery Joe's salad days were done.

George Caster, a tall right-hander who broke in with the A's in 1934, was a starter who until 1942 had never had a good year. From 1942 through 1944, though, Caster did an excellent job as number-one man in the St. Louis Browns' bullpen. He appeared in 116 games, all in relief; he won more games than he lost; and his ERA for the three years was a nifty 2.46. Contrast that with his record of 1940: 4–19, with a 6.56 ERA.

In a memorably bad relief outing that year, Caster replaced A's starter Ed Heusser in the first game of a doubleheader with the Red Sox. It was the fourth inning, and five Bostonians had already crossed the plate. Caster allowed two more for good measure, then got the final out of the frame. In the fifth the Sox took a breather and rang up only one score. But in the sixth against Caster, they resumed the onslaught. Ted Williams, Jimmy Foxx, and Joe Cronin hit consecutive home runs, and then Bobby Doerr slugged a triple; the Associated Press report of the game said Doerr "was stopped at third though observers thought he could have reached home." Then Jim Tabor hit the fourth home run of the inning, putting Caster in the record books with seven other unfortunates for most four-baggers allowed in one inning. Only the caution of Boston's third-base coach deprived Caster of exclusivity. After the sixth inning, he retired for the day—having allowed ten hits and ten runs in two and a third innings' work.

While we're on the subject of arson jobs, let's not overlook the wartime debut of Joe Nuxhall, who in later years would be quite an effective pitcher. But on June 10, 1944, he was a scared fifteen-year-old called in to mop up a game against the Cardinals. Signed out of high school by the Cincinnati Reds, he took the mound in the ninth inning with the score 13–0 against him; when he left, the score was 18–0. Nuxhall allowed five walks and two hits while registering two outs. Manager Bill McKechnie excused Nuxhall from class and permitted another pitcher to close out the inning. The shell-shocked Nuxhall returned to high school, was restored to amateur status so he could participate in interscholastic sports, and didn't reappear in the majors until 1952.

Another senior citizen who prolonged his baseball career during these years was Joe Heving, a relief pitcher whose sinkerball brought him his league's relief-win crown in 1930, 1939, and 1940. Yet his finest years were 1943 and 1944, when he notched personal highs in saves. In 1944, at age forty-four, he set an American League record by appearing in 63 games in relief.

The major-league record was the province of Ace Adams of the Giants, who the previous year had pitched 70 times, surpassing Ed Walsh's mark set in 1908, and relieved 67 times, eclipsing Clint Brown. Adams was a wartime star who broke in with the Giants as a twenty-nine-year-old in 1941. His first measure of success came the next year, when he led the N.L. in games for the first of three straight years and games finished for the first of four straight. In 1945, he was tops in both relief wins and saves, but in 1946 the wartime flash fizzled. Called on three times in April, he was touched for nine hits and five runs in only two and two thirds innings. After that he jumped to the Mexican League. (Tied with Adams for the 1945 lead in saves was the Phils' Andy Karl, who established a record for innings worked in relief that stood 28 years.)

No better indication of the wartime shortage of able players exists than the presence on major-league rosters in 1945 of two disabled players—Pete Gray, the one-armed outfielder of the Browns, and Bert Shepard, the one-legged pitcher who relieved in a game for the 1945 Senators.

Shepard's P-38 had been shot down over occupied France in

1944, and his right leg was mangled in the wreckage. German doctors had no choice but to amputate just below the knee. Shepard's hopes for a postwar career in baseball were seemingly dashed. But in 1945, one week after being fitted with an artificial limb at Washington's Walter Reed Hospital, he asked the Senators for a tryout. He pitched in an exhibition game against the Dodgers, and won. But Clark Griffith signed him up primarily because he thought Shepard's presence on the roster would be an inspiration to other crippled vets. All Shepard was permitted to do was pitch batting practice, until on a July day when the Senators were taking a pasting from the Red Sox, manager Ossie Bluege called the left-handed Shepard into the game. Amazingly, he went five and a third innings, allowed only one run and three hits, and fanned two batters.

Not long after the game, his right leg began bothering him, and he checked into Walter Reed again. Though he rejoined the Senators later that season, he did not pitch another game.

After the season, Shepard requested his release so he could pitch in the minors and make the majors on merit. In 1946, he won two and lost two in the Southern Association, but he never returned to the big leagues. No matter—by pitching in one major-league game, he had accomplished enough for a lifetime in baseball.

In the National League in 1946, the most memorable relief work was performed by Pittsburgh starter Preacher Roe, whose economy in gaining a relief win on May 5 approached that of Nick Altrock 40 years earlier. Altrock had won a game in relief without throwing a single pitch to the plate; Roe strained himself to the tune of one pitch, and that a pitchout.

The setting was game two of a Sunday twin bill with the Dodgers in Pittsburgh. Pennsylvania blue laws of the time forbade ballplaying after 6 P.M. As the clock neared the witching hour, the Dodgers were sending three runners across the plate to tie the score in the top of the sixth. Brooklyn's Bob Ramazotti was at third with two out when Roe was summoned in to replace Nick Strincevich. On the first pitch, catcher Bill Salkeld called for a pitchout to foil a potential squeeze play. Salkeld's guess was right, and Ramazotti ran right into the catcher's waiting tag. The Pirates came back with a run in the bottom of the frame, the game was called for curfew, and Roe had his one-pitch win.

The American League's top fireman that year was Earl Caldwell, another of the after-forty set who had dominated the war years. "Teach" Caldwell had seen his first major-league action as a twenty-three-year-old in 1928, then dipped back down into the minors for six years before resurfacing with the Browns in 1935–

1937. Then, incredibly, after saying adios to the big leagues in mid-1937, he bobbed up again in 1945. In 1946, at age forty-one, he had the season of his life, winning 13 games in relief and saving eight more. Although he pitched two more big-league seasons, he never again approached those heights. He returned to the minors, where he pitched until he was forty-nine. At one point, his catcher was his son!

Teach Caldwell was by no means the last of the old-timers who made the bullpen their special fiefdom. But that trend was slowing, and baseball would not see a return to the dominance enjoyed by elder hangers-on during the war years. In the next era of relief pitching, 1947–1958, there was a broad return to the pattern established with Marberry and Murphy: Find a young pitcher with the arm and the disposition suited to bullpen work, and use him as a fireman virtually from the outset of his baseball career. This practice netted great results with two of the game's top ten relievers who began their relief careers after World War II: Hoyt Wilhelm and ElRoy Face.

# 8

# The Ten Best: Wilhelm

In 1914, in a book entitled *How to Play Baseball,* John McGraw wrote about the knuckleball: "It is one of the hardest to pitch and has been mastered by very few twirlers. . . . I would not advise anyone to try this." Fortunately, this book escaped the attention of a sixteen-year-old schoolboy pitcher named Hoyt Wilhelm, who was wondering how he would ever make it to the pros without an outstanding fastball or curve.

Instead, the ace of North Carolina's Cornelius High happened upon a newspaper article about the Washington Senators' Emil "Dutch" Leonard* and the knuckler that vaulted him to stardom in 1939. The article illustrated the 20-game winner's grip: the tips of the index and middle fingers dug into the seams, not the first joints of the fingers squeezing down on the ball, as pitchers did when McGraw wrote the cautionary words above. The pressure applied to the seams, Wilhelm learned, causes the ball to float homeward, rotating imperceptibly if at all. With the ball virtually still as it hurtles forward, air currents hit the raised seams and push the ball suddenly to one side or the other, and generally down, by as much as a foot.

The young right-hander tried it. The rest is history. Hoyt Wilhelm went on to become the greatest relief pitcher of all time. In a

* No relation to Hub "Dutch" Leonard, discussed briefly in Chapter Four.

21-year big-league career with as many moves up, down, and sideways as any knuckler he ever threw, Wilhelm pitched in 1,070 games, more even than Cy Young; he won 123 games in relief, saved 227 more, and finished 651 games—all major-league records. He captured the ERA crown of each league, a singular feat, and his lifetime ERA of 2.52 is second only to Tom Seaver among pitchers who broke in after the introduction of the lively ball and pitched 1,500 innings. The records go on and on, as Wilhelm himself did. He came to the majors late, as a twenty-eight-year-old rookie with the Giants, and left late, cut adrift by the Dodgers five days short of his forty-ninth birthday.

Hoyt Wilhelm, the greatest of all firemen, photographed near the end of his career.

When Wilhelm first tried to throw the knuckler, he found that while it would break sharply, the break often carried it out of the strike zone. All pitchers who experiment with the pitch come to this discovery, and most abandon it at this point. But Wilhelm persevered, and gradually he learned to control it, mostly by giving up the notion of pitching to spots. Hoyt could safely throw the ball belt-high down the middle, knowing that the pitch would hardly ever cross the plate where he aimed it.

Upon graduation from Cornelius High in 1942, Wilhelm signed on with Mooresville in the North Carolina State League, a Class-D outfit. Early in the season, the team's manager and catcher—perhaps acting out of self-preservation—told Hoyt to can the trick pitch and go with the stuff that he could control. Wilhelm followed orders in his next game and got creamed. Upon restoring the knuckler to his repertoire, he won nine starts in a row before being drafted into the army. Control? He walked two men per game, only half as many as he fanned.

Wilhelm spent the next three years with the 99th Division and was wounded in the back and right hand at the Battle of the Bulge. The wounds were not serious, however, and he returned to Mooresville in 1946.

Now going on twenty-three-years-old, Wilhelm was as far from being a major-league pitcher as a professional could be. And though he went 21–8 in 1946, at season's end he found himself no closer to his goal. Any major-league team could have picked up his contract in the draft for a mere $2,500, but none was willing to take a chance on a bush-leaguer who relied on a knuckler; a freak pitch was respectable only for a veteran who had lost his fastball and was trying to hang on.

A disappointed Wilhelm returned to Mooresville in 1947—his sixth year on the same roster—and again won 20. This time the Boston Braves bought his contract and elevated him to Evansville in the Three-I League. But before he pitched a game for Evansville, he was drafted by the Giants, in whose system he languished for four more seasons. Despite his winning record all the way through Triple-A ball, New York did not think enough of Wilhelm to protect him from the draft. As it turned out, it didn't matter—there were no takers.

In the spring of 1952, the lanky North Carolinian was at last invited to train with the big club. The Giants were just coming off their miracle finish in the 1951 season, when Bobby Thomson's last-minute heroics obscured the fact that it was the pitching staff—the league's best—that had been the main ingredient in the team's success. Larry Jansen, Sal Maglie, Jim Hearn, and Dave Koslo comprised an impregnable first four; Wilhelm's only chance to make the ball club would be as bullpen help for George Spencer.

Forty-two-year-old knuckleballer Dutch Leonard, the man whom Wilhelm took as a model in 1939, had been a highly successful reliever for the Cubs in 1951. Why not Wilhelm, manager Leo Durocher reasoned in inviting him to camp. The Lip knew he had something when he saw the six-footer's floater and his jerky, deceptive motion—Wilhelm would release the ball somewhere between three quarters and sidearm, and as his arm came around, his head would tilt disquietingly to his left.

Before the regular season was one month old, Wilhelm had shown himself cool in the tight spots, able to get the ball over, and just plain nasty to hit. Supplanting Spencer as the Giants' number-one fireman, Wilhelm went on to pitch 71 games, all in relief; he won 15, lost only 3, and saved 11. He led the league in games, relief wins, winning percentage, and earned-run average. Not only was Wilhelm the first rookie ever to top his league in both winning percentage and earned-run average, he was also the first and thus far the only full-time relief specialist to win the ERA title. What's more, in his first major-league at bat, Wilhelm walloped a home run (21 years and 431 trips to the plate later, he still had not collected his second). Despite these accomplishments, he lost out in the balloting for National League Rookie of the Year to the Dodgers' Joe Black, whose comparable achievements helped his Dodgers win the pennant.

In 1953, Wilhelm did not match his record-setting pace of the year before, but he was nevertheless effective. He topped the league in games once more, and upped his saves total to 15. Nineteen fifty-four was more satisfying, as the Giants blasted their way back to the top of the National League and in the World Series knocked off the favored Cleveland Indians in four straight. Hoyt's contribution was a 12–4 mark, with seven saves and an ERA of 2.10. The only record he had anything to do with that year was one of ignominy, as catcher Ray Katt, in the eighth inning of a game on September 10, permitted four knucklers to dance to the backstop. Over in the American League, the record for passed balls in an inning is three, shared by four catchers—all of whom accomplished their "feats" while forming a battery with Wilhelm. Baltimore catchers Gus Triandos and Joe Ginsberg each waved at three of Wilhelm's butterflies in one inning in 1960, and the Orioles' Charlie Lau also turned the trick two years later. It was this sort of experience that prompted Wilhelm, with Paul Richards, to design the oversized (38-inch-circumference) floppy catcher's mitt that is used to catch most knuckleballers today. Most embarrassed of the four record-holders was the California Angels' Joe Azcue, who came up empty-handed on three straight Wilhelm tosses on August 30, 1969. Perhaps coincidentally, Wilhelm was shipped to Atlanta one week later. Braves' catcher Bob Didier, who had caught knuckleballer Phil Niekro all year, said, "Catching Hoyt may be tougher. I've detected a pattern with Phil's knuckleball. It usually breaks down. But Hoyt's jumps a lot of different ways."

In 1955, Wilhelm's knuckler began to fail him. Marv Grissom, with whom he'd shared bullpen duties in the championship year, now became the first fireman Durocher would call. Wilhelm continued to work, but rarely when the decision was on the line. Although he appeared 59 times, he recorded not a single save.

In 1956, Durocher was replaced at the helm by Bill Rigney, who waved for Wilhelm in more meaningful spots. But due to the previous year's inactivity, Wilhelm had lost confidence in his ability to get his out pitch over. He'd get behind on the count, come in with the fastball, and get nailed. Recalls Wes Westrum, Wilhelm's principal catcher in all his years with the Giants: "Hoyt began to worry and try different things, and the more he changed, the worse it got."

During the winter, he was packed off to St. Louis. There he worked a mere 55 innings in 40 games, and was waived to Cleveland before the season was out. Every N.L. team passed on him. Becoming a vagabond pitcher was a signal that the end of the line was near; Wilhelm struggled to recover the knack before he ran out of chances. With Cleveland in 1958, however, Hoyt's record was 2–7. In late August, he was waived again.

In fact, Wilhelm had not pitched all that badly for the Indians, who briefly tried him as a starter. Though he failed to notch a victory, he pitched well enough for his name on the waiver list to rouse the interest of Baltimore manager Paul Richards; in 1936–1937, the former catcher had been the battery mate of—guess who—Dutch Leonard. Richards took a flyer on Wilhelm, and, at the knuckleballer's request, continued to use him as a starter.

Wilhelm lost his first three decisions as an Oriole regular, which gave him a starter's log of 0–6 for the year and for his career. On September 20, a Saturday afternoon home date with the Yankees, Richards gave Wilhelm another chance to get off the schneid. Hoyt knew that if he did not show the Orioles something soon, he might well be cut loose in 1959. Operating under that kind of pressure, all he did was throw a no-hitter against the league's best team, before a national television audience. Paradoxically, it was this first victory as a starter that enabled him to stay in the majors, and to create his unparalleled record in relief.

In a drizzle that continued throughout the ball game, Wilhelm matched blanks with Yankee starter Don Larsen (just two years past the game of *his* life) through six innings, in which Larsen himself allowed only a bunt single. In the bottom of the seventh, Big Don was relieved by Bobby Shantz, who was nicked for a run. Wilhelm's catcher, former Yankee Gus Triandos, walloped a drive over the wall in dead center, and all Wilhelm had to do was to put six more pinstripers down.

The spell was very nearly broken with the Yankees' first batter in the eighth. Norm Siebern drove a hard ground ball past the mound, seemingly headed for center field. But second-baseman Billy Gardner, who had been playing the left-handed batter to pull, ranged far to his right, whirled, and threw to first in time. The next two outs were routine. Wilhelm was but one inning from immortality and, more importantly in the short term, a measure of job security for next year.

It all came down to the last batter, veteran right fielder (and future Oriole manager) Hank Bauer. Bauer stunned the hometown crowd, and Wilhelm too, by bunting at the first pitch. Had the ball not rolled foul, there would have been no play at first.

Still dazed by the enormity of what he was about to accomplish, Wilhelm offered up another knuckleball and trusted to fate. Bauer wafted the ball into short right field, and fate guided it into Gardner's waiting glove.

His self-esteem buoyed by that late-season triumph, Wilhelm came back all the way in 1959. Thrust into the starting rotation at season's outset, he won his first nine games; before Detroit beat him in June, his ERA was 0.99. Overall, he garnered 15 wins for the sixth-place Birds, and took the ERA crown with a splashy 2.19. Against his no-hit victims of the previous September, he tossed a one-hitter in April and ran up a streak in which he allowed the Bronx Bombers only two earned runs through five starts. Oddly, in the bullpen's greatest year—the year of Sherry, Face, McDaniel, McMahon, Lown, Staley—Wilhelm recorded no relief wins and no saves.* At the age of thirty-six, when so many starters were being relegated to bullpen work, Wilhelm had a new career as a starter—and bucking conventional wisdom, a one-pitch starter at that.

Wilhelm would throw an occasional fastball or curve or slider for its surprise value, or would try to get by with the "natural" pitches on days when there wasn't enough wind to give action to

---

* He did, however, pitch one remarkable game in relief. On August 6, he relieved against the White Sox with the score tied 1–1 in the ninth. For the next eight and two-thirds innings, he did not allow a hit. After he concluded his tenth inning of shutout relief, the game was called on account of curfew.

his knuckler. But on most occasions, nine of every ten pitches he threw were butterflies. "The secret of the pitching business is variety, all right," Wilhelm once said, "but of speeds, not type of pitches." And Hoyt did throw the knuckler at varying speeds, obtaing the smallest, most sudden break when he threw the hardest.

In 1960, Paul Richards's Baby Birds put it all together and shot up from sixth to second. Kids like Milt Pappas, Steve Barber, Jack Fisher, and Chuck Estrada were too good not to start, and besides, *they* were the future of the franchise, not a thirty-seven-year-old starter for whom things might fall apart as suddenly as they had come together. Besides, the Orioles' top fireman of 1959, Billy Loes, had been traded to the Giants; where one year earlier Richards's vacancy had been in the rotation, now it was in the pen. Despite his excellent 1959, Wilhelm started only 11 games in 1960, while relieving in 30. Without fanfare, he became the first man to pitch in 400 games in relief—as he would become the first to relieve in 500, 600, 700, 800, 900, and 1,000.

The one year spent exclusively as a starter had been therapeutic. Restored to relief duties, Wilhelm was to be even more effective than he had been with the Giants. In 1961, he reached a lifetime high (to that point) of 18 saves and 27 relief points. The next year his ERA dipped below two runs per game for the first time, and he fanned men at a career-peak rate of one per inning. Asked how he felt about his return to the bullpen, Wilhelm replied with all the conviction of a recent convert, "Anybody can start. That isn't the question. It's whether or not you can finish."

In 1962, Wilhelm was finished with the Orioles. They wanted someone younger, or at least less ancient, and found him in the thirty-six-year-old Stu Miller. Wilhelm was dealt to the Chicago White Sox, with whom he made good the claim that life begins at forty. In his first year with the Sox, Old Sarge, as he had come to be called, posted a new career high of 21 saves and with Jim Brosnan combined to give Chicago the best bullpen it had ever had. What's more, he began to teach the knuckleball to Eddie Fisher, a willing pupil who went on to have phenomenal success with the pitch over the next few seasons.

Brosnan departed after the 1963 season, and Wilhelm took up the slack. In 1964 he saved 27 games, his most ever, and won 12 more to combine for his highest total of relief points in any season. Strangely, this man who leads all relievers in total saves and relief points never led his league in either category. His ERA was 1.99, which turned out to be the *highest* figure he would produce over the next five years (in 1967 his ERA plummeted to 1.31). The older he got, the better he pitched; the knuckler placed so little strain on his arm and shoulder that it seemed he might stay on the mound until he could collect Social Security.

From 1965 through 1967, Old Sarge was close to unhittable. During that span of 161 games, he permitted an average of 5.6 hits per nine innings. Few pitchers have ever posted lower marks in any *one* season, and only Ryne Duren was able to sustain the pace over three years. Lifetime, Wilhelm doled out 7.02 hits per nine innings, the third least among pitchers who hurled 1,500 innings.

In 1968, his last year with the White Sox, the forty-five-year-old wonder was paired up in the Sox pen with his new pupil, the left-handed knuckleballer Wilbur Wood. While Wood was appearing in a record 88 games, Wilhelm himself strolled out of the pen on 72 occasions, his most ever.

After the season, A.L. clubs were compelled to expose several of their roster players to the draft that stocked the new Kansas City Royals and Seattle Pilots. White Sox management couldn't see protecting a forty-five-year-old and letting a young prospect go; besides, why would an expansion team select a pitcher who by all rights should have been sent out to pasture long ago?

The answer came as the Royals selected Wilhelm in October and traded him to the Angels in December, receiving two promising youngsters in return. With the Angels in 1969 Wilhelm continued to act like a colt. In September, however, with California out of contention, Wilhelm became available to the highest bidder among the six teams who were struggling for two spots in the N.L. Championship Series. After a 12-year absence from the National League, Wilhelm returned with the Atlanta Braves. It was quite a homecoming, too: Old Sarge pitched eight times for the Braves in the last month, winning two, saving four, and whiffing 14 in only 12 innings' work. He proved instrumental in the Braves' final spurt to the Western Division title, but was ineligible for postseason play. His presence would not have altered the Braves' fate in the play-offs, though—the Mets were destiny's darlings that year.

For a pitcher who in 1959 found himself perhaps one start away from enforced retirement, the 1960s had been a remarkable decade. Wilhelm established lifetime American League records for relief appearances, wins, and games finished. His ERA for the ten years was 2.18.

But in the 1970s Old Sarge's fountain of youth dried up at last. The forty-year-old marvel was only adequate with the Braves in 1970, experiencing control problems for the first time since his early years with the Giants. When the Braves fell out of the pennant running early, the stage was set for another late-season transfer to a contender—this time the Cubs. In three September games with Chicago, he did not show enough to figure in their plans for 1971, so he was dealt back to Atlanta. The ominous pattern of team-hopping that had set in during the late 1950s was recurring; this time, there would be no last-minute stay of execution. On June 29, 1971, after only three appearances for the Braves, Wilhelm was handed his unconditional release. No major-league team had seen fit to pay the $20,000 waiver price for a pitcher one month short of forty-eight.

But Wilhelm himself was not convinced he was through. He signed a minor-league contract with Spokane of the Pacific Coast League, where one month's work earned him a recall to the big time with Los Angeles, his tenth major-league team. The Dodgers offered him uniform number 48, to match his age, but a testy Wilhelm refused, saying, "The whole country seems to know how old I am. What difference does it make?"

In 1972, finally, it made a difference. Not working often enough to keep his knuckler in top form, Wilhelm walked more men than he fanned, and was rocked for 4.68 runs per nine innings. Five days short of his forty-ninth birthday, he was given his fifth and final release. This time he accepted the verdict.

Although Rollie Fingers or Mike Marshall or Sparky Lyle may soon exceed Wilhelm's career total for saves, or relief wins, or relief points, his stature will be undiminished. He was the greatest reliever of his long day in the sun, and one of the great pitchers the game has produced, an equal of many of the hurlers enshrined in Cooperstown. Most of the modern-day (post-World War II) relievers I questioned believe Wilhelm belongs in the Hall of Fame. Dave Baldwin, a fireman with the Senators while Wilhelm was starring for the White Sox and Angels, perhaps says it best: "Wilhelm was the best reliever I ever saw. He was the best pitcher in the American League (starters included) for a number of years. If any pitcher from the sixties deserves to be in the Hall of Fame, he's it."

9

# The Ten Best: Face

Another reliever of this period who belongs in the Hall of Fame is ElRoy Face. Yet his chances of being inducted in the foreseeable future seem remote. In the 1978 vote, Wilhelm's first year of eligibility, Face attracted only 27 votes to Old Sarge's 158; election required 285 ballots. Perhaps his stock will go up once Wilhelm is safely in.

Face made his fame and fortune with the forkball, a pitch delivered by wrapping the index and middle fingers around the ball where there are no seams. Thrown high, Face's forkball would break in toward a left-handed batter (Face was a righty); aimed low, the ball would shoot down suddenly. The pitch is something of a cross between the knuckler and the sinker: Like the knuckler, it "slips" out of the pitcher's hand and sails plateward with little or no rotation; like the sinker—and even more like its disreputable cousin, the spitter—it drops explosively at the last instant, seemingly at a right angle to the plate. Although the extent of the drop could be varied by changing speeds, Face almost invariably threw his forkball hard, thus achieving a sharper and tighter break. This is the way today's Bruce Sutter of the Cubs throws his forkball, or "split-fingered fastball."

Face did not possess the forkball in 1949, when he was a carpenter/mechanic pitching in his spare time in Stephentown,

New York, where he had come into the world 21 years earlier. He used only a fastball and curve, but those were impressive enough for Phillie scout Fred Matthews to sign him up in 1950. A professional contract would have been accomplishment enough for one who had had to overcome life-threatening rickets and five cases of pneumonia. But Face did so much more.

In 16 years as a major-league reliever, the gritty 5-feet-8 right-hander led the National League in games twice, relief wins once, saves three times, and games finished four times, the latter a league record. He is, at this writing, third among all firemen in career wins and relief points, and fourth in saves and games pitched. His fabulous 18–1 mark in 1959 gave him the all-time top winning

Roy Face. He went 18–1 in 1959, and that wasn't his best year.

percentage for a single season (15 decisions or more) by any pitcher, starter or reliever. And that wasn't even his best year.

After signing with the Phils' organization, Face worked his way up from Broford to Pueblo to Dallas, off whose roster general manager Branch Rickey drafted him for the Dodgers in 1950. Two years later Rickey, now general manager of the Pittsburgh Pirates, noticed that the Dodgers had left Face on the Fort Worth roster for the winter. Rickey again drafted the little hurler and brought him up to the big club.

The Pirates of 1952 had been a stupendously awful team, winning 42 games, losing 112, and finishing 22½ games out of seventh. It was a well-deserved finish—they were last in hitting, fielding, and pitching. This was a team in need of any kind of help in 1953, but Face didn't supply much of it. The Pirates lost eight fewer games, but the club was again dead last, and Face took his share of the credit for that. On a pitching staff that compiled an atrocious ERA of 5.22, Roy brought up the rear with his mark of 6.58. Somehow he won six games against only eight losses, but Rickey recognized that Face was not a major-league pitcher, not even by the Pirates' relaxed standards. He threw only two pitches —the fastball and the curve—and could not change speeds on either. Rickey foresaw a time when the warm bodies filling out the Pirates' staff would become good young pitchers; if Face were to be one of them, Rickey decided in spring training 1954, he would have to go back to the bushes and learn a change-up.

But before Face headed west for New Orleans, he sought guidance from one of the veterans in camp—fading fireman Joe Page, attempting a comeback with the Bucs after three years' absence from the majors. Page showed Face how to throw the forkball, and Roy seemed to take to it right away. Though he was small, his fingers were long enough to surround the ball and grip it firmly. The pitch that was supposed to be a change of pace for his fastball and curve soon became the dominant weapon in his arsenal. His record in the Southern Association was only 12–11, but the year spent down south gave him the confidence to come back and contribute to the Pirates' improvement in 1955.

Though they finished last again, the fourth time in four years, the young players gave signs that they might be on the verge of something. Bob Friend led the league in ERA, Vern Law was a .500 pitcher, and the roster was peppered with names that would draw acclaim in the years to come: Roberto Clemente, Dick Groat, Dale Long, Frank Thomas, Bob Purkey—and Roy Face, who was only 5–7 in his 42 appearances, ten of them as a starter, but lowered his earned-run average by a full three runs per game.

In 1956, the Pirates abandoned the cellar, barely. First-base-man Dale Long hit eight home runs in eight successive days to set a record, and Face pitched in nine straight games, which also set a record (later broken by Mike Marshall). He led all N.L. pitchers in games, 68, and of these only three were starts. He won 11 and saved six, modest totals to be sure, but it is rare for a fireman to put together impressive numbers while pitching for a club that's well under .500.

The next year, in which Face started a game for the last time in his career, was something of a step back for Face and the Pirates both. But 1958 was the year of breakthrough: the Pirates shot up from last to second as the team's bullpen created a new league mark for saves with 41. Of these, Face and his forkball accounted for an N.L. high of 20. After losing his first two decisions, he won his last five to give him supremacy in relief points. Who could have predicted that these five consecutive wins would be the foundation for a 22-game winning streak? Between May 30, 1958, when he won his first game of the season, and September 11, 1959, when he finally lost, Face marched out of the bullpen 98 times.

One week after the first All-Star game of 1959 (they played two that year, one in July and one in August), Face's record was 14–0 and his ERA was an incredible 0.90. Over his next 23 appearances he was hit hard enough to lift his final ERA to a mere mortal's 2.70, yet he ran his record to 17–0. There were a few hair-breadth escapes when he surrendered the tying or go-ahead run only to have his teammates storm back to give him the win; but to go unbeaten for the better part of two seasons, you have to be lucky as well as good. The Dodgers burst his bubble on September 11 with a 5–4 loss, but Face took his last decision to finish 18–1 and establish himself in the public eye as the game's top reliever.

Although the Bucs slid back to fourth in 1959, they had been only three-and-a-half games off the lead on the last day in August. And there had been a tip-off that the team was primed for a real pennant push in 1960: In one-run games, the Pirates were 36–19, and in extra-inning contests an amazing 19-2. These Buccaneers, young as they were, did not beat themselves with the big mistake at a critical moment. And having a Roy Face to call on in the late innings of a tight game gave the team a substantial edge over any opponent.

Most experts predicted that the 1960 Pittsburghers would again finish fourth; a few brave souls saw a third-place finish, con-tingent on an improved performance from Bob Friend, a big disappointment in 1959. The consensus was that the Pirates had lacked the punch to prevail in 1959, so how could they expect to improve by standing pat in 1960? Well, the punchless Pirates went on to lead the league in hitting, and Friend, Law, and Face all had fine years; Pittsburgh waltzed to the pennant past the favored Braves.

Face contributed 10 wins and 24 saves, exceeding the relief-point total of his 18–1 year. He led the league in games and contributed mightily to the Pirates' thrilling seven-game victory over the Yankees in the World Series. The Pirates had last participated in the fall classic in 1927, when the Murderers' Row gang had demolished them in four straight. This time, the Yanks demolished the Pirates in Games Two, Three, and Six by scores of 16–3, 10–0, and 12–0. Overall in the Series, they outbatted the Bucs .338 to .256, outscored them 55 to 27, outhit them 91 to 60, and outhomered them ten to four—but they neglected to win four games, and the Pirates exacted revenge for their humiliation in 1927. Of the four Pittsburgh wins, Face saved the first three for a new World Series record.

After bailing out Vern Law in Game One with two innings' work, Face came back to relieve Law in the seventh inning of Game Four. The score was 3–2 in favor of Pittsburgh, but the Yankee bats were warming up. They had already tallied one in the inning, and two men were on with only one out when manager Danny Murtaugh decided Law could no longer be counted on to keep order. Face came in and put down eight pinstripers in succession to wrap up the game.

With the Series now squared at two games apiece, Harvey Haddix took a 4–2 lead into the seventh, when with one out he too gave evidence of fading. For the second time in as many days, Face was called upon to get eight outs, and get them he did, again without interruption by a lone base hit.

The one time Face got blasted was in the wild and woolly seventh game, when he was brought into the midst of a sixth-frame Yankee rally. Pitching with a 4–1 lead, starter Vern Law yielded a single to Bobby Richardson and a walk to Tony Kubek. Face came in to relieve Law for the third time in the Series, but his luck had run out. He was smacked for a run-scoring single by Mickey Mantle and a three-run homer by Yogi Berra. Murtaugh must have regarded the pounding as a momentary aberration, for he left Face in to hold the line while his teammates struggled to draw even. But the Yanks solved the forkballer for two more runs in the eighth and appeared to be home free. Veteran Bobby Shantz, now given a 7–4 margin, had blanked the Pirates since entering the contest to start the third inning. But the Bucs stormed back for five runs in their half of the eighth, knocking out Shantz and taking Face off the hook.

The Yankees were left with the task of scoring two in the ninth to tie. That is precisely what they did, as Bob Friend failed to retire a batter in his attempt to save Face's win. Harvey Haddix put out the fire at 9–9, and Bill Mazeroski put an end to the seesaw battle with his lead-off home run in the bottom of the ninth.

In 1961, the Pirates came back to the pack as Deacon Law missed virtually the whole year and no other starter picked up the baton. Led by Roberto Clemente's N.L. high of .351, the Bucs again led the league in hitting, and Face tied for the league lead in saves. But in truth, Roy did not have a season equal to his previous three. He was belted for nearly four runs per game, and lost twice as many as he won.

This slip from the heights seemed to spur him to what most observers regard as his finest year—1962, when he lowered his ERA to 1.88 and amassed eight wins and 28 saves. The latter was a new N.L. record, and only one off the major-league mark (established the previous year by his former bullpen mate, Luis Arroyo).

At age thirty-four, the forkballing fireman had reached his peak, and the next three seasons witnessed a decline that threatened to put him on the sidelines a bit before he cared to go. He surrendered leadership of the Pittsburgh pen to Al McBean. Yet after injury limited Face to only 16 appearances in 1965, he bounced back at age thirty-eight to pitch in 54 ball games, saving 18 and winning six. Once again he was the man who received the first call in the pen; ably abetted by McBean and Pete Mikkelsen, the Pirate bullpen was the league's best, and very nearly carried the team to the top.

The next two seasons were disappointments to Pirate rooters, and the manager's chair became a hot seat. With the team going nowhere, front-office thoughts had to be for the future. And the future held no place for a forty-year-old relief pitcher, no matter how effective.

Although Face had saved 13 and won two for the 1968 Pirates, his name was placed on the waiver list late in the season in hopes of fetching a few dollars from a contending club, for whom one month's bullpen help could spell a pennant. On August 30, the last day of the waiver period, the Detroit Tigers put in a claim. They could not actually purchase his contract, however, until September 1 without bumping a current Tiger off the team; on the first, league rules permitted expansion of the roster from 25 men to 40.

At the time the Tigers claimed Face, the veteran was only one appearance short of Walter Johnson's record of pitching 802 games for a single team. On the day of the thirty-first, manager Larry Shepard suggested that Face start the game, throw one pitch, then give the mound over to Steve Blass, whose starting turn it was. Shepard did not want to tell Face that this would be his last chance to pitch for the Pirates, but the import of his proposal must have been plain.

Face asked instead to pitch to one batter in relief, since he had put together an unbroken chain of 613 bullpen efforts since 1957. Shepard went along with the request and Blass, after opening the game by retiring the first batter, went out to left field as Face came in. One pitch to Felipe Alou produced a groundout, and Face exited; Blass resumed his chores.

After the game, Face was officially notified that he was headed for the other league. "I'm sad leaving the Pirates," he said, "and glad I'm going to a team in first place." Fifteen years with one club is a stretch matched by no other relief pitcher, and of the great ones only Johnny Murphy came close. So many relievers have burned themselves out quickly that the tendency among front-office people is to move the bullpen bodies around at the first sign of slippage, or even in anticipation of it. Face had become a Pittsburgh institution.

He pitched in only two games for the Tigers and was not a factor in the pennant drive. He was released and found a new home with the first-year Montreal Expos. There he combined with lefty Dan McGinn to give the Canadians a respectable bullpen on an otherwise (understandably) poor team. But Face had gained employment as a stopgap measure, an attempt by the Expos to win enough games in their first season to prevent the town from souring on the team. Toward the end of the year, the Montreal brass judged that it had enough good young talent lined up for 1970 to dispense with the forty-one-year-old Face, and they did.

Roy Face returned to his adopted home of Pittsburgh and resumed his family trade of carpentering. As a National League fireman, there had been no better at whittling bats into sawdust over such a long stretch. He holds his league's records for career relief wins, saves, and games finished, and his place among the top ten relievers of all time is unchallenged.

# 10

# Gaining Respectability: 1947-1958

Nineteen forty-seven saw a relief explosion in the American League, as complete games dropped by 10 percent from the previous year and saves increased by almost 45 percent. Leading this charge was the Cleveland Indians, who finished fourth in 1947 by utilizing the bullpen more than any other contender and first in 1948 as the pattern was repeated. Number one in the Indian pen of 1947 was Babe Klieman, whose 17 saves tied him for the league lead with Yankee Joe Page.

Page, in his first year as an emergency specialist, tied the 21-year-old mark for relief points (31) and, as mentioned earlier, excelled in the World Series that focused public attention on the Yankee and Dodger bullpens. The left-hander with the explosive, rising fastball and deceptive motion followed in a great tradition, rising from the coal mines of Pennsylvania to become a big-league hurler. He came to the Bronx in 1944 and was an immediate sensation, winning five of his first six starts. In July, he was named to the American League All-Star squad. But on the day of the game, played in Pittsburgh, his father died. Page could not snap back from the blow and dropped his next six decisions. He ended the year with the Newark Bears.

In 1945 and 1946 he pitched well enough. But his repeated inattention to curfew rules irritated manager Joe McCarthy, who didn't like to see talent wasted. In a shouting match between the

Joe Page, the first fireman to post a 40-point season (1949).

two on an airplane in May 1946, McCarthy threatened to bury Page in Newark if he continued to flout his authority. The next day, however, instead of Page saying good-bye to New York, it was McCarthy. Weary of wheedling and cajoling his players, who had finished third and fourth the previous two years, old Joe resigned the post he had held since 1931. Bill Dickey was appointed to run the team, but he too departed before year's end.

In 1947, the new Yankee skipper was Bucky Harris. When he saw the hop on Page's heater, Harris recalled his relief star of two decades back, Firpo Marberry. Page, who had always had a problem with confidence as a starter and would frequently run out of stuff in the late innings, soon became supremely confident whenever he marched out of the bullpen.

But the transformation was not instant. In Page's first few fireman calls, he poured gasoline on the blaze, generally because of poor control. The turning point came in May, when the defending A.L. champion Red Sox came to Yankee Stadium. New York starter Spec Shea was clipped for three early runs and was in danger again in the third inning. With men on first and second and nobody out, Page was called on to face Ted Williams. He jammed him with the first pitch, and Williams sent a nubber down to first-baseman George McQuinn, who was fooled by the backspin on the ball and booted it. Visibly upset, Page missed the plate with his first three pitches to the next batter, Rudy York. A free pass might trigger a big inning and produce a parade of pinstriped pitchers.

Page threw one down the middle, knowing York would be taking. Next, a swinging strike on Joe's best fastball, and then York watched one go by for strike three. Page felt better now. Harris felt better. But against Bobby Doerr, Page reverted to form and threw three straight wide ones. An impatient Harris had one foot on the top step of the dugout, an unmistakable message. Page responded by zipping the next three by a stunned Doerr for out number two. When Eddie Pellagrini popped up to strand three Red Sox, Page left the hill to an ovation. He had held the line, and the Bronx batsmen came back to score nine for the win.

After the game, Harris volunteered to the press that "one more ball to either York or Doerr and he would've been a goner. I'd had it with him." Bucky was not talking about a trip to the showers but a one-way ticket out of New York.

Page went on to tie the relief-point record set by Marberry in 1926. But in a winter on the banquet circuit, he added 30 pounds, all of which had to come off in spring training. Harris was beginning to see what it was about Page that had driven Joe McCarthy to quit. The crash diet and heavy workouts left Page feeling weak all season, he was later to say, and the result was an off year. Though he again led the A.L. in relief points, his won-lost record slipped from 14–8 to 7–8 and his relief ERA doubled. The Yanks finished two and a half games off the pace, and Harris was shown the door.

Perhaps feeling that Page's off-season excesses had cost him his job, Harris was later to say that Marberry had been a greater reliever than Page. But Fireman Joe had his supporters, too. After Page's phenomenal results in 1949, Connie Mack said that as a reliever, "he is the best I ever saw." And Connie saw them all.

Nineteen forty-eight saw more fine performances by superannuated savers such as Harry Gumbert (38) and Satchel Paige

(42, perhaps), and comparative youngsters Russ Christopher and Earl Johnson.

Johnson, a 6-feet-3 left-hander, manned the Boston Red Sox bullpen brilliantly, leading the A.L. in relief wins with nine. To look at his 4.53 ERA, one would think hitting against Johnson was pretty much a day at the beach. As a starter that was true enough: 34 earned runs in 19 innings—ERA 16.11. However, in 32 relief turns his earned-run average was a minuscule 1.49.

Over in Cleveland, fearing that Babe Klieman would not live up to his 1947 form, owner Bill Veeck went out and got some bullpen help. First he acquired the tall, slender right-hander Russ Christopher from the A's, where he had been an effective reliever in 1947. Although Christopher was frail—he was to die at age thirty-seven—he did manage to conquer illness and chip in 45 games and a league-leading 17 saves to the Tribe's pennant drive (consummated in a one-game play-off with Boston).

Veeck's other acquisition was Satchel Paige, the oldest rookie in baseball history when he joined the Indians midway through the 1948 campaign. That he had not "come up" sooner was not his fault, of course; the color line that had existed since the 1880s had been broken only the year before.

Satchel first pitched professionally way back in 1926, in the Negro Southern Association, and by the early 1930s many major leaguers, who had the chance to face him in exhibition games, considered him the finest pitcher alive. In one barnstorming game, Paige fanned Rogers Hornsby five times; on other occasions he fanned Jimmy Foxx and Charlie Gehringer three times each. In 1934 he won a 1–0, 17-inning duel with Dizzy Dean.

Even as an over-the-hill rookie in 1948, Paige showed signs of his former greatness. In his first big-league appearance, before a record crowd in Cleveland on July 9, he started and threw a three-hit shutout. But Veeck knew that, apart from Satchel being a great gate attraction, his prime value to the Indians could be as a relief pitcher. He had pitched three innings a day for years on the road, where the fans at each backwater stop came to see the advertised appearance of the great one. Indeed, it could be said that Paige proved the efficacy of Mike Marshall's pitching theories before Marshall was born.

Paige's best years as a major-league reliever came not with the Indians but with the St. Louis Browns, whose owner Bill Veeck—the man got around—hired him in 1951 after Paige had returned to the exhibition circuit in 1950. "Everybody kept telling me he was through," Veeck said, "but that was understandable. They thought he was only human." In 1952, Satchel led the A.L. with eight relief wins, and added ten saves. "I'd rather face any other pitcher in the league in a pinch situation," Mickey Mantle said at the time. Whenever the Yankees would find themselves in a tight game with the Browns, Casey Stengel would see Paige warming in the bullpen and he'd pace the dugout, saying, "Get the runs now! Father Time is coming!"

Paige was still an effective hurler when he parted ways with St.

Satchel Paige, the oldest "rookie" in major-league history.

Louis after the 1953 season (as the Browns themselves did, moving to Baltimore). He made his last appearance in a big-league uniform in 1965, when in a publicity stunt at age fifty-nine he started a regular-season game against the Red Sox. Father Time held them scoreless for three innings, allowing only one base hit.

Harry Gumbert had been a successful National League starter for a decade before Cincinnati converted him to relief in 1946. In 1947, he led N.L. bullpenners with ten wins, a total he duplicated in 1948 to go with his league-high 17 saves. That was Harry's last hurrah, however, for old age caught up with him in 1949, and one outing with the Pirates in 1950 proved to be his swan song.

Oddly, all four of the firemen who prospered in 1948 faded in 1949. Gumbert's relief points tailed from 27 to 10, and his ERA shot up by more than two runs. Paige's won-lost record fell from 6–1 to 4–7. Christopher was too ill to play at all, and Johnson was clobbered for an ERA of 7.48.

But the fireman for whom 1948 had been an off year, Joe Page, bounced back in 1949 to have one of the great relief years of all time. The Yankee left-hander who had tied Marberry's relief-point record of 31 two years earlier, now obliterated it. Responding to new manager Casey Stengel's fire alarm 60 times, Page recorded 13 wins and 27 saves; all three figures led the American League, and his 40 relief points more than doubled the total of any other reliever in baseball. He so dominated relief pitching that he won recognition in the postseason balloting for Most Valuable Player; although Ted Williams was the writers' choice, no fireman had ever merited serious consideration for the honor.

In the 1949 World Series with the Dodgers, Page was as brilliant as he had been in 1947, when he and Hugh Casey had stolen the show. For his third-game win and final-game save, he landed the first Babe Ruth Memorial Award, given to the top player in the Series.

In 1950, Joe retreated from brilliance to become just another body in the Yankee bullpen. Though he still finished second in the A.L. in saves, he was hit so hard so often that Stengel lost faith in him. When World Series time rolled around, Tom Ferrick and Allie Reynolds were used in relief while Page sat by the bullpen phone.

After a couple of years in the minors, Joe bounced back to the big time briefly in 1954, but seven games with the Pittsburgh Pirates were proof enough that the fastball of old was gone forever.

Over in the National League in 1949, the top fireman was Ted Wilks of the Cardinals, who almost never lost a game. In 1949 he

Jim Konstanty, the only relief pitcher ever to win Most Valuable Player honors (1950). (*George Brace Photo*)

went 10–3; in earlier years he had put together winning streaks of 10 and 11 games, going undefeated for all of 1944–1945. By 1950, after seven years with St. Louis, the little right-hander nicknamed "Cork" had put together an exalted won-lost record of 51–20.

Challenging Wilks for 1949 N.L. relief honors was a thirty-two-year-old virtual rookie named Jim Konstanty. Before coming to the Phils in September 1948, the big bespectacled right-hander had had a wartime tryout as a starter with the Reds, and a cup of coffee with the 1946 Braves. Otherwise he had toiled in the minors without distinction since 1941, when he broke in with a 4–19 thud. Obviously, he had not yet mastered the palmball learned from former major-leaguer Ted Kleinhans, Konstanty's coach at Syracuse University.

But as the years went by and Jim added a slider to his palmball and fastball, he began to enjoy a measure of prosperity. With Toronto at the Triple-A level from 1946 to 1948, he had pitched under the tutelage of manager Eddie Sawyer. When Sawyer was elevated to the helm of the Phillies in mid-1948, he resolved to give Konstanty a shot as a reliever when major-league rosters expanded in September. Big Jim was no disappointment, either, giving up only one run in six relief turns.

He stuck with the big club throughout 1949, posting nine wins and seven saves in 53 contests. But nothing that had come before could have prepared him for the season he would have in 1950. Leading the Phils from a distant third in 1949 to a last-day pennant victory in 1950, Konstanty set a major-league record for games, 74; games finished, 62; and relief wins, 16. He set a National League record for saves with 22, and his relief-point total of 38 was to stand as a league record for 20 years. After the season, he was rewarded with the first—and thus far the only—Most Valuable Player Award ever to go to a fireman. The election was no contest—he outdistanced second-place finisher Stan Musial 286 votes to 158.

At one point in the regular season, Big Jim put together a skein of 23 scoreless innings before giving up a solo home run to the Pirates' Ralph Kiner—then he came back and added 15 more frames without allowing a run. This kind of pitching was reflected in his 2.66 ERA, lowest on the Phils' staff and second lowest in the league.

In a surprise, the brawny native of Oneonta, New York, was named to start Game One of the World Series against the Yankees. He had not started a single game in 1950, and his last big-league start had been a losing effort four years earlier. Nonetheless, Konstanty performed brilliantly, allowing only four hits while dropping a 1–0 duel with Vic Raschi. Although the Phils went down in four straight, they didn't make it easy for New York, losing three one-run games before absorbing a definitive beating in the fourth and final game.

Konstanty was never to reach the heights again. After two years that could be characterized at best as mediocre, the Phils tried Jim as a starter 19 times in 1953, and he responded with a 10–7 mark in that unfamiliar role. But the Phils were fading out of the pennant picture year by year, and in September 1954 they sold the thirty-seven-year-old Konstanty to the Yankees, who were making a futile run at Cleveland.

With New York he regained some of the touch he had displayed in 1950. His 1955 record for the Yanks in 45 appearances was 7–2, with a creditable 11 saves. But in 1956 Stengel chose to go with young bullpenners Bob Grim and Tom Morgan, and Konstanty found himself back in the National League with the Cards. Big Jim was now thirty-nine, and while he never had much of a fastball to lose, he recognized that he had been slowly slipping for years, despite the respite in 1955. After 27 games with St. Louis, he returned to Oneonta, where in later years he ran a successful sporting-goods store.

As Big Jim Konstanty was showing a glimmer of his future greatness in 1949, so was Little Bobby Shantz, a rookie left-hander with Connie Mack's A's. Standing only 5 feet 6 and weighing less than 140 pounds, the Lilliputian made baseball take notice of him on May 6. In a game against Detroit, he relieved starter Carl Scheib with none out in the third inning and proceeded to pitch nine straight innings of no-hit, no-run ball. Though he weakened in the twelfth inning and allowed two hits and a run, the A's Wally Moses hit a two-run homer in the bottom of the inning to give Shantz his memorable relief win. Shantz went on to become an outstanding starter for the A's, winning 24 games and the Most Valuable Player Award in 1952.

Another remarkable relief story was furnished by Ellis Kinder of the Red Sox. In 1949 he was one of the top starters in the A.L., winning 23 games against only six losses and throwing a league-high six shutouts. He fell back to 14–12 in 1950, but in double duty from the bullpen added a team-high nine saves. The Red Sox had barely missed the pennant three straight years, and a large reason for this, Boston management felt, was the lack of a fireman on the level of Joe Page or Jim Konstanty. Reliever Earl Johnson had pitched well for them in 1948, when the Red Sox were beaten in the play-off by Cleveland. But good as Johnson had been that year, he was not the durable type who could be relied upon 60 times a season.

Boston asked Ellis Kinder if he would step out of the rotation in 1951 and try to fill that role. The transplant took: At age thirty-five, in his first year as a specialist, Kinder relieved a league-high 61 times and topped the A.L. in both saves (14) and relief wins (10) while losing only one of his bullpen efforts. Injury held him back in 1952, but in 1953 he returned with a performance almost the equal of Joe Page's in 1949. "Old Folks" recorded 27 saves, tying Page, and 10 relief wins. His ERA of 1.85 was remarkable in a hitter's year, when the league ERA was a fat 4.00, and his games total of 69 established a new A.L. mark. When he retired in 1957 at age forty-three, he was pitching nearly as well as ever.

The National League's top fireman of 1951 was Clyde King of the Dodgers, whose 13 relief wins included two in one day against the Cardinals. Of his six saves, the most gratifying was "coming in to pitch against the Phillies," he said. "The bases were loaded, two men were out, and the Dodgers were leading by one run in the ninth. Del Ennis was the batter, and the count was three balls and no strikes. The first pitch was a called strike. Ennis fouled off the next one, then bounced to me for the last out."

When the Dodgers blew the 1951 pennant to the Giants, in the crucial spot in the last game of the play-off, manager Charley Dressen went to starter Ralph Branca instead of to a bullpen operative. The second-guessing of that move will never end, for the result was thoroughly disastrous. Leading 4–1 going into the bottom of the ninth, the Dodger starter, Don Newcombe, permitted one run to score and put two men on base before being relieved. Branca threw a gopher ball to Bobby Thomson, and that was that.

No situation more eloquently expresses the exquisite tension of the reliever's task. If Branca retired Thomson, the Dodgers would be N.L. champs; a base hit might deadlock matters and defer resolution of the conflict; a home run would bring a flag to the Giants. One pitch could turn the game and the season 180 degrees, and of course it did.

Would the outcome have been different if Dressen had brought in a relief specialist? The question cannot be answered. But were the situation to repeat itself today, it is extremely doubtful that any manager would pass over his firemen to go with a starter. This is not to imply that Charley Dressen was less than astute; it is simply to point out that times have changed. Dressen broke into major-league baseball in the year that Bucky Harris refused to pull Walter Johnson out of the seventh game of the World Series, preferring to "go down with my best," as Harris put it then. The idea that a manager's "best" might not be best in a given situation is a concept not universally upheld until the 1960s.

Dressen's star reliever in 1952 was twenty-eight-year-old rookie Joe Black. All he threw was a fastball and a hard curve with a narrow break, but that was enough for him to go 15–4 with 15 saves and a 2.15 ERA. That earned him Rookie-of-the-Year honors and a third-place finish in the MVP balloting.

With eight days left in the season, Dressen gave the 6-feet-2, 220-pound right-hander the first of two starts designed to ready Black for use as a starter in the World Series. Dressen felt that in a short series an ace in the bullpen was a wasting asset—thinking that is quite the opposite of today's, when managers stress over and again how the bullpen makes the difference when the stakes are the greatest.

Black started the first game, and bested the Yanks' Allie Reynolds, 4–2. Reynolds took revenge in Game Four by a count of 2–0, and again in Game Seven, which Black lost 4–2. As a reliever and as a starter, Black had enjoyed a phenomenal 1952. But in spring training the next year, Dressen determined that Black could not get by much longer with his limited repertoire and tried to teach him a big curve, a screwball, and a forkball for his change of pace. Black became confused and lost his ability to control the two pitches he had commanded so beautifully in 1952. Never again did he enjoy a good season, though he managed to hang on with the Reds and Senators till 1957.

Black's nemesis in the 1952 World Series, burly right-hander Allie Reynolds, was a great starter with the Indians and Yankees who to that date had rarely doubled as a reliever. But when he did come in from the bullpen, he was terrific. In 1952 the Oklahoma Superchief, called upon to put out a fire on only six occasions, picked up six saves—without allowing a run. And in World Series play between 1949 and 1953, he was similarly summoned in six times—with a resulting record of four saves and two wins!

In Game Four of the 1949 World Series, Reynolds had saved the win for Eddie Lopat by putting down ten Dodgers in succession, five of them on strikeouts. In 1950, he had come in to strike out the final batter in the final game as the Phils were staging a last-minute uprising. In 1952, in addition to shutting out the Dodgers in Game Four after losing the opener, Reynolds saved Game Six and won the finale in long relief.

When Reynolds was pinch-hit for in the seventh inning of that game, Stengel called on Vic Raschi to bail out Reynolds, as Reynolds had bailed out Raschi the day before. But Vic could get only one out before loading the bases, and the Yanks were in a deep hole what with Duke Snider coming up. Snider had already hit four round-trippers in the Series and was batting a resounding .357. Stengel took the ball from Raschi and waved in left-hander Bob Kuzava, who had been used little during the regular season and not at all in the Series. Stengel no doubt recalled the 1951 Series, when he also had kept Kuzava on ice until the final game; on that occasion, Bob had responded by getting three straight Giants to fly out and thus save the game.

Kuzava got the dangerous Snider on a pop-out, with no advance by the runners. Next was Jackie Robinson, whom the lefty induced to lift a 3–2 pitch high into the air near the pitcher's mound. First-basemen Joe Collins lost sight of the ball in the sun, and both Kuzava and catcher Yogi Berra seemed paralyzed. Out of nowhere, seemingly, raced second-baseman Billy Martin to grab the ball a foot off the grass. Had the ball dropped, the game would have been tied, at the least, for all runners were off with the pitch in the full-count, two-out situation. But the ball was caught, and the Dodgers' assault blunted. Retiring the next six batters was duck soup for Kuzava, and the Dodgers once again had to wait till next year.

In 1953, the little-used lefty worked even less than he had the previous two years. But the thirty-eight-year-old Allie Reynolds now began to work more frequently as a fireman than as a starter. With the incredible efficiency that marked his whole career in relief, the Superchief came in from the pen but 26 times, yet recorded seven wins and 13 saves against only a single loss.

Fleeting as fame was for Joe Black, the losing pitcher in that seventh game of the 1952 Series, the drop from the heights was even more meteoric for another rookie reliever, Eddie Yuhas. This Cardinal freshman attained stardom by going 11–1 with six saves as the right-hander in the St. Louis bullpen. (The lefty was Al Brazle, who topped the circuit in saves in 1952–1953.) A real flash, Yuhas followed up in 1953 by pitching in two games for the Cards and then disappearing from the big-league scene forever.

The third notable freshman fireman that year was Hoyt Wilhelm, who owed his belated entrance into the big time in large measure to Dutch Leonard. Apart from his role as a trailblazer for Wilhelm, Leonard himself was quite a reliever for the Cubs in 1952, equaling if not surpassing his heroics of the season before, when he had won ten games in relief. At forty-three, Dutch saved 11 games while being nicked for only 2.16 earned runs per nine innings.

Leonard had been almost exclusively a starter from the time he joined Washington in 1938 (following four seasons in Brooklyn) until his second year with the Cubs, 1950. Looking back on that transition, Leonard says today, "I got to where I'd get just as big of a thrill if I pitched one ball and got the out, or saved the game, as I used to get pitching a full nine innings." His biggest thrill as a reliever came in a game against the Dodgers, when he was called in to protect a one-run lead. "It was the ninth inning, no outs, and the bases loaded. The three hitters I had coming up were Jackie Robinson, Gil Hodges, and Roy Campanella. Jackie popped out. I struck out Gil. Roy hit a grounder. No score; we won the game, 2–1."

Leonard at last began to fade in 1953, but new blood for the

Ryne Duren. No reliever was ever more feared.

manager Ralph Houk's tutelage he found the plate and himself. A local doctor helped him to correct his vision problem, which had stemmed from childhood rheumatism, and in half a season the newly confident Duren was 13–3 for Houk.

In 1958 he made the big club and was an immediate sensation, leading the American League in saves and striking out more men than innings pitched—the first time any reliever had ever done so. Also, his 4.76 hits allowed per nine innings is one of the lowest ever recorded by any pitcher in frequent use as a starter or reliever.

Batters dared not dig in with Duren on the mound. His wildness was legendary, with the witting assistance of Duren himself. Ryne would come in from the bullpen, search out the mound, take off his thick glasses and wipe them clean, put them back on and squint, then often as not fire his first warm-up pitch over the catcher's head to the screen. In many cases he quelled a crisis before throwing his first pitch in earnest.

Duren pitched every bit as well in 1959, at one point being unscored on for better than two and a half months, covering 18 games and 36 innings. In one game during this streak, on June 26, he came in to pitch the last three innings of a game with the White Sox. Of the nine outs he obtained, eight came on strikes. Of the last 19 batters he faced before his scoreless streak ended in the latter part of July, he fanned 15.

The strikeout was Duren's enduring trademark, even in the years after 1959, when he was not effective. In 1961 the Yanks, content with Luis Arroyo in the bullpen, unloaded Ryne onto the expansion Los Angeles Angels. Although he again struck out more men than he pitched innings, he was pounded for an ERA of 5.19. The two bright spots: a complete-game shutout as a starter, and an unprecedented loss to the White Sox. On May 18, 1961, Duren relieved starter Ronnie Kline in the seventh, with the score tied 4–4. He struck out Minnie Minoso and Roy Sievers, but catcher Del Rice let the third strike to Sievers get by, allowing the slugger to reach base. Then Jim Landis tripled, scoring Sievers. Duren next whiffed J. C. Martin for what should have been the third out of the inning, with no runs having crossed. But then Sherm Lollar singled, scoring Landis. At last Sammy Esposito became the fourth Chicago batter to fan in the inning, and thus the game ended, 6–4.

Beset by alcoholism and deteriorating physical skills, Duren drifted from the Angels to Philadelphia to Cincinnati, back to Philly, to Washington, and in mid-1965, out of baseball. Looking back on his career today, Duren cites the sixth game of the 1958 World Series as his greatest relief performance.

Actually, Duren had been great throughout the Series. In Game One, he was nicked for a tenth-inning run and absorbed the loss, but he did strike out five Milwaukee Braves in his two and two-thirds innings of work. He threw two hitless innings to save Game Three for Don Larsen. And in Game Six, with the Yankees trailing 2–1 after five frames and facing elimination, Ryne came in to throw beebees past the Braves, fanning eight in four and two-thirds innings, an unaccustomedly long stint. He held the Braves to one hit from the sixth through the ninth, enabling the Yanks to tie the score and eventually go ahead by two in the top of the tenth.

In the Braves' half of the tenth, however, a weary Duren wavered and allowed a run on a walk and two singles. The final out had to be registered by Bob Turley, who had pitched a shutout the game before. While winning 21 during the regular season, Bullet Bob had relieved only twice. In Game Seven, Stengel called him out of the bullpen for the second time in two days, and Turley responded with one of the great World Series relief performances. In six and two-thirds innings he allowed but two hits, thus permitting the Yanks to recover from a 3–1 deficit in games and take the championship.

Relief pitching had made remarkable strides in this brief period of 1947 to 1958. In 1946, major-league starters completed 42.7 percent of their games, and relievers recorded saves in 9.2 percent of all contests. By 1958, these percentiles had, respectively, contracted to 30.2 and expanded to 16.4. The historical trend toward greater reliance on the bullpen was acclerating; by 1970 the major leagues' number of saves would *exceed* its number of complete games.

But recognizing the statistical evidence of a trend does not itself dramatically affect that trend; events do. Baseball's biggest event is of course the World Series, and what happens there tends to alter strategy on the field and in the front office in the years immediately following. The 1947 battle of Joe Page and Hugh Casey, for example, spurred other teams to develop specialists in their bullpens and added enormous prestige to the fireman's calling. The 1958 World Series touched off no such explosion, for the most memorable relief performance was that of a starter, Bob Turley. The fall classic of 1959 would be the trigger for relief pitching's next advance.

**11**

# The
# Ten Best:
# McDaniel

Although he pitched 21 years in the major leagues, tying Hoyt Wilhelm, Lindy McDaniel never got a chance to display his considerable talents in the grand October arena. Nevertheless, by the time he hung up his spikes after the 1975 season, McDaniel had secured his place among the top ten relievers of all time. Despite seeing his fortunes skyrocket and then plummet and then skyrocket again several times during his career, he gathered impressive lifetime marks. He came to the rescue in 913 games, won 119 of them, and put together 291 relief points—all figures second only to Wilhelm (though Lyle or Fingers may have passed the latter mark by the time you read this). He topped the National League in saves three times and, ten years after his last saves title, captured the most relief wins in the American League.

Lindy's main weapons were the forkball, which was a devastating change of pace after his good fastball, and an over-the-top pitching motion that tended to negate the advantage left-handed batters ordinarily enjoyed with right-handed hurlers. But when he first came to the majors in 1955, after having received a $50,000 bonus from the St. Louis Cardinals, all the nineteen-year-old right-hander threw was a fastball and a sinker, both delivered from a three-quarters position. That was enough, for as a starter in 1957 McDaniel blossomed into a 15-game winner, leading the Cardinals to a surprising second-place finish. What made that year particu-

Lindy McDaniel. His fortunes were constantly soaring and plummeting, but when he called it quits, he could look back on a glittering career.

larly enjoyable was being joined in the starting rotation by his eighteen-year-old brother, Von, who chipped in with seven wins, two of them shutouts.

Nineteen fifty-eight was not a good year for the McDaniel boys or the Cardinals, who slipped to sixth. Von lost his control and faded out of the majors for good, while Lindy somehow lost his sinker and got kicked around for nearly six runs per ball game; year's end found him in Omaha trying to regain his equilibrium. His 4–1 record in the American Association belied the fact that he was still less than a puzzlement to opposing batters, who reached him for better than one hit per inning.

Back with the pitching-hungry Cards in early 1959, McDaniel recalls, "I was pitching only about once a week, used as a spot starter, with very average success. On May 23 I asked to go to the bullpen, and on that same day I swtiched to straight overhand pitching, as suggested by coach Howie Pollet, and I pitched five and two-thirds innings against the Cubs, allowing two hits and no runs and picking up the win. In the next three months, throwing straight overhand, I picked up 25 wins and saves." His season's total of 28 relief points tied Roy Face for the N.L. high, and his 15 saves matched Milwaukee's Don McMahon.

Nineteen fifty-nine had been McDaniel's introduction to relief work, and it was a great year for many other firemen—Face, Mc-Mahon, Sherry, Lown, Staley, Elston, Henry, Duren, Loes, Fornieles. But for McDaniel 1960 would be even better.

At the close of the 1959 campaign Lindy went home to work on a change-of-speed pitch that would prevent hitters from laying back for the fastball. Fooling around in his backyard, McDaniel came up with a forkball. No one showed him how to throw the pitch, though ElRoy Face's success with the pitch the previous year might have provided the inspiration. Unlike Face's forkball, which broke in to left-handed batters, McDaniel's dropped straight down to both left-handed and right-handed batters because of his overhand motion. This feature kept him in games where another right-hander might have been pulled in a strict percentage move.

McDaniel appeared in 65 games for the Cards in 1960, all but twice in relief. As a fireman, his record was phenomenal: 12 wins, 2 losses, 26 saves, and an eye-popping ERA of 1.29. (In his two starts, both losses, he was blasted for 12 runs in 12 innnings, lifting his season's ERA to 2.09.) His 38 relief points tied the league record set by Jim Konstanty in 1950, and his 26 saves set a new N.L. record. "Except for the two games I started," McDaniel says, "I did not have a bad outing in 1960, which I never came close to duplicating."

In 1961, he was very far off that form, indeed: His relief ERA nearly quadrupled, his strikeouts slipped badly, and only good fortune enabled him to close the books on the season with a 10–6 record. The following year, when he pitched somewhat better, his luck evened out, and he went 3–10. Persona non grata in St. Louis, he packed his bags for Wrigley Field.

The 6-feet-3, 195-pound right-hander with the militarily erect bearing on the mound had seen his fortunes rise in 1957, fall in 1958, rise in 1960, and now fall again. The pattern would continue throughout his career, the good years far outweighing the bad in the end. Straining to recover his abilities with the Cubs in 1963, he pulled muscles in his elbow. Yet he bounced back to lead the National League in saves once more while adding 13 wins. His heroics helped the Cubs to finish over .500 for the first time since 1946 and briefly to challenge for the top spot.

McDaniel's most fondly remembered win of that season occurred on June 6, at Wrigley Field against the Giants. "It was a
capacity crowd," McDaniel recalls. "We were one game behind
the league-leading Giants in the standings. Entering the game in
the top of the tenth with the bases loaded and one out, I picked
Willie Mays off second base, struck out Ed Bailey, and received a
standing ovation as I walked off the mound. I was the lead-off
hitter in the bottom of the tenth, and on a 2–2 count I hit a home
run which decided the game, enabling us to sweep the four-game
Series and tie us with the Giants. Another standing ovation."

There was no applause to be heard in 1964, as the on-again,
off-again bugaboo resumed its course. Though he was able to log
15 saves, his won-lost record of 1–7 buried him in the bullpen behind Ted Abernathy the following year. Lindy pitched well in
1965 while making his all-time high of 71 appearances; but when
the game was on the line, the call went out for Abernathy. The
submariner saved a record 31 games; McDaniel saved two. Now,
*that's* expendable.

McDaniel was duly expended, to San Francisco in a deal that
brought the Cubs Bill Hands and Randy Hundley. For the Giants
in 1966 Lindy had a quietly good season, going 10–5 with six saves
in support of Frank Linzy. Although only thirty years old, McDaniel
had completed his twelfth year in the big time, and was becoming
tagged as a fading veteran, a part he lived up to in 1967. Tempo-
rarily short of starters, Giant manager Herman Franks handed the
ball to McDaniel for two successive turns. In the second outing
Lindy hurt his arm and was out of action for six weeks or so. Now
he was tagged as a sore-armed fading veteran.

In his first outing of 1968, McDaniel was pounded for four
runs on five pitches by the Pirates. The Giants tried to move him,
but couldn't get anything in return as the trading deadline passed.
No one would believe that McDaniel's arm was sound, though in
fact it was. You could hardly blame the National League clubs for
being suspicious, for through mid-July, Lindy had been used only
as a mopup man of last resort; in his 12 games, he registered no
wins, no losses, no saves, and a grotesque ERA of 7.58.

McDaniel was despondent. He thought about quitting. Franks
wouldn't use him because he was being hit hard—yet how could he
regain his command without game action? Then, on July 12, a deal
was worked out with the Yankees. Bill Monbouquette cleared
waivers in the American League, McDaniel cleared in the National,
and the two swapped teams.

As with Wilhelm, whose career had been hanging by a thread
when he switched leagues in 1958, the crossover worked miracles

for McDaniel. Manager Ralph Houk understood that Lindy was rusty, and assured him that he would be given a fair chance to work himself back into sharpness; the Yanks weren't going anywhere that year, anyway.

In two and a half months with the Yankees, the man whom no National League club would take saved ten games, won four against a lone loss, and posted an ERA of 1.76. One month after donning pinstripes, McDaniel tied an American League record by retiring 32 batters in succession without a base hit, walk, hit batsman, or error in the field (the record has since been upped to 33, by Steve Busby and John Montague). Lindy's feat encompassed four ball games: Beginning on August 18, he retired the last eight men he faced; continuing on the twenty-first, he was called on to retire only two batters, and did; culminating on the twenty-third, in a spectacular display he retired all 21 men he faced in long relief; and ending with one batter retired on the twenty-fifth.

Nineteen sixty-eight had been, by general agreement, the "Year of the Pitcher." Capping a trend that had taken shape in the early 1960s, the earned-run average of each *league* dipped under 3.00; ten years earlier, no single team had posted so low a mark. The American League produced only one .300 hitter, Carl Yastrzemski, and his league-leading average was only .301. As a team, the Yankees batted an unfathomable .214 to bring up the rear, but of the 19 other clubs, only one batted for more than .252. This was also the year when Bob Gibson's ERA was 1.12, Lius Tiant's 1.60, and five other qualifiers finished under 2.00.

Something had to be done if batters were to avoid the endangered species list. For 1969, the pitching mound was lowered and the strike zone narrowed—a small step, seemingly, but its effect was profound. Batting averages shot up, as did bases on balls and earned-run averages. Not a few of the pitchers who had been brilliant in 1968 were casualties in the new climate of 1969.

McDaniel was one of these. It took him more than half the year, in which he was generally ineffective, to realize that he had been trying to guide the ball into the newly restricted strike zone, that he wasn't cutting loose as he had in previous years. Result: His pitches were coming to the plate in good locations but were being whacked; he had sacrificed an essential measure of his stuff. When he caught on to that fact late in the year, he determined to go more to his fastball, still swift at age thirty-three, and not worry so much about whether his forker might drop below the redefined strike zone.

In 1970 he rode back up on the roller coaster with a marvelous year for the Yanks, who revived en masse and made a good run at the Tigers for the flag. Lindy matched his previous best relief-point total of 38 and picked up a personal-high 29 saves. This was for McDaniel "probably my most rewarding year."

A devout Christian and off-season preacher, McDaniel had the even temperament that has characterized most relief pitchers and that has enabled them to ply their treacherous trade. As McDaniel had already seen, you could go from toast of the town to out of town in a hurry, and you had to be equally prepared for accolades and brickbats.

McDaniel had not enjoyed two good seasons back to back since 1959–1960, and he was not about to repeat the trick in 1971. In many respects, his showing that year was the poorest full-season performance since 1958, when he had merited a demotion to Omaha. To a 5–10 won-lost log he added only four saves, and the Yankees who had shown so much promise in 1970 returned to mediocrity. With McDaniel failing as the stopper, the Yanks had no one to turn to but Jack Aker, who was past his peak years with the A's. As a team, the 1971 Yankees compiled only 12 saves—no team had had fewer since the infamous 1962 Mets, who won but 40 games.

If there was a virtue in the bullpen collapse that McDaniels's off year precipitated, it was that it prompted the Bronx brain trust to go out and steal Sparky Lyle from the Red Sox. In 1972 Lyle saved 35 games while McDaniel, though pitching effectively again, notched nary a one. At age thirty-six, he was called on fewer than 40 times for the first time since 1958. The end of his fine career was drawing near.

Or so one thought. In 1973, Lindy got up off the canvas, to mix a metaphor, and led the American League in relief wins with 12. What's more, to Lyle's 27 saves he added 10 of his own. In a remarkable performance for a fireman seemingly just padding his pension, Lindy worked more innings in relief than he ever had before. "Numerous times," Lindy says, "I came into a ball game in the fourth or fifth inning, finished the game giving up no runs, and picked up the win." On August 4, 1973, against Detroit, he pitched 13 relief innings to get the win.

McDaniel's last two years were spent with the Kansas City Royals, playing out the string. There were a few sparks that showed how great a pitcher he had been over the years, but McDaniel was nearing his fortieth birthday and found it hard to convince others that these so-so years were just another slump, the kind he'd always bounced back from before. He left the game after 21 years. Although his record is uneven, few relievers can match his accomplishments, and none his indomitability.

# 12

# The Ten Best: Perranoski

When Ron Perranoski was a boy growing up in Fair Lawn, New Jersey, he was a Yankee fan whose idols were left-handers Joe Page and Tommy Byrne. Perhaps he thought that someday he too would become a Yankee star. He was left-handed, and he threw a surprisingly good curveball for a fourteen-year-old; the trouble was that Ron stood 5 feet 5 and weighed a horrifying 75 pounds.

As he moved through high school, he filled out to a comparatively beefy 130 pounds, but he also grew to 5 feet 11, so the net effect was much the same; Ron's high-school teammates called him "Bad Body." Yet the anemic-looking left-hander with the precocious curveball took his team to the state championship, along the way hurling 56 straight scoreless innings and attracting the attention of major-league scouts. In the expectation that as he added weight he would also add a major-league fastball to his repertoire, the White Sox offered him $4,000—the maximum amount that a team could award without carrying the player on the major-league roster for two years. But Perranoski rejected the bid in favor of a scholarship award from Michigan State.

There, under the guidance of coach John Kobs, Perranoski polished his act and won the Spartan award as top pitcher in both 1957 and 1958; in the latter year he and his roommate were both Big Ten first-team picks. His roommate was Dick Radatz. Incredibly, three of the ten best major-league relievers of all time are Michigan State alumni (the third being Mike Marshall, who signed a pro contract at eighteen and never played for MSU).

At the conclusion of the Spartans' 1958 season, Perranoski—now filled out to a solid 180 pounds—signed with the Chicago Cubs for a reported bonus of $21,000. Bonus restrictions had been eased since the White Sox had made their offer in 1954, and the Cubs were able to farm him out. One of the main reasons Perranoski chose the Cubs was that unlike the Dodgers, who ran three Triple-A teams, the Cubs had only one. Already twenty-one, he was in a hurry to reach the majors and the Cubs figured to provide him quicker entry.

The calculations were astute, but events overtook logic. After

Ron Perranoski. A star in each league, he is one of three firemen to post more than one 40-point season.

a fairly routine record as a starter in the Cub chain, Perranoski was traded to the Dodgers in April 1960, along with two other players who were destined never to wear Dodger blue. The Cubs sweetened the pot with $25,000 to get the object of their desire, infielder Don Zimmer, who had hit .165 for Los Angeles the season before.

While Zimmer played for the Cubs in 1960, all three players the Dodgers acquired went to the minors. Perranoski was assigned to the Triple-A Montreal club, where he opened the 1960 season with an 0–5 record. Montreal manager Clay Bryant was seriously contemplating lowering the lefty to Double-A when in mid-June Perranoski finally won a game and earned a reprieve. But Ron was relying almost exclusively on his fastball, for his curve had deserted him: It was breaking out but not down as it came to the plate. Teammate Ralph Mauriello, who had pitched in three games for the 1958 Dodgers, showed him his own curve—delivered with the pressure applied to the ball by the middle finger rather than the index finger. This unconventional or "incorrect" method restored the drop to Perranoski's curve and the glow to his record. Used as a reliever and spot starter, Ron threw four shutouts.

In September, when he thought he might be summoned to L.A. to aid in the pennant drive, he instead was moved to St. Paul in the American Association, another Dodger Triple-A outfit. There he started for manager Danny Ozark until the play-offs, when suddenly he was sent to the bullpen. Perranoski was disappointed until he learned from Ozark that the move had been dictated by the Dodgers, who planned to bring him up in 1961 as a relief pitcher.

In winter ball before the 1961 season, Ron developed a sinker, that necessary ingredient for all firemen but the flamethrowers. He was now ready to take on National League hitters.

But Walter Alston thought he was ready only for left-handed hitters, and in the opening weeks of the season would yank Perranoski for Larry Sherry or Dick Farrell whenever the opposition put up a couple of righties in a row. By season's end, when he compiled a record of seven wins, six saves, and a 2.65 ERA, manager Alston was convinced that the rookie could be tough on any batter. Dick Farrell was allowed to go to Houston in the expansion draft, and Sherry became number-two man in the pen. Perranoski's saves total jumped from 5 to 20, while Sherry's sank from 15 to 11. In 107 innings of work, Ron allowed only one home run, evidence of the effectiveness of his recently developed sinker. His 70 games led the National League and established a new record for a left-hander. There were only 25 games all season in which he did not warm up at least once, and in some games he was up five times in the bullpen; he even warmed up once during Sandy Koufax's no-hitter. Yet when the chips were down in the final, pennant-deciding game of the season, Perranoski was passed over.

With seven games left to play in that 1962 season, the Dodgers led the Giants by four games and were making plans for their World Series checks. L.A. was losing almost every day, but the Giants were keeping pace. With three games left, all the Dodgers had to do to clinch the flag was win one. They couldn't. A two-of-three play-off, reminiscent of the 1951 affair, was necessary.

Just as in 1951, the Giants took the first game, the Dodgers the second, and the Bums brought a lead into the final inning of the final game. And just as in 1951, they couldn't hold it. In the last National League game of 1962, Alston chose not to bring in Perranoski to protect a two-run lead that a weary Ed Roebuck had already nursed through three innings. With one man out, one run in, and the bags full of Giants, the Dodger pilot called on Stan Williams, primarily a starter that season, and watched him walk the lead run across the plate. Once the damage had been completed, Perranoski was called in to get the final out.

Next season, Alston went with Perranoski whenever the issue was in doubt, and Ron responded with a record of 16–3, 21 saves (Larry Sherry was next high on the Dodgers with three), and a 1.67 ERA. He led the league in games, relief wins, and winning percentage. During one stretch of 30 days in June and July, Perranoski allowed not a single run over 13 appearances. Perhaps his finest single performance under pressure came in a September series with the red-hot St. Louis Cardinals who, on the strength of winning 19 of 21 games, had come from nowhere to challenge the Dodgers. If the Cards could sweep the three-game set in St. Louis, they would overtake the Dodgers by a full game.

On September 16, the Cards suffered a disappointment as Johnny Podres beat them 3–1. On the seventeenth, Sandy Koufax shut them out, 4–0. Still, if the Cards could take the final contest, they would be only three games back with two weeks to go. The score was 5–4 in favor of the Cards in the eighth inning of this key game when Ron Perranoski came in and got the side out. In the top of the ninth, L.A. first-baseman Dick Nen, just up from Triple-A, wrote his name large in Dodger history with a long home run to right center—tying the game with his only hit ever as a Dodger.

In the bottom of the twelfth, however, Cardinal shortstop Dick Groat led off with a triple. "I enjoy the challenge more with men on base," Perranoski once said, "than with the bases empty and a three-run lead." Here was a chance for real enjoyment. He fanned

Gary Kolb, then intentionally walked Bill White and Ken Boyer, since their runs meant nothing. The strategy looked good after Curt Flood's grounder forced Groat at the plate. Then Perranoski closed out the brilliant display by inducing Mike Shannon to bounce out to third. The Dodgers pushed a run across in the thirteenth to win 6–5, and Ron stayed in all the way to get the win.

Perranoski had such an outstanding season in 1963 that he positively exuded confidence as he took the ball from the manager and set to work. He was so loose on the mound that he would smile at the batters, stick his tongue out at base runners, and cheerfully cut their hearts out. His imperturbability earned him the nickname "Nonchalantski" from his teammates, who marveled at the way he would drop that curve of his in, no matter what the count, no matter how many men were on base. He would not give in to the batter and toss him a meatball just because the situation demanded a strike. "I can throw my curve anytime. I can control it. I pitch everyone the same way. When I see the plate I never see the middle—I see only the corners, and I'm going to throw either low inside or low outside. I'm a low-ball pitcher and I don't care if he's a low-ball hitter. He's going to have a tough time hitting my pitch."

Nonchalant, but aggressive; unconcerned, yet confident—those attributes characterize most of the great relievers. All felt they were better than any hitter, and would throw their strength against his strength, if it came to that.

Before the opening of the 1963 World Series against the Yankees, Perranoski said: "Their left-handers I don't worry about. [Their left-handers included such as Roger Maris, Yogi Berra, Joe Pepitone, John Blanchard.] I don't worry about any left-handers." But in the Dodgers' four-game demolition of the Yankees, Perranoski got little chance to manifest his disdain on the mound. Three of the four L.A. wins were complete games; in the other, Johnny Podres took a shutout one out into the ninth inning before manager Alston decided to call in his relief ace and sew up the win. Ron got the save, but permitted a single to Elston Howard that brought in one of only four runs the Yankees could muster in the whole Series.

When award time rolled around, Perranoski's achievements were not ignored. He finished second in the balloting for the Cy Young behind Sandy Koufax, and fourth in the MVP count, again behind his teammate.

Nineteen sixty-four was a disappointing year for Perranoski and the Dodgers, as he fell from 37 relief points to 19, and they finished far back in the pack behind the Cardinals. And 1965 started out no better for Ron, whose ERA ballooned to more than 4.00

by the All-Star break. He was nearing thirty, and two successive off years would undoubtedly precipitate a change of scenery. Already the Dodgers were leaning more and more on right-handed reliever Bob Miller.

In the last seven weeks of the season, however, Perranoski caught fire. In 21 appearances covering 47⅓ innings, the left-hander with the compact motion allowed only one earned run. The Dodgers clinched the pennant on the last day of the campaign, averting a third play-off with the Giants.

In the World Series, Perranoski pitched two scoreless innings in the opening-game loss to the Minnesota Twins. In Game Two, he entered with the Dodgers trailing by 2–1 in the seventh. When he departed one inning later, L.A. was down 5–1. That was the last action he saw in the Series, and his benching provided a harbinger of what was to come in 1966.

The Dodgers acquired a failed starter named Phil Regan from Detroit in the off-season. The Vulture, as he came to be known, dominated the Dodger bullpen as he swooped away with N.L. relief honors. Perranoski saw little action when it mattered, and his relief-point totals dropped to the level of his rookie year. The highlight of this otherwise forgettable regular season took place on September 12, when he entered a game in the fifth—he never used to see such early action—and fanned the first six men he faced, tying a league record.

In the Series that year his two appearances were poor, but of no great moment, for the Dodgers were blown away in four straight by the Baby Birds of Baltimore: After the third inning of the first game, Los Angeles scored no runs. That winter Sandy Koufax stunned baseball by announcing his retirement, and the Dodgers began rebuilding.

Although Ron, now thirty-one, rebounded with a good year as Regan faded, the Dodgers finished 16 games below .500, their worst record in over three decades. They were determined to clean house. Bullpen mates Miller and Perranoski were traded to Minnesota in the winter, and Regan too was banished shortly after the 1968 season opened.

Ron's first season in the American League was a period of adjustment. After a fairly idle April, he started the month of May with eight bullpen calls in ten days, during which he permitted no earned runs and garnered three victories in four days. That early flash turned out to be the highlight of a lackluster season, in which he took a back seat to the Twins' longtime relief ace, Al Worthington. Although he pitched in 66 games, many of these appearances involved just pitching to one or two lefties, then retiring in favor of Worthington or Miller. Perranoski's career was going in reverse gear; being the left-handed "percentage pitcher" was a role he had not played since he was a rookie.

Perranoski himself attributed his declining effectiveness to inactivity. Like many sinkerballers, he needed to work often or he would get too strong and his sinker would come in straight as a string. "The more tired I get," he said, "the more my ball sinks." Perranoski wasn't wearing out, he felt; he was rusting out.

The Twins changed managers in 1969, dismissing Cal Ermer and taking on Billy Martin. Martin would last only one year in the Twin Cities, but in his brief tenure he brought Cal Griffith a Western Division title and restored to usefulness a disgruntled thirty-three-year-old fireman. Martin discovered that what Perranoski had always said about his need for frequent work was true: "You've got to warm him up every day until his arm falls off," the skipper said, "and then you can pitch him. His sinker isn't effective until his arm is about dead." Pitching 32% more innings in 1969 than he had in 1968, Perranoski gave up fewer base hits; his saves total shot up from six to a league-high 31, and his wins rose from eight to nine.

In 1970, Martin was gone, replaced by the more serene Bill Rigney. The Twins took their division again, as Rigney's bullpen posted an American-League-record 58 saves. Perranoski claimed 34 of these while Stan Williams and Tom Hall divvied up most of the rest. Adding seven wins to his A.L.-record number of saves, Perranoski became the only pitcher besides his old college roommate, Dick Radatz, ever to enjoy more than one 40-point season in relief (Rollie Fingers in 1978 also accomplished the feat). His exploits even earned him one of the 24 first-place votes for Most Valuable Player. In his tenth year in the majors, when his skills should have been on the wane, Ron Perranoski reached the pinnacle of his career.

The descent from the pinnacle was swift. On July 30, 1971, after 36 games in which he posted a 1–4 record and a monstrous ERA of 6.75, the Twins released him on waivers. Minnesota was nose-diving into the second division, and the bullpen of Perranoski, Williams, and Hall bore much of the blame. Just as the Dodgers had cleaned house after the 1967 season, so did the Twins; none of the three was with the club in 1972.

The man who picked up Perranoski's contract was Billy Martin, now managing Detroit. "They're not handling him right over there," Billy declared, and set about resuscitating Ron's career once more.

This time he couldn't do it. Perranoski's arm was shot. He pitched 11 games for Martin in 1971 and 17 more the next year, then was given his outright release. The Dodgers re-signed him in

August, and he won two games for them, but he was the proverbial shadow of his former self. They too released him after the season.

Dreams die hard; baseball had been Perranoski's occupation and preoccupation for 20 years. He gave it one more shot in 1973 with the Angels, but eight nondescript appearances convinced him to call it quits.

Today he remains in baseball as minor-league pitching instructor for the Dodgers.

**13**

**The
Ten Best:
Radatz**

The inclusion of Dick Radatz in the pantheon of relief pitching may be disputed: He lasted only seven years in the big leagues, and the last three of these are best forgotten. If longevity is a prime criterion for this honor roll—and it is—the question naturally arises why Radatz and not, say, Stu Miller or Don McMahon? And the answer must be, simply, that while he was at his peak, he was a better relief pitcher than anybody ever has been.

Nicknamed "The Monster," Radatz terrified American League hitters more with his awesome fastball than with his awesome size (6 feet 5, 245 pounds). For three years in a row, he led American League firemen in relief points, a feat matched only by Marberry and Page. In that period, pitching for a club that finished eighth, seventh, and eighth, he *averaged* 72 games, 13 relief wins, 26 saves, and an ERA of 2.17. Over his career, even taking into account the three poor years, the big right-hander struck out more men per game (9.67) than any pitcher who ever played the game, reliever or starter.

Until his final year at Michigan State University, Radatz was not considered a great major-league prospect. Growing up in Berkeley, Michigan, a suburb of Detroit, he starred in baseball, basketball, and football. He pitched three no-hitters, and drew an offer of $4,000 from the Orioles. Yet the hometown Tigers did

Dick Radatz. For a short stretch, The Monster was the best ever.

not send anyone to look at Radatz until he was a sophomore at East Lansing, at which time the Detroit scout judged that for Radatz's size, he ought to have a better fastball. Verdict: He was lazy.

In truth, the young Radatz was simply experiencing the typical growing adolescent's difficulty in becoming comfortable with his body. Awkward, sluggish, and uncertain in his movements, he just couldn't master the mechanics of a well-timed pitching delivery. It seemed he was pitching entirely with his arm, Spartan teammate Ron Perranoski observed at the time, rather than getting his body into the release. In truth, Radatz did not yet possess as much body as he was later able to apply to his fastball—he was tall, yet did not fill out until he was out of his teens. Tall and slim as a high-schooler, he came to MSU on a basketball, not baseball, scholarship.

Though he gave up basketball for baseball after his freshman year, he did not impress the scouts until he was a junior, when he and Perranoski were both first-team Big Ten selections. As a senior, with his roommate departed for the pro ranks, Moose, as he was known then, blossomed into an All-American. He won ten games while losing but one, with an ERA of 1.12 and 106 strikeouts in 96 innings. Radatz put a price tag of $20,000 on his professional services, and the Boston Red Sox were the only team who thought he was worth it.

At the conclusion of the school year in 1959, Radatz joined the Red Sox farm team at Raleigh, North Carolina, where he continued to start, as he had in college. Though he opened the 1960 season with Raleigh, he soon was promoted to Minneapolis, Boston's top minor-league club. There he did a bit of relieving in addition to his regular turn on the mound, and the bug was planted in manager Johnny Pesky's ear.

Next year, training in Florida with the same club (shifted to Seattle as Minneapolis became a major-league city), Radatz fanned 11 Rochester Redbirds in five innings of an exhibition game. After the contest, pitching coach Harry Dorish, himself a fine reliever in the 1950s, suggested to Pesky that Radatz might make the big club sooner as a fireman than as a starter. Although Dick was developing a slider, he had displayed no aptitude for the curveball and was still basically a one-pitch pitcher. Boston's front office had seen in Ryne Duren how effective a late-inning fireballer could be, and in Radatz they had the prospect of a strikeout artist *with* control.

Dick was not happy at the "demotion," as he referred to it at the time. He even asked Pesky to send him to a lower classification where he could pitch every fourth day. "Don't worry," his manager responded. "I'm going to pitch you every day." Radatz went on to give the Pacific Coast League a taste of what American League batters would have to contend with the next year. In 54 games and 71 innings, he fanned 74, allowed only 50 hits, and notched an ERA of 2.28 in what has always been regarded as a hitter's league.

Now he was ready for Boston. Manager Mike Higgins brought Radatz to Beantown as ace of the bullpen, replacing a fading Mike Fornieles. Dick appropriated for himself the nickname formerly reserved for Fenway Park's imposing left-field wall—"The Monster."

Radatz created an immediate stir with his tight, deceptively slow windup and smoking fastball. Hitters knew what was coming nine pitches out of ten, but couldn't do anything about it. Bill Rigney, then manager of the Angels, said, "Radatz throws the 'heaviest' ball I can remember." Besides leading the American League in games, relief wins, and saves his rookie year, Radatz undoubtedly led in broken bats as well. On a pitching staff whose ERA was 4.22, his was the reverse—2.24. Perhaps his most amazing statistic in that rookie year was that while he struck out better than ten batters per nine innings, he walked fewer than three; such a combination of speed and control had not been seen since the days of Walter Johnson.

In late August of that rookie year, Radatz entered a tie game with the Yankees in the eighth inning. For nine frames he held the World Champions scoreless until his teammates could push a run across in the sixteenth to give him the win. From that point on, Radatz had no greater admirer than Yankee pilot Ralph Houk, who later called him "the greatest relief pitcher I have ever seen." He cited Radatz's ability to retire left-handed and right-handed batters with equal dispatch, and his unsurpassed strikeout capacity.

Radatz confessed to going for the strikeout almost all the time, distrusting the conventional wisdom that prescribes throwing sinkers and hoping for the ground ball. Perhaps, given the Boston infield in 1962–1964, Radatz had greater incentive to get the strikeout—Boston was dead last in double plays two of those three years. Nonetheless, going for the strikeout all the time meant that Radatz was throwing an incredible number of pitches in comparison to his innings worked, for not only did he fan better than one man per inning, but he stretched the count out to four or five pitches on seemingly every batter. This may have had a lot to do with his failure to extend his success over many seasons.

In 1963, Radatz came back even stronger, as Johnny Pesky took the helm of the Red Sox. In a one-month period prior to the All-Star break, he pitched 33 innings over 14 games without allowing a run. Ralph Houk named him to the All-Star squad, saying, "I want those Natioanl Leaguers to get an idea of what we have to face over here. Let them get a taste of Radatz for a couple of innings." And they did—pitching the last two frames of a 5–3 American League loss, Radatz fanned Willie Mays, Dick Groat, Duke Snider, Willie McCovey, and Julian Javier.

That was the form he exhibited throughout the 1963 season, in which he won 15 games—10 of them in a row—lost only 6, added 25 saves, and posted an ERA of 1.97. For the second straight year, he led the American League in relief points. His 15 wins out of the bullpen tied the league record set by Luis Arroyo in 1961.

By this time, Radatz had established himself as the most feared reliever in baseball. Perranoski and McDaniel could get you out with depressing regularity, and Wilhelm could make you look foolish chasing one of his butterflies. But Radatz would humiliate you, dispose of you as if you were a Little Leaguer. In 1964 he pitched more games and more innings than ever before, and The Monster was nourished by the work. In a season in which the hapless Red Sox could gather only 72 wins, Radatz won or saved an amazing 45 of them—62.5 percent, a record little noted, which no one has yet surpassed. He won 16 games to set a new A.L. record and tie Jim Konstanty's major-league mark, and he tied Arroyo's all-time high of 29 saves. He established a new major-league mark for relief points, since exceeded only once, by John Hiller in 1973. He also created a new mark for games pitched, 79, only to be passed in the same season by K.C.'s John Wyatt.

In the All-Star game that year, Radatz breezed through the seventh and eighth and seemed certain to protect the American League's 4–2 lead through the ninth. After being blown away by Radatz on three pitches, Hank Aaron said, "He struck me out on three identical low fastballs. I couldn't believe it. But you can't get set on him with that slow-fast delivery trick." But The Monster couldn't complete this job unscathed, as Johnny Callison hit a three-run homer to beat him and hand the A.L.'ers their second of what would be nine straight All-Star losses.

With two games left in the 1964 season, Johnny Pesky handed the reins of his Red Sox over to Billy Herman. In two years, Pesky's teams had not been able to win more than 76 games, and the natives were restless. Radatz had been great, propping up an otherwise wretched pitching staff, but Boston needed players. The Sox had not taken a pennant since 1946 and had not been in contention for over a decade.

After the 1965 campaign, however, Pesky's performance started to look better in hindsight. The Red Sox fell to ninth place while losing 100 games, and even Radatz was caught in the quicksand. Though his 31-point performance would have been the highlight of many a reliever's career, it was substantially off the pace Dick had set the previous three years. He continued to fan batters at about the rate he always had, and continued to allow fewer hits than innings pitched, but he was being victimized by the long ball; his ERA soared to 3.91.

After 1965, the decline was as steep as the ascent had been. On June 2, 1966, Boston traded him to Cleveland; on the year, he failed to win a game for either club. Though he lingered for two more seasons in the majors, with a one-year hiatus in 1968, Radatz was throwing only the memory of his fastball up to the plate. His speed was still major-league-quality-plus, but the ball did not dart or rise or sink in the unpredictable and wonderful way it once had. And he was not able to change styles, to learn a breaking ball that would set his faded fastball off to better advantage. Over his last three years, Radatz won three games, lost 11, and saved 22. In a series of interleague waiver deals and releases, Radatz managed brief stays with the Tigers, Cubs, and expansion Expos, with whom he finished up as a bullpen mate for Roy Face, also playing out the string.

But let's remember The Monster who stilled rallies as soon as his entrance was announced over the public-address system, whose fastball left Hank Aaron standing at the plate openmouthed, who was virtually unhittable even in a ball park in which everyone else was eminently hittable. Let's remember the Dick Radatz who, in his brief shining moment, was the best of the best.

14

Full
Speed Ahead:
1959-1973

The year 1959 saw no explosion of bullpen activity, no departures in relief strategy, no statistical leap in the long trend of greater reliance on relievers. In fact, the number of complete games in 1959 decreased by a mere tenth of a percent from the previous year, while saves bucked the trend and also decreased. And yet, 1959 was the most important year for relief pitching since 1905.

Every club had a relief specialist, while the better teams generally had more than one capable arm in the pen. And 1959 saw more fine individual performances than any previous year, from old-timers like Turk Lown and Gerry Staley enjoying their finest years, to up-and-coming firemen making their reputations, like ElRoy Face, Lindy McDaniel, and Don McMahon. The roll call of top bullpen performers in this year goes on to include Don Elston, Ryne Duren, Billy Loes, Mike Fornieles, Bill Henry—and a rookie brought up to the Dodgers in July by the name of Larry Sherry.

Despite all the fine performances that made 1959 the "Year of the Reliever," it was the late-season work of this twenty-four-year-old righthander that captured the spotlight for all relief pitchers as never before. After dropping his first two decisions upon being recalled from St. Paul, Sherry won his next nine, including postseason play. He added five saves, two of these also coming in the Series.

Sherry began the 1958 season with the freshly transplanted

Larry Sherry. He *was* the 1959 World Series.

Dodgers, but five outlandishly bad outings in relief won him a speedy return ticket to the Pacific Coast League. Disappointed, there he went 6–14 with an ERA of 4.91. It was his sixth minor-league season without once cracking the .500 barrier.

When the Dodgers retrieved him from St. Paul the next year, his won-lost mark was an unexciting 6–7, but what stirred Walter Alston's imagination was Sherry's 109 strikeouts in 115 innings. The Dodgers were making a surprising run at the pennant after being a seventh-place flop in their debut year on the West Coast; if the Braves were to be prevented from repeating as N.L. champs, the pitching staff needed bolstering. Roger Craig was recalled from Spokane in mid-June, and Sherry followed soon after.*

* Craig contributed mightily to the Dodger pennant drive with an 11–5 mark, mostly as a starter. One of his two wins in relief took place on July 9 in Milwaukee, when Craig pitched eleven innings of shutout relief, throwing only 88 pitches. Only Bob Osborn of the 1927 Cubs hurled more consecutive scoreless frames in a relief win.

Sherry was a fastball pitcher recently converted to the joys of the slider. An apt pupil, he learned how to throw the slider at different speeds, and with his newfound weapon added to a good fastball and adequate curve, he baffled batters in both leagues.

Used nine times as a starter and 14 times in relief, Larry posted a regular-season record of 7–2, with three saves and a 2.19 ERA. In his 36⅓ innings as a fireman, amid the pressure of an extremely tight pennant race, Sherry coolly pitched for an ERA of 0.74. On August 15 at St. Louis, for example, he relieved Johnny Podres in the first, hurled eight and two-thirds innings of shutout ball, and hit two singles and a home run to win his own game. To cap what Walter Alston later called "the greatest one-man show I ever saw," Sherry preserved his one-run lead in the ninth by fanning Stan Musial, Bill White, and Ken Boyer!

But the real fun did not begin until the regular season ended, with the Braves and Dodgers tied for the top spot. In Game One of the best-of-three play-off, Sherry replaced starter Danny Mc-Devitt in the second inning, yielded one unearned run, then slammed the door on the Braves for the next seven and two-thirds innings to win. Reliever Stan Williams took Game Two, and the Dodgers advanced to the Series against the A.L. champion Chicago White Sox. And it was in the World Series that Sherry accomplished what no pitcher had accomplished before or has accomplished since—winning or saving every one of his team's four victories.

The "Go-Go" Sox embarrassed the Dodgers in Game One, winning 11–0 behind Early Wynn and Gerry Staley. But in Game Two L.A. took a 4–2 lead with a three-run burst in the sixth. Johnny Podres had been pulled for a pinch hitter during the rally, and the lead was given to Sherry to protect. He did, allowing one harmless run in his three innings. In the next game, Don Drysdale was nursing a 2–1 lead when he opened the eighth by putting two Sox on base. Sherry again saved the day, stranding the runners and holding Chicago scoreless in the ninth as well.

Two more scoreless innings in Game Four this time netted Sherry a win, as Roger Craig had frittered away a 4–0 advantage in the seventh. Larry's action in the fifth contest was limited to a fruitless pinch-hitting effort in a 1–0 loss in which Chicago employed three hurlers. And Game Six went down in the win column for Sherry, too, in recompense for his five and two-thirds innings of shutout relief. This was the rookie's fifth postseason contest in 11 days; his record—three wins, two saves, and an ERA of 0.44.

How do you top that act? You don't. Larry Sherry returned

in 1960 to post 13 wins in relief, leading the National League, and went on to be a solid major-league reliever until his retirement in 1968. But as long as pitching exploits are recited, Sherry will be remembered for his phenomenal World Series.

What many observers noted about the 1959 Series besides Sherry's brilliant work was that, for the first time, neither team allowed a starting pitcher to complete a game. An interesting oddity, it was proclaimed, but that fact actually signaled a revolution in the making. The time would not be far off when a route-going performance in a highly important game would itself become the oddity.

In 1960, in the wake of Sherry's exploits, *The Sporting News* instituted its weekly tabulation of saves, for the purpose of presenting a Fireman of the Year Award to the top relief-point collector in each league (Sherry never did manage to land one of these prizes himself.) Also in 1960, major-league complete games hit an all-time low, while saves reached an all-time high (to that date, of course).

The vanquished White Sox of 1959 made it as far as they did on defense, speed, and pitching, particularly relief pitching. With veteran right-handers Turk Lown and Gerry Staley on call in the bullpen, manager Al Lopez was quick to employ the hook. While the pitching staff as a whole posted by far the lowest ERA in the American League, they also posted the fewest complete games and the most saves. At age thirty-five, after eight years in the senior circuit, Turk Lown appeared 60 times in his newly adopted league and led in both saves and relief wins. The thirty-nine-year-old Staley, a longtime Cardinal starter, led in appearances with 67 and trailed his teammate in relief points by only two. Both these old codgers proved to have a few more years of usefulness left in their right arms, though as a tandem they never matched their 1959 peak.

The team that suffered the heartbreak of the play-off defeat to L.A. had its own bullpen ace in Don McMahon, an admirably durable and consistent fireman who broke in with the Braves in 1957 and didn't stop pitching till 1974. Like Lown a Brooklyn-born right-hander, McMahon was trained in the minors as a reliever. He pitched well though sparingly in the Braves' pennant-winning years of 1957–1958, and in 1959 he stepped up the pace, appearing in 60 games and topping the National League in saves with 15. Although he went on to compile more than ten times that number, never again did he take saves honors. (At age forty, however, he did lead the N.L. in relief wins while enjoying perhaps the

Luis Arroyo, a one-season marvel for the 1961 Yankees.

best season of his career.) A fastballer to the end—and the end didn't come until he was forty-four—McMahon finished among the top ten firemen in lifetime wins, saves, and games.

Like Lown and Staley for the Sox in 1959, right-hander Jim Brosnan and left-hander Bill Henry combined for the Reds in 1960 to form one of the best "multiple bullpens," to use Larry Shepard's phrase, that baseball had seen. Henry notched 18 relief points to go with Brosnan's 19; Jim's ERA, had it not been for two no-decision starts, would have been a tidy 1.71.

Both pitchers were even better in 1961, as the Reds surprised N.L. pundits and won the pennant. Manager Fred Hutchinson played pretty strict percentage baseball with his bullpen pair, record for a reliever, set by Walter Johnson in eleven and a third innings of relief against the Browns on July 24, 1913.

Another remarkable bullpen feat, though of a smaller magnitude, was accomplished in 1962 by Houston sinkerballer Russ Kemmerer. "I came in against the Braves with the bases loaded and one out," he recalled. "We were ahead by one run. I threw one pitch to Frank Bolling and he ended the game with a double play. The next evening we were playing the Cards. The situation was the same as in the previous game. Musial came in to hit, and though I was right-handed, I was brought in to pitch to Stan. The first pitch, he hit into a double play to end the game." Two games, two pitches, four outs, two saves.

Also on that Colt crew in its first year was Hal Woodeschick, a tall thirty-year-old left-hander who had enjoyed little success as he bounced around the American League from 1956 on. Houston gave him his best shot at showing what he could do as a starter, and he responded with a 5–16 mark and an ERA of 4.39. Nerves were Hal's problem. He'd work himself into a dither between starts planning what he was going to do. When it came time to do it, he was without confidence.

The Houston organization was sympathetic only to a degree: They dropped Woodeschick from the 1963 roster, but gave him an opportunity to make the club in spring training—as a fireman. Hal survived the final cut and went on to win 11 and save 10 while better than halving his 1962 ERA. Although he went on to enjoy three more fine seasons as a reliever, Hal today looks back on 1963 as the year "everything just seemed to go my way. In a four-game series in Milwaukee, I saved two games and won the other two. Then we played in Pittsburgh the next day, and I pitched eight scoreless innings in relief and won the game in the seventeenth."

In 1959, Cincinnati had dumped a veteran reliever to the minors, where he was rescued by an American League club with whom the veteran became a star. That year the man had been Luis Arroyo; in 1964 the scene was reenacted, with the protagonist being Al Worthington.

"Red" Worthington had broken into the majors with a bang in 1953, throwing shutouts in his first two starts for the Giants. The rest of his career had been only so-so, spiced by his quitting the White Sox in 1960 because they "cheated"—tipped off their batters to opponents' signs through use of a peephole in the Comiskey Park scoreboard. He returned to the majors in 1963 as a bullpen operative for the Reds. But when he got raked for 11 runs in his first six innings of 1964, Worthington was released to the Pacific Coast League. There the Twins scouts thought they spotted a flicker of life and brought him back to the bigs.

The big Alabaman was duly grateful, rewarding Minnesota with five outstanding seasons, culminating in his leading the American League in saves in 1968, at the age of thirty-nine. He was the bellwether of the Minnesota bullpen from 1964 through 1968, the constant source of strength as various veteran firemen came and went, lending fine support along the way. Among these were Johnny Klippstein, Ron Perranoski, Ron Kline, and Bob Miller.

Klippstein had been the A.L. saves leader in 1960 with the Indians; Perranoski has been discussed earlier; Kline had recorded a league-high 29 saves with a very poor Senators club in 1965; and Miller had led the National League in games in 1964. Cal Griffith's revolving-door operation for relievers was very successful in the mid-1960s, and continues successful to the present day.

The last mentioned of these firemen, Bob Miller, presents an interesting case. He was the ultimate vagabond, pitching for ten teams in his 17-year career, two of them twice. His most-traveled year, 1971, turned out to be his best. Pitching for three N.L. clubs, Miller posted an ERA of 1.64 in 56 games, winning eight and saving ten. But he did not always have such success. With the expansion Mets of 1962, only a win in the last week of the season sullied an otherwise perfect 0–12 mark.

In one game that distressing year, Miller entered with the bases loaded and no one out—the classic reliever's dilemma—and handled the situation with the utmost aplomb: He threw one pitch, which was hit into a triple play. Amazingly, he repeated this feat in 1968 with the Twins! (Others who have turned this rare relief trick are Si Johnson with the Reds in the early 1930s, and Don Nottebart of the Reds in 1967, who entered a game against Pittsburgh with men on first and second, threw one pitch for the triple play, and thus protected a 1–0 win.)

An incredible relief performance by two entire bullpens occurred on May 31, 1964, in the second game of a twin bill between the Mets and Giants. Rallying from a 6–0 deficit, the Mets tied San Francisco in the seventh on a three-run homer by Joe Christopher, and the game went into extra innings . . . and extra innings . . . and extra innings. Finally, the Giants scored two in the top of the twenty-third to end what had become, from a standpoint of time elapsed, baseball's longest game. Gaylord Perry won the game with ten innings of scoreless relief, while Galen Cisco lost it after having held the Giants at bay through eight innings. In all, Met relievers Cisco, Larry Bearnarth, Frank Lary, and Tom

Sturdivant combined for 19⅔ shutout frames, while Giant relievers Perry, Ron Herbel, Bob Shaw, and Bob Hendley threw goose eggs for 16⅓.

Nineteen sixty-four produced a fine relief performance by Al McBean of the Pirates (N.L.-high in relief wins, 30 relief points, 1.97 ERA); a better one by Bob Lee of the Angels (19 saves, five wins, plus an almost invisible ERA of 1.29 in 59 relief outlings); and a record-setting one by John Wyatt of the Kansas City A's (81 appearances). Each of the three firemen was able to sustain this level of success for two more seasons, and Wyatt got a chance to apply his best season to the pennant drive of the Boston Red Sox in 1967.

But the most appealing relief story of 1964 was supplied by a thirty-eight-year-old knuckleballer named Barney Schultz who had only two months in the sun, and made the most of them. Schultz had first pitched professionally in 1944, when he broke in with Wilmington of the Inter-State League. After 11 years of riding the buses with 11 minor-league outfits, he got his first big-time shot with the 1955 Cards. But his 7.89 ERA in 19 games buried him in the bushes again until 1959, when the Tigers gave him a cup of coffee. Then back down once more until 1961, when he landed with the Cubs, who kept him until June of 1963. Rejoining the Cardinals, his original big-league team, he did a respectable job; at age thirty-seven, however, he did not loom large in Cardinal long-range plans. Offered the post of pitching coach for the Cards' farm team at Jacksonville, Schultz accepted.

Having given up his 20-year pursuit of major-league success, Schultz could not give up pitching cold turkey. In 42 games covering 86 innings, Barney went 8–5, saved numerous other games, and logged a sensational ERA of 1.05. On July 31, the Cards called the old man back up, and in the final two months of the campaign he was as tough on the National League as he had been on the International. In 30 games, he saved 14 and won one more, with an ERA of 1.64. He wrapped up the final-day, pennant-clinching win for Bob Gibson, and in the World Series against the Yanks he saved the opener for Ray Sadecki. But next year Barney lost the knack he had possessed so briefly, and returned to his job with Jacksonville.

The fourth game of the 1964 World Series produced one of the finest relief performances in Series history. After the Yanks blasted Ray Sadecki for four hits and three runs with only one out in the first, Roger Craig came in and pitched four and two-thirds innings of two-hit, eight-strikeout, scoreless ball. Pulled for a pinch hitter as the Cards erupted for four runs on Ken Boyer's grand slam in the sixth, Craig got the win as he gave way to Ron Taylor, who allowed no hits and no runs in the Yankees' final four turns.

The Canadían-born Taylor left the Cards the following year for Houston, where his career faltered badly. But in 1967, Met general manager Bing Devine "took me off the Houston scrap pile," Taylor says, and "Wes Westrum gave me the chance to pitch." Ron put together four fine years in New York. "My biggest thrill in baseball," he says, "was in the 1969 National League play-offs, when I saved Game One and won Game Two." He also picked up a save in the World Series that year. In six postseason games, Taylor's ERA was 0.00.

In 1965 the Chicago White Sox bullpen gathered a record 53 saves and enabled the Sox to give the Twins a run for the flag. The star fireman that year was knuckleballer Eddie Fisher, who had learned his floater at teammate Hoyt Wilhelm's knee as Old Sarge was putting together year after year of sub-2.00 ERA's. At last in 1965, the twenty-nine-year-old pupil surpassed the master. Fisher set new American League records for games with 82 and relief innings with 165, and led A.L. firemen with 15 wins and 39 relief points. Eddie never approached those figures again, but he did remain a capable reliever for another decade. The third member of the Sox relief contingent was rookie Bob Locker, who went on to have several fine years on the South Side of Chicago, and in 1973 had his finest year on the North Side with the Cubs.

Over in the National League in 1965 the top fireman was Ted Abernathy of the Cubs, a "submariner" whose rising fastball and curve and top-notch sinker befuddled hitters who had had no experience against such an unorthodox style; Abernathy's delivery was once fairly common in major-league baseball, but that was in the years preceding the lively ball.

Abernathy came to the majors in 1955 with a conventional delivery, but in three years with the Senators showed little ability to control the ball or get much on it. An arm injury in 1957 turned out to be his salvation, for it forced him to experiment with an underhand delivery or call it quits.

Ted's new style was not an instant success. He bounced around the minors for five years, except for two games with Washington in 1960. His return to the big leagues with Cleveland was solid but not spectacular, and control problems there in 1964 precipitated his sale to the Cubs just before Opening Day, 1965.

All Abernathy did for Chicago was set a new major-league record for games with 84 and a new major-league saves record with 31, and walk off with Fireman-of-the-Year honors from *The*

*Sporting News.* But how soon they forget: The Cubs unloaded him on Atlanta in May of the very next year. After the season, the Braves put the thirty-three-year-old hurler on their Richmond roster, from which he was shrewdly plucked by the Cincinnati Reds, sadder but wiser after their experiences with Arroyo and Worthington.

For the Reds in 1967, the submarining right-hander again became the N.L.'s top reliever, with 34 relief points and an ERA of 1.27 while working 70 games. He allowed a mere 5.33 hits per nine innings.

That was Ted's last super year, but he did continue as one of the game's best, finishing up his career where he had started it, in the junior circuit. At age thirty-nine, bolstered by the addition of a knuckleball for use as a change-up, Abernathy posted an ERA of 1.71 in 45 games for the Royals—who released him after the season.

Two youngsters who stood out in relief in 1965 were rookie Frank Linzy of the Giants and second-year man Billy McCool of the Reds. The right-handed Linzy and the left-handed McCool each posted nine wins and 21 saves; sinkerballer Linzy specialized in inducing grounders, while fireballer McCool fanned more men than he pitched innings. Linzy proved the more durable as McCool, a star at twenty, succumbed to arm trouble at twenty-six.

The top A.L. fireman of 1966 was Kansas City's Jack Aker. A twenty-six-year-old right-hander who relied on his sinker, Jack exploded onto the major-league scene with a 40-point, 1.99-ERA performance, after opening the previous season in Vancouver. Next year he slipped to only 15 points, and though he went on to enjoy several fine seasons in each league, he never again approached the levels he attained in 1966, when "everything seemed to go right," he reminisces. "I had my good sinker in nearly every game I entered. Whenever I didn't, it seemed the balls that were hit hard went right to a fielder. I had great desire and concentration that year, and complete confidence in my ability."

Pitchers like Aker, McCool, and Linzy represented the trend toward developing young pitchers into firemen; the old tradition of retreading a fading starter into a shiny new relief pitcher was represented by Phil Regan. Regan had once won 15 games as a starter with Detroit, but had fallen on exceedingly hard times in 1964–1965. In both years his ERA zoomed over 5.00, and his combined won-lost record was a dismaying 6–15. In mid-1965, the twenty-eight-year-old right-hander was optioned out to Syracuse, a humiliating fate for a six-year vet. There he pitched well as a starter. In a stroke of genius, Dodger scouts saw his potential as a fireman and acquired him in an off-season exchange for Dick Tracewski, a spare infielder who was coming off a .215 season.

The Dodgers put Regan to work 65 times, all in relief, and he responded with league-high totals of 14 wins (13 of them in a row) and 21 saves. He suffered only one defeat, and his ERA of 1.62 was less than a third of what it had been during his last years in Detroit. He acquired his colorful nickname of The Vulture for his ability to swoop down upon a close game in which a starter had pitched well to no avail, and earn a win with only an inning's work—ElRoy Face had displayed this knack in winning 22 straight in 1958–1959.

The Vulture was afforded slim pickings in the 1966 World Series as the Dodgers went down quietly in four. In the opening game, L.A. drove Oriole starter Dave McNally from the mound in the third inning by loading the bases with one gone. As it turned out, one man would cross the plate on a walk, and that would be the last run the Dodgers would score in the entire Series.

The muffling of Dodger bats began as veteran reliever Moe Drabowsky took the mound in place of McNally. Moe had bounced back with a 6–0 season for the O's after ending 1965, his tenth major-league campaign, with Vancouver in the Pacific Coast League. He fanned Wes Parker, walked Jim Gilliam to force in a run, then ended the ruckus by getting John Roseboro on a foul pop. Over the last six frames he allowed only one hit while fanning ten more Dodgers—six of them in a row. All 11 strikeout victims went down swinging, most of them fooled by Moe's hard slider. Quite a show from a man who had been considered washed up at the same time the previous year.

Drabowsky continued his fine work into the 1967 season, but The Vulture came in for a hard landing; early the next season, the Dodgers practically gave him to the Cubs. Wrigley Field proved a tonic, and The Vulture flew high once more, winning his second Fireman of the Year Award. Oddly, both Regan and Drabowsky saw their careers end in late 1972 with outright releases by the Chicago White Sox.

Minnie Rojas of the Angels swept A.L. relief honors with 39 points in 1967, the one great year of a career that, due to a tragic accident, was ended just as it seemed to be on the ascent. In Chicago that same year, Wilbur Wood's career was still in the germinal stage. With Eddie Fisher departed for Baltimore, the White Sox filled their third bullpen slot with the twenty-five-year-old left-hander they had bought from Columbus, where he had spent all of 1966. Previously he had seen some major-league action with the Red Sox and Pirates in every year since 1961, without notable success. He was fast on his way to becoming that classic and sad baseball phenomenon—the Triple-A terror whose skills are just short of major-league quality.

But in Chicago Wood came under Wilhem's wing, and just as Eddie Fisher had blossomed with the old knuckleballer's instruction, so did Wood. In 1967 he made a capable though not indispensable addition to the Sox bullpen, but he was already looking to the future. Every day he and Wilhelm would stand in the outfield, throwing butterflies and discussing the theory and practice of the pitch; by season's end, Wood was a complete convert to Old Sarge's principle that to have an effective knuckleball you had to throw it nine pitches out of ten.

In 1968 the rotund lefty made 86 trips from the bullpen, and added two starts; the record for games pitched was now his, though briefly. He won 12 in relief and saved 16 others, topping the American League and garnering Fireman-of-the-Year honors. And he was nearly as good the next two years, in each of which he led the league in games.

In 1971 Chuck Tanner became the new Sox manager and, having seen knuckleballer Phil Niekro win 23 games as a starter in 1969, thought that Wood might do just as well. Wilbur did, winning 20 or more games four times running. The man who had led A.L. relievers in games in 1968–1970 now led in starts from 1972 to 1975. Like his mentor Wilhelm, Wood disproved the axiom that relievers do not make good starters.

A question seldom asked these days is, Do strong-armed outfielders make good relievers? In the change-pitcher days of Harry Wright and Jack Manning, many did. But in modern times, a Dave Kingman or Vic Davalillo or Jim Hickman has taken the mound only when his manager, in the midst of a fearful beating, has chosen not to waste any more pitchers on a lost cause.

This was the choice Yankee manager Ralph Houk made on August 25, 1968, as he waved Rocky Colavito in to pitch in the opener of a doubleheader with the Tigers. The thirty-five-year-old outfielder possessed probably the strongest throwing arm in the American League, but had toed a major-league rubber only once before, in a similar situation ten years back. On that occasion he had turned in three hitless, scoreless innings; on this one, he again pitched three shutout innings, allowing one hit. In one of the most surprising developments of Ralph Houk's career, the Yanks stormed back from way behind and won the game for the reluctant reliever.

More conventional relief exploits were turned in the following year by Houston's portly right-hander Fred Gladding, who led the National League in saves, and the Dodgers' screwballer Jim Brewer,

who surpassed the 25-point mark for the first of five straight years,
an enviable level of consistency. Brewer went on to have a truly
remarkable 1972 season, in which his ERA dropped to 1.26 and his
4.69 hits allowed per nine innings established an unofficial all-time
major-league low.

The pennant-winning Orioles of 1969 had an excellent bullpen, as did the N.L. champion Mets. The Birds' foursome of Eddie
Watt, Dick Hall, Dave Leonhard, and Pete Richert combined for
an ERA of 2.09. The Mets' combo of Ron Taylor, Tug McGraw,
and Cal Koonce was not nearly as effective, nor were the Mets
nearly as solid a team as the Orioles—they were simply good
enough to beat you. The Mets took the Orioles in five, with their
bullpen recording two saves and allowing not a single run.

For the twenty-five-year-old McGraw, 1969 had been his fourth
year in the majors but his first as a full-time fireman. He was
number two in the pen behind Ron Taylor who, because of his
World Series experience with the Cards in 1964, appeared twice
against the Orioles while McGraw spectated. By 1971, however,
the situation changed. Taylor faded and Tug came on like a
whirlwind. The screwballing left-hander (who also threw a fine
fastball and curve) posted a 1.70 ERA, which he equaled the next
year, and 19 relief points, which he nearly doubled in 1972. Typical
of the sensational way he could rip through a batting order was
an outing in August of 1971, when he was called on to protect a
two-run lead through four innings. When the first batter he faced,
San Diego's Nate Colbert, hit a mammoth home run, Tug still had
twelve outs to go, but the margin was now the minimum. He
steeled his nerve to the task at hand and proceeded to retire the
12 men in order, nine of them on strikes.

Where most relievers were reserved, even-tempered types,
McGraw was flamboyantly open. "I get very excited when I do
well," he says, "and very ticked off when I don't." A run-scoring
hit off him would produce a minor tantrum in which he'd wave
his arms, pace the mound, and kick at the dirt. An inning-ending
strikeout with men on base would produce a tight-lipped but
clearly satisfied grin and repeated glove-slaps to his thigh as he
marched to the dugout.

McGraw's 1973 season gave him little cause for celebration,
until it was almost over. In a deep and protracted slump, Tug let
game after game slip through his grasp as he became the most

Tug McGraw. "You gotta believe!" he chanted as he led the 1973 Mets
from last place to first in two months. (*Paul H. Roedig*)

notorious arsonist since Nero. At wit's end, manager Yogi Berra reversed the traditional practice of sending a troubled starter to the bullpen, and gave McGraw a start. It seemed to work. Although Tug did not win that start, or his next one, he appeared looser, and his return to the bullpen was triumphant. In less than three weeks, beginning on August 22, Tug appeared 17 times, picking up an unbelievable 12 saves and four wins. The Mets soared from last place to first, and very nearly won the World Series as McGraw extended his miraculous comeback into post-season play.

The magic of late 1973 failed to transfer to 1974, and the Mets moved McGraw over to Philadelphia in 1975. He continues to be a valuable member of the excellent Phillie bullpen, which includes Ron Reed, Rawly Eastwick, and Warren Brusstar. But it is hard to believe that he will ever again experience the exhilaration of those last six weeks in 1973, when both he and the Mets performed a little miracle.

In 1970, for the first time, the number of saves recorded in the major leagues exceeded the number of complete games. A prime reflection of that trend was Cincinnati, where manager Sparky Anderson allowed the starters of his N.L. champion Reds to complete only 32 contests while he called on the bullpen to deliver a record 60 saves.*

The men primarily responsible for the Cincinnati record were Clay Carroll, Wayne Granger, and Don Gullett. Granger was a stringbean right-hander with a great sinker. He had come to the Reds by trade after a half-season in St. Louis, where he had pitched well enough, but done nothing to presage his accomplishments of 1969. In that year Granger appeared 90 times, a record until Mike Marshall came along, and was National League Fireman of the Year with 36 relief points. In the pennant-winning year he slacked off from 90 games to 67, and from 145 innings to a mere 85—yet his relief points soared to 41, and he repeated as Fireman of the Year. His 35 saves were the all-time N.L. high until his teammate Carroll notched 37 in 1972.

---

* Purists may choose to view the 53 saves registered by the 1965 Chicago White Sox bullpen as the record and may insist that saves have not exceeded complete games in *any* season. The statistical waters have become a little muddied for the period 1969–1973 because of the liberalized save rule adopted by the major leagues at that time. The rule has since been tightened, but earlier totals have not been revised to conform to the new standard (see Chapter One for a detailed explanation of the save requirements). At some point this should be done, just as the inflated batting averages of 1887, when bases on balls were counted as hits, have been revised downward by applying modern standards to the old box scores.

Granger fell off a bit in 1971 and was traded to Minnesota —that overnight stop for all veteran firemen, it seems—and there in 1972 he rebounded with 23 points. But then he began bouncing around frantically—from the Twins to the Cards to the Yanks in 1973; the White Sox in 1974; and the Astros in 1975, his last big-league outfit. He spent 1978 in the Mexican League.

Carroll, basically a fastballer, also arrived in Cincinnati via trade, from the Braves in early 1968. Over the next nine years the right-hander became the mainstay of a bullpen that saw Granger and Gullett go (Gullett to a starter's role) and Pedro Borbon, Tom Hall, Rawly Eastwick, and Will McEnaney arrive. Carroll's great year was 1972, but his lifetime record in postseason play was also remarkable: In 22 games he won four, saved two, and posted an ERA of 1.39. Like Granger he drifted after his exit from Cincinnati in 1975, pitching for the White Sox, the Cards, the White Sox again, and most recently landing with the Pirates after spending nearly all of 1978 in the minors.

Gullett was a nineteen-year-old rookie when he contributed his fastball to the Cincinnati bullpen of 1970. Remembering the fate of Billy McCool, the Reds limited the young left-hander to 44 appearances, in which he was able to pick up six saves and five wins (one of these as a starter). His best regular-season performance came against the defending champion Mets at Shea Stadium on August 23. Entering the game in the sixth inning as the Reds trailed by one, Gullett fanned the first six men he faced and retired the other six in order; the Reds rallied to give him the win. In the divisional play-offs against the Pirates, he saved two of the three Red wins. But next year, when he developed a major-league curveball, he left the fireman's fraternity for good.

Other frat brothers who shined in 1970 were cellar-dwellers Claude Raymond, who posted 23 saves and six wins with the Expos, and Ron Herbel, who worked similar wonders for San Diego, including a game against the Reds when he came in with the bases loaded, no one out, and fanned Pete Rose, Tony Perez, and Johnny Bench in order.

Also that year, right-hander Dave Giusti came to the Pirates. The graduate of Syracuse University—where he had learned his out pitch, the palmball, from Ted Kleinhans, who had been Jim Konstanty's mentor—had been a starter in all his previous years with the Astros and Cards, enjoying middling success. The Pirates made him a fireman right off, and Giusti responded with nine wins and 26 saves.

Dave matched that total the next year and won the Fireman of the Year. He capped his season by throwing scoreless ball while

Dave Giusti. He prospered through use of the palmball he learned from Jim Konstanty's instructor, Ted Kleinhans.

appearing in all four games of the divisional play-off against San Francisco, and saving all three Pirate wins. He added another three scoreless outings in the World Series, saving the only Pirate win that was not a route-going job by the starter.

Dave continued as one of the league's very best firemen through 1973, but began to slip a bit in 1974. He closed out his fine career in 1977 with the Oakland A's and the Chicago Cubs.

A comparison of Stan Williams's 10–1 record for the 1970 Twins and Darold Knowles's 2–14 record for the Washington Senators that year might seem a case of the sublime and the ridiculous. Yet it's debatable who was the better fireman that year. For the veteran Williams, "1970 was a near perfect year," he says today. "For over half the season I never allowed runners to score when I entered the game, nor did I allow any runs in a situation where we were tied or close. I did allow some, at times, once we expanded our lead." In addition to his 10 wins, Stan saved 15 and had an ERA of 1.99 in what proved to be his last hurrah.

The left-handed Knowles, pitching for a last-place club, saved 27 games while logging an ERA of 2.04. All season long he allowed but 27 earned runs, yet these accounted for an all-time-high 14 relief losses. While Williams participated in 26 percent of his team's wins, Knowles took credit for 41 percent of his.

Washington gave Knowles a break in 1971 by trading him to Oakland, with whom he picked up winners' shares of the World Series loot in 1972–1974. In his first full year with the A's he had his best ERA, 1.36, as he combined with Rollie Fingers to give Oakland one of the best righty-lefty bullpen combos baseball has ever seen. In the 1973 World Series, Knowles saved two games and set a record by pitching in all seven contests, giving up no earned runs. Although in recent years he has had to keep his suitcase packed, he has remained a successful reliever.

Another instance of how deceptive a reliever's won-lost record can be occurred in 1971, when Milwaukee's Ken Sanders was 7–12 yet was American League Fireman of the Year, and received votes for the Most Valuable Player and Cy Young Awards. A sinker-slider pitcher, Sanders had a checkered career before being rescued from the Pacific Coast League by the Brewers in 1970. In that year, his fourth in the majors since 1964, he posted an ERA of 1.76 in 50 games to establish himself as a quality fireman. But in 1971 the right-hander became an entire bullpen, registering 31 of his team's 32 saves and finishing 77 contests, still the American League record. In a game against Baltimore that year, Sanders recalls, "We had a one-run lead in the top of the ninth inning. The bases were loaded, and there were two balls and no strikes on Don Buford. I came in and got Buford to pop up, struck out Paul Blair, and then Frank Robinson grounded out to short."

In a player poll taken at the end of the season by *Sports Illustrated*, Ken was named the top reliever in the major leagues. Never again did he approach such heights, but he was an effective hurler for the Mets in 1975–1976 before returning to the American League to close out his career.

The top single-game relief performance of 1972 belonged to a starter, Oakland's Vida Blue, who suffered through a 6–10 campaign on the heels of winning both the Cy Young and the MVP the year before. Prior to the play-off with the Detroit Tigers, manager Dick Williams named his three starters, and Blue was not one of them. Depressed and grumbly, he contributed only a meaningless one third of an inning through the first four games. But in the final contest, Blue Moon Odom handed his 2–1 lead over to Vida, who held the Tigers right there through four innings. Recording the first save of his career, he led the A's to the Series—where in Game One he recorded save two!

Nineteen seventy-three was marked by the introduction of the designated hitter into American League play, and it had a dramatic effect on the league's complete-game totals, which jumped more than 15 percent, even allowing for the increased number of games played (1972 had been the year of the player strike and a truncated season). Strangely, though relievers were being used less, the per-

John Hiller. He came back from a heart attack to post an all-time mark for relief points (48) in 1973.

centage of games in which a save occurred *increased*. Seemingly, the major effect of the d.h. was to permit more starters to absorb route-going defeats where previously they might have been pulled for pinch hitters.

The d.h. had no notable influence on the Detroit pitching staff in 1973. Manager Billy Martin allowed only 39 starters to go nine that year, as against 46 the previous season. The reason: John Hiller. When you have a gun, you shoot it, Billy reasoned, and Hiller was a very hot pistol indeed. In a league-leading 65 appearances, the hard-throwing left-hander won 10 and saved 38; the latter remains a major-league record, as do his 48 relief points. Striking out a man an inning, Hiller logged an ERA of 1.44. He accounted for 56 percent of Detroit's victories through a win or a save, and finished fourth in the balloting for both the Cy Young and the MVP.

Coming up to the Tigers in 1965, Hiller labored as a swing man for the next five years, with only occasional success. Then in 1971, at the age of twenty-seven, he was struck down by a heart attack. He sat out all of that year and had to strong-arm his doctors into letting him pitch batting practice for the Tigers in 1972. By July, he had bounced back so impressively that Martin restored him to the active roster and employed him judiciously to build up his stamina. It was remarkable that he had returned at all, yet Hiller compounded the feat with a 2.05 ERA, his best ever. Then came his fabulous 1973 effort.

The following season he was hit hard on occasion, as reflected in his major-league-record 14 losses (a tie with Knowles and Marshall). Still, he pitched well enough to win 17, a new A.L. mark. A liver disorder threatened to end his career in 1977, but Hiller bounced back again as one of the top relievers of modern times.

Nineteen seventy-three had been a notable year for relief pitching: Hiller had set records for saves and relief points, Mike Marshall had set a record for games with 92, and Tug McGraw had captivated the nation by compressing a whole season's heroics into six weeks' work. The current era of relief pitching would be sparked by Marshall's monumental achievements for the 1974 Dodgers, which expanded the parameters of performance for all firemen.

# 15

# The
# Ten Best:
# Marshall

In 1974, his first year with the Los Angeles Dodgers, Mike Marshall stunned baseball by relieving in 106 games and 208 innings, both all-time highs. Leading his team to the World Series, he also led his league in relief wins (15) and saves (21), and set major-league records for games finished (83) and consecutive games pitched (13). For his prodigious accomplishments, the thirty-one-year-old right-hander was presented with the N.L. Cy Young Award, becoming the first fireman to win it, and with *The Sporting News* N.L. Pitcher of the Year Award, joining Jim Konstanty as the only firemen thus honored.

This was Marshall's third outstanding year in a row, the previous two having come with Montreal, and many in baseball were hailing him as the greatest relief pitcher of all time. But that praise proved premature, as in the ensuing years he slowly slid out of baseball before the Twins snatched him from the brink of oblivion in mid-1978. His career back on track, Marshall can no longer be classed a three-year marvel like Dick Radatz, and he may yet pitch long enough and well enough to depose Hoyt Wilhelm as the top fireman (if Sparky Lyle or Rollie Fingers doesn't do it first).

When Marshall signed his first pro contract, with the Phils in September 1960, it was as a shortstop. He had pitched for his high school and in sandlot ball in his hometown of Adrian, Michigan,

Mike Marshall, in the uniform of the Dodgers for whom he pitched in 106 games in 1974.

but he wanted to play every day, and pitching didn't seem to offer that chance.

Marshall attended Michigan State University, alma mater to Perranoski and Radatz, but he never played a game for the Spartans. Instead he reported in 1961 to Dothan of the Alabama-Florida League, where he played shortstop, or rather, shortstop played him; in 118 games he committed a league-leading 53 errors.

Undaunted, he continued to play the infield the next three

years, leading in errors twice more. In 1965, his second year with Chattanooga, the 5-feet-10, 180-pound right-hander took the mound eight times as a reliever and did well; moved up to Eugene, Oregon, that season, he continued his schizophrenic duties, taking the hill 36 times and batting .316 while playing the field. The Phils didn't know what to make of him, and at the end of the 1965 campaign let him go over to Detroit's Montgomery club in the Southern League. There he and manager Wayne Blackburn made a bargain: Mike, who was getting nowhere fast by position-hopping, would open the season at short, play there one month, then pitch in relief the next month. Afterward, they would decide which would be the better route to the majors.

In his last 13 at bats before the end of the first month, Marshall got eight hits, sorely tempting Blackburn to keep his hot bat in the lineup. But Blackburn was a man of his word, and Marshall took the mound in relief the very next game. He won it and has been a reliever ever since.

Marshall proved a first-rate fireman with Montgomery, and before the 1967 season he was elevated to the roster of the Toledo Mud Hens, Detroit's top farm team. Training with the big club down in Florida in the spring of 1967, Marshall impressed Tiger pitching coach Johnny Sain, who said, "He's definitely big-league material, and what's so amazing is that he's never really had anyone help him with his pitching and he's got a variety of pitches." Even at this stage of his career, Mike threw a fastball, curve, slider, and sinker, and was beginning to experiment with the screwball.

After Marshall pitched only 15 innings with Toledo, Mud Hen manager Jack Tighe recommended that the Tigers call him up for what was shaping up as a tight pennant race. The race did turn out to be the dizziest in years, with four teams going into the final week with a chance to emerge on top, and Marshall did do a good job. In 37 appearances he logged an ERA of 1.98 while saving ten, winning one, and losing three. But two of these losses came on late-season gopher balls served up to the Chicago White Sox, whom the Tigers were fighting for the flag. Manager Mayo Smith objected to the variety of pitches Marshall threw coming out of the bullpen —like most baseball men, Smith felt a reliever ought to go at the opposition with his single best pitch in the tight spots. After Marshall lost a game on a homer by Chicago's Ken Boyer, Smith was heard grumbling something about "these bright college boys," and Mike was kept on the shelf for the rest of the season.

Smith could not fathom Marshall's ethereal view of pitching as a competitive exercise in concentration, not a personal struggle between individuals in which winning is all-important. And he had to be puzzled by if not downright distrustful of a man who, before coming to the Tigers, had completed his master's degree with a thesis entitled "An Investigation of the Association between Sexual Maturation and Physical Growth and Motor Proficiency in Males." Moreover, Marshall had combined with MSU baseball coach Danny Litwhiler to write articles for the *Athletic Journal* on training methods for baseball players, a subject traditionally the domain of managers and coaches.

In the spring of 1968, Marshall reported late to camp from East Lansing, where he was working on his doctorate in physiological psychology. Mike didn't throw hard the first two weeks of camp, preferring to work on a few problems he had identified the previous season. He was planning to put his act together and throw hard in the last week before breaking camp. But by the time the final week rolled around, Marshall found himself back with Toledo.

Smith had cut him ostensibly for being "behind the others" because of his late arrival. But the demotion probably had more to do with his being a "bright college boy." It would not be the last time Marshall's erudition would give him trouble.

Mike was converted to a full-time starter in 1968. Though he went on to lead the International League in innings pitched and complete games while going 15–9, the Tigers let him molder in Toledo the whole year, recalling him at season's end only so they could expose him to the expansion teams—and get $75,000 for his contract instead of the $20,000 they would have yielded had he been chosen in the minor-league draft.

The Seattle Pilots selected Marshall but forbade him to use the screwball he had perfected in Toledo. Thus disarmed, Mike posted a record of 3–10 with a 5.13 ERA, mostly as a starter; before October, he found himself down in the sticks again. He was twenty-six years old, and after that promising beginning in 1968, his career had foundered disastrously.

Not all his problems originated on the mound. In Mike's first training camp with the Detroit organization, in 1967, a reporter had learned of his research in kinesiology (the study of how the body acts in motion and how motion acts on the body). Marshall's theories about proper conditioning for a pitcher involved: no wind sprints, only long-distance running; working with weights; muscle-stretching exercises; and above all, a lot of throwing to maintain muscle strength at its peak rather than foster the body's tendency to atrophy at lower levels of use. When it was suggested that he might be an invaluable aid to the Tigers' conditioning program, Marshall had replied, "That's none of my business here. I just keep my mouth shut, do what I'm told, and play where I'm told." Yet when Marshall was told to play in Toledo in 1968, it was because he had followed his own ideas about how he should prepare himself for the regular season.

Marching to his own music in Seattle hastened his departure there as well. Despite orders that he not use his unconventional pick-off move—a clockwise ("wrong") turn, a transfer of weight to the back foot, and then the toss—Marshall flouted manager Joe Schultz and used the move to nab eight runners off first and nine off second in half a season. On one occasion he picked Bert Campaneris and Rick Monday off second in successive innings.

His next major-league stop was Houston, where he lost no time tangling with manager Harry Walker. Harry the Hat had developed a comprehensive set of on-field and off-field rules for his players, which he recited at length to the newly arrived Marshall. Mike was silent for some ten minutes—he could hardly have been otherwise—and then, when Walker paused to take a breath, he asked, "How many times a week am I allowed to make love to my wife?" Not waiting for an answer, he walked out of the manager's office and thus sealed his fate; after pitching in four games for the Astros, Marshall was sent down to Oklahoma City. Winnipeg, Montreal's Triple-A team, then acquired him in a trade for outfielder Don Bosch, and soon the Expos called him back to the big time.

He did not exactly find instant success north of the border, but that could hardly have been expected of a man who had worn the uniforms of six teams in one and a half seasons. What Marshall did find was a manager who would let him be, who would let him use his screwball, his pick-off move, and his conditioning methods. Gene Mauch, said Marshall, "was not afraid of a college education like most of the others." Perhaps the greater stimulus to tolerance was Mauch's desperate need for bullpen help.

Mike took over as the Expos' main man in the pen in 1971, posting 23 saves and five wins. At age twenty-seven, he had finally completed a full season on a major-league roster and settled into the pitching pattern that would bring him stardom over the next three years: four pitches out of ten, the fastball; four more, the screwball; the other two divided between the slider and the palm-ball.

In 1972, he started off at a pace that threatened another retreat to the bushes. In his first 22 innings he allowed 20 hits and 18 walks. He had developed a control problem in the latter stages of spring training because he wasn't getting enough game action. So, Marshall was forced to work his problem out in the regular season —not by grooving his pitches to avoid the bases on balls, but by continuing to go for the black part of the plate and accepting increased walks in the early weeks as the price for success later in the season. As it turned out, Marshall knew what he was doing, for he finished with 14 wins, 18 saves, and his career-best ERA, 1.78.

April proved the cruelest month again in 1973, as Marshall's first five games produced no wins, two losses, and an ERA of 8.78. Many observers speculated that the Expos had missed the boat by not trading Marshall to a contender after his fine 1972 effort, and the boobirds at Jarry Park made their sentiments clear. How did Marshall react to his fickle supporters? "I'm personally unaffected," he said at the time. "Booing me is as inappropriate as cheering me." Marshall had always scorned hero worship, or at least the worship of mere baseball players as heroes. "Kids who worship an athlete are worshiping a false god," he said. "Let them pay homage to their teacher, their scoutmaster, the policeman on the beat, or whoever has a more meaningful role in their lives." As an extension of this conviction, he refused to sign autographs, a choice for which he took a lot of heat in the press.

Marshall's early-season difficulties in 1973 melted away as rapidly as they had the previous year. Pitching 92 games, then a major-league record, he won 14 and saved 31 to take Fireman-of-the-Year honors and very nearly take his Expos to the N.L. East title. While he was putting out all those fires there had to be a lot of flaming faces over in Detroit, Houston, and Milwaukee (where the Seattle franchise had shifted after one year).

For the second straight year, Marshall was named the Expos' most valuable player by the O'Keefe Brewery, who awarded him a Cadillac Eldorado one year and $5,000 the next. Marshall accepted the car, though he stated that he thought the gift inappropriate and would feel pompous driving it. Accommodatingly, the O'Keefe people changed the award to straight cash the next year; Marshall refused it, writing the brewery president, "I can't imagine players on the same team competing for this kind of award." Marshall played baseball because he loved competition, but individualistic as he was in so many ways, he believed that on the field there was no place for personal goals except insofar as each individual, by performing to the maximum of his capabilities, could contribute to the team goal.

Philosophically appealing as Marshall's pursuit of pure competition may have been, his rejection of the prize was a public-relations gaffe that may have contributed to his surprising departure from Montreal before the 1974 season. Other causes: The Montreal office recognized that its need for a center fielder could not be filled by the nascent farm system, and they felt that by pitching 92 games

Marshall might well have pitched himself out for 1974; thus the trade of Marshall to the Dodgers for thirty-four-year-old center fielder Willie Davis.

What Montreal didn't know, or didn't care to know, was that Marshall had become convinced that, by using the muscles correctly, there was no reason a pitcher could not pitch virtually every day. His investigations into the science of kinesiology had led him to the writings of Daniel Bernoulli, the Swiss mathematician and physicist who had developed a key principal of hydrodynamics, and those of Hans Selye, an expert on the effects of stress; they helped him to formulate his view that by specifically training muscles or muscle groups to do the things of which they were capable, the body could perform feats of which it had been thought incapable.

Case in point: pitching in 106 games in the regular season of 1974, plus two in the play-offs and all five World Series games. In addition to the statistics and honors he gathered that season, Mike highlighted his string of 13 straight appearances by winning five games in six days. And if his 21 saves seem a skimpy total for a man who finished 83 games, remember that the tighter save rule had just come into effect; had the older rule prevailed in 1974, Marshall would have rung up more than 35.

Marshall's skein of 13 games in a row began June 18 against Pittsburgh, in a losing cause, and ended on July 3, with a save in the first game of a doubleheader against the Reds. On June 21 he got a win by setting down all nine Giants he faced and watching his Dodgers rally from a 3–0 deficit. Next day he mowed down six more Giants in succession and won as Bill Buckner homered in the tenth. On the twenty-third, Ken McMullen's ninth-inning hit gave Marshall the win as he hurled two more scoreless frames. On the twenty-fourth, Marshall went one and two-thirds without allowing anything, but L.A. lost. On the twenty-fifth, he pitched a 1-2-3 ninth and his mates rallied for two runs to prevail over the Braves. On the twenty-sixth he won again, though not in classic fashion; he gave the Braves their lead run in the ninth, but then watched the Dodgers score two in the ninth yet again.

On September 9, in a game against Cincinnati, Marshall trekked in from the bullpen for the ninety-third time, breaking his record of 1973. And he did it with a flourish, snuffing out a Red rally in the eighth and fanning the side in the ninth to preserve the victory.

In the last weeks of the season, Mike did not perform up to the levels he had attained earlier; his won-lost record, at one point 11–3, tailed off to a final 15–12. But when play-off time rolled around, he returned to his early-season form. Although the situations in which he was called upon to pitch were not tight enough for him to gain credit for a save, Mike finished two Dodger victories, allowing but one harmless hit in four innings. In the World Series he extended his scoreless string through seven more frames before giving up a homer to Joe Rudi that decided the fifth and final game. Over the Series, Marshall pitched nine otherwise impeccable innings, saving Game Two in dramatic fashion by picking "designated runner" Herb Washington off first base with one out in the ninth, then fanning the final batter to end the game.

After winning the Cy Young and the Fireman of the Year and being beaten out—unjustly, many claimed—for the MVP by teammate Steve Garvey, Marshall announced that he might not return to baseball in 1975. He didn't really like being a major leaguer, he intimated, not the way he liked his research and teaching at East Lansing. "I wish," he said, "I could get the great hitters of today—Joe Torre, Willie McCovey, Hank Aaron—to drop by Michigan State so I could pitch against them on weekends."

The Dodgers offered Marshall a contract for 1975 that made him baseball's first $100,000 fireman, and he returned to the fray. But Marshall's 1975 was sabotaged by injury, limiting him to only 57 appearances in which he went 9–14 with 13 saves. Never a popular man with the press, Marshall got it with both barrels from writers who were glad to see him get his comeuppance. And many baseball people who bristled at hearing Marshall say things like, "I know more about pitching than anyone in the game or anyone who's played the game," were delighted to see Mike's body seemingly give the lie to his theories.

When he failed to bounce back 100 percent in 1976, the Dodgers tried to trade him, but found there were no takers. Marshall was still baseball's highest-paid reliever, was coming off an injury, and had developed a rep as a troublemaker. On June 23, 1976, after Mike had won four and saved eight for the Dodgers, they gave him to the Braves for the waiver price of $20,000. Columnist Jim Murray, who bore no love for Marshall, wrote at the time, "There isn't a team in baseball that wouldn't have wanted Mike if it could keep the right arm and throw the rest away."

For the Braves Marshall was an experiment that failed—he added only two wins and six saves to his Los Angeles totals, finishing with a 4.00 ERA and being sidelined on the disabled list for all of September. He aroused considerable consternation over a petty feud with MSU, which had arisen during the off-season, regarding Marshall's alleged improper use of an athletic facility. Marshall was arrested by the university, whom he in turn sued.

Twice during the 1976 season Mike was obliged to leave his team and fly to East Lansing to settle affairs.

Nineteen seventy-seven opened with Marshall in Atlanta, but after pitching ineffectively in four games, he found himself back in the American League, waived to Texas. No National League club had wanted him. He pitched briefly and badly for Texas, troubled with a knee injury that was to knock him out for the last three months of the season.

At season's end Marshall became a free agent and his name went into the reentry draft pool. All teams but the White Sox passed on the opportunity to negotiate with him, and the White Sox proved halfhearted suitors at best.

If this was to be the end of his career, at least Marshall had given plenty of thought and effort to planning a second career. By May 1978 he had finally completed his doctoral dissertation, "Maturation at Adolescence in Males," and he had been teaching courses in his specialty, child growth, during the off-season for several years. But no major-league batters ever took Marshall up on his offer to square off on weekends in East Lansing; if he still had the competitive itch, he would have to come to them.

The best experience Mike had ever had in the majors, he felt, was playing for Gene Mauch, a man who respected ideas and did not try to tamper with Marshall beyond exercising the on-field authority of a manager. On May 10, 1978, Mike came to Chicago to audition for Mauch, now manager of the Minnesota Twins. It looked to be an ideal situation for Marshall: Mauch had remained an admirer of Marshall's even after they parted company in 1974, and Minnesota owner Cal Griffith (a) was inclined to view veteran relievers favorably, for example, Stan Williams, Ron Perranoski, Al Worthington; and (b) was badly strapped for a fireman, with his 1977 ace, Tom Johnson, injured.

In 30 minutes of throwing to four Twins batters at Comiskey Park, Marshall was "unhittable," according to Craig Kusick. "We had a pile of broken bats behind the cage that you could have started a bonfire with. I think he broke eight of them. Jose Morales and Glenn Adams said he threw harder than he had in the National League." Mauch emphatically recommended that Griffith hire him. But Griffith balked, saying, "There is nothing in his record to indicate he would help us. It doesn't make good sense to me."

These remarks didn't make good sense to the Twins players, particularly Rod Carew, who said, "The situation is ridiculous, a joke. It's demoralizing for everyone. . . . I'll play out my option and become a free agent. And if Griffith tries to trade me, I'll veto the deal. If he's going to stick it to us, I'm going to stick it to him."

Next day, Griffith reconsidered and hired Marshall to a low-sala-ried, incentive-leveraged contract that, as it developed, brought Marshall nearly $100,000 after all.

Marshall put on the uniform of the last-place Twins for the first time on the night of May 15. One week later, Minnesota had won seven of eight, and Marshall had picked up four saves and a win in his five appearances, allowing one hit and no runs in eight innings. On the season, despite having missed the first five weeks of the campaign, he finished third among American League reliev-ers for Fireman-of-the-Year honors, with 10 wins and 21 saves. Marshall was back, to reclaim his reputation as one of the game's great relievers of all time.

**16**

**The
Ten Best:
Lyle**

In 1977, Albert Walter Lyle, better known as Sparky, became the second man to win a Cy Young Award as a relief pitcher. Upon learning that he had received the award, he said, "I'm thrilled with this award not only for myself, but for all relief pitchers. Maybe they will get more recognition from now on."

Sparky may have been reflecting back on one of the disappointments of his career, not being named to the American League All-Star team in 1972, when he had had an even better year than the one he enjoyed in 1977. At that time Earl Weaver of the Orioles, manager of the A.L. contingent, had declined to nominate any relievers because their skills were "too specialized."

The Baltimore pilot's stance may in turn have stirred other recollections of rejection, for Lyle had been signed to his first pro contract by Baltimore. At the age of nineteen, the 6-feet-1, 195-pound lefty attracted the O's attention by fanning 31 batters in a 17-inning sandlot game. His hometown was Reynoldsville, in the coal country of Pennsylvania that has produced so many outstanding major leaguers. "The biggest thing I wanted to do as a kid was get out of school, get a job, and get out of my hometown." The motivation to succeed must have been much the same for Ed Walsh and Joe Page, to name two coal-country products who starred in relief in years past.

Lyle reported to Bluefield in the Appalachian League, where he pitched in only seven games before showing enough to warrant a promotion to Fox Cities in the Midwest circuit. Used as a starter, Lyle put in 68 innings' work on the year, producing 95 strikeouts and, even more impressive for a fastballing youngster, only 43 walks. If ever a pitcher were marked for stardom from the outset, Sparky seemed to be it. Yet the Orioles were flush with young pitching prospects in their farm system and young stars in Baltimore (Jim Palmer, Dave McNally, Milt Pappas, Wally Bunker). Deciding they could not protect Lyle on the 40-man roster preparatory to the winter draft, they put him on the list of the Triple-A Rochester Redbirds, from whom he was joyfully plucked by Boston.

With Winston-Salem in the Carolina League the next year, he was made a fireman, more by accident than design. "The team had a left-handed reliever," Sparky recalled, "but he got hurt and I won the job." He has never started a game since.

Nineteen sixty-six was spent close to Boston, with Pittsfield, where he continued to strike out batters at the rate of one an

Sparky Lyle—from Cy Young in 1977 to sayonara in 1978.

inning. This was the year bullpen king Dick Radatz's bubble burst in Boston, and the Red Sox settled on Sparky as the heir apparent, though they relied on Don McMahon and John Wyatt in the interregnum. Sparky opened the 1967 campaign with Toronto in the International League, Boston's top farm club. After sparkling in 16 games, he came to Beantown.

A month short of twenty-three, Lyle still relied heavily on his fastball and mixed it with only one other pitch—the slider or the curve, whichever happened to be working better that day. He went out after the strikeout, like Radatz, and also like Radatz, he had extraordinary control. The key to Sparky's longevity, however, is that unlike Radatz, he was able to develop another pitch—the slider—to the extent that today it has entirely supplanted the blazer in his repertoire. The Sparky Lyle of today will throw the hard slider 19 pitches out of 20; if at age thirty-four his fastball has slipped a few miles per hour, who's to notice?

Sparky pitched well in limited action with the pennant-winning Sox of 1967, winning one and saving five while posting a commendable ERA of 2.28. But he injured himself in the late going and was unable to participate in the World Series. John Wyatt was the head honcho in the Boston bullpen that year, unexpectedly bouncing back from a weak 1966 with the best season of his life. Sparky would have to wait his turn.

It was in 1969 that he really came on, appearing 71 times, saving 17 and winning eight. While Lyle had performed well enough his first two years, Boston manager Dick Williams now showed more faith in him than ever before, bringing him in and leaving him in whether the batters due up were right-handed or left-handed.

In 1970 Eddie Kasko became the new Boston pilot, and he played the percentages closer to the book. While Sparky's total appearances only declined from 71 to 63, his innings pitched plummeted from 102⅔ to a mere 67. He started the season in fine style, at one point saving four wins in four days against Oakland. But that success soon evaporated—whether poor outings led to his inactivity or inactivity caused his poor outings is not clear, but the result was a wretched mark of 1–7 and a large ERA of 3.90. Nonetheless, in a year everyone in Boston regarded as calamitous, Lyle managed to save 20 games, the most he was ever to collect in a Red Sox uniform.

Sparky's use as a left-handed specialist intensified in 1971 as he pitched fewer innings than any of the other three men in the pen—Ken Tatum, Bob Bolin, and Bill Lee. Although with 16 saves he again led the club, Lyle felt that he could do more if only management would let him. And in 1972 they did, but in New York. Boston had been impressed with the showing of lefty Bill Lee in his first full year with the team; Lyle became expendable, and less than a month before the 1972 season opened, he was traded to the Yankees for Danny Cater, a competent major-league hitter, and Mario Guerrero, then a minor-league shortstop.

Nineteen seventy-one had been a year of utter collapse for the Yankee bullpen, with a pitiful team total of 12 saves—a figure Tug McGraw was to equal in 20 days in 1973. Lyle came in and restored the bullpen to health single-handed. He saved 35, won nine, and his ERA was 1.91. He copped A.L. Fireman-of-the-Year honors and finished fourth in the MVP vote. Two years of being called in to throw the breaking ball to left-handers had sharpened his slider to a point where now he scarcely threw anything else. To the right-hander, slider down and in; to the left-hander, slider low and away.

In a memorable tight spot against Texas that year, Lyle was called in to put down a ninth-inning uprising that had placed Rangers on second and third with no one out. Frank Howard was at the plate and Lyle, deciding that discretion would be the better part of valor, gave the giant a purposeful pass. Then he set to work, throwing ten pitches and fanning the side.

It was that kind of flourish that made him an instant favorite of the New York fans. Lyle's cocky strut to the mound upon exiting from the bullpen car, to the accompaniment of the organist playing "Pomp and Circumstance," galvanized Yankee Stadium. Sparky oozed confidence and determination. If the issue was in doubt before Sparky marched in, one cheek distended with a chaw of Red Man tobacco, there was no doubt in the crowd's mind once he took the mound. He would do the job, and that was that.

Apart from his on-field heroics, Lyle won the affection of the fans with his quirky manner. "Some people say you have to be crazy to be a reliever," he once said. "Well, I was crazy before I ever became one." Lyle was lionized in the press for episodes that might have been banned in Boston, such as his penchant for sitting naked on cakes that had the misfortune of being delivered to the Yankee clubhouse. "I like chocolate the best," he declared. Reporting late to spring training, as was his custom, after a highly successful season, he showed up at the Yankee camp with a cast on his left leg and left arm. The Yankee brass was horrified that Sparky had gone out and cracked himself up without ever notifying the club. But by day's end, the truth was out—the fractures were a hoax.

In 1973, Lyle's won-lost record slipped to 5–9, but his ERA

remained low, and he did contribute 27 saves. Manager Ralph Houk no longer put all game-saving situations into his hands, but parceled out the work between McDaniel and Lyle, with Lindy generally taking on the longer stints. If Lyle suffered a bit from his reduced work load, the net result was that the Yankees gained. In the 1978 season, Rich Gossage came along to share the work, the Yankees prospered, and Sparky suffered again.

McDaniel moved on in 1974, and so did Houk. The Yankee manager was now Bill Virdon, who had played with Pittsburgh when Roy Face had been a one-man bullpen. Virdon handed Sparky the ball, said, "Go get 'em," and Lyle complied, posting a 1.66 ERA and 15 saves as the Yanks fell only two games short of the flag.

Nineteen seventy-five saw Virdon hand the reins over to Billy Martin in midseason, and Lyle go on to have his poorest year. Inactivity in spring training had brought Sparky into the regular season out of shape and lacking his customary control, and he never hit his stride. He posted only five wins and six saves, his lowest full-season total ever. Many advocated that he be traded while he still had some value, especially since newcomer Tippy Martinez looked so good in the late going. But the Yankees recalled that Boston had been burned by similar reasoning in 1972, and determined to keep Sparky around a bit longer.

It paid off as New York marched to the A.L. pennant for the first time in a dozen years, and Lyle was once again the dominant figure in the pen. In 64 games, he posted seven wins, a league-leading 23 saves, and an ERA of 2.25. And in his first exposure to postseason play, Lyle was immaculate, with one scoreless appearance for a save in Game Two of the play-off with Kansas City and two more scoreless outings, to no avail, in the Yanks' four-game wipeout by the Reds.

Then came the year of the Yankees' World Series revenge and of Sparky Lyle's preeminence among American League pitchers. Oddly, though Sparky won the Cy Young Award for his 13 wins and 26 saves, he did not win the Fireman of the Year—that went to Bill Campbell, whose 44-point heroics had kept the Boston Red Sox in the race till the end.

The A.L. play-offs rematched the contestants of 1976, when Kansas City had gone down to defeat on Chris Chambliss's dramatic ninth-inning home run. Lyle was not impeccable this time around—he was better. Though touched up for a run in Games One and Three, both Yankee losses on which Lyle bore no impact, he was sensational in Games Four and Five.

With their backs against the wall, the Yankees took an early

4–0 lead in Game Four. But starter Ed Figueroa gave all those runs back in the fourth frame. Dick Tidrow replaced him but was unable to put out the fire and, with men on first and third and two out, Tidrow handed the ball over to Lyle. Sparky got the third out, and threw blanks at the Royals over the next five innings, limiting them to two hits and gaining the win.

Next day, it was the Royals who showed the early foot, running up a lead of 3–1 after three. In that third inning, Martin pulled starter Ron Guidry, not up to par with only two days' rest, and brought in Mike Torrez. Big Mike, who would go on to be the pitching star of the World Series, kept the Yanks in the game over the next five and one-third innings, holding the Royals scoreless while the Yanks crept to within one. But when Mike faltered with two down in the bottom of the eighth, in came Sparky to get the out. Three Yankees crossed the plate in the top of the ninth, and Lyle set down the dazed Royals in the bottom of the frame to win his second critical contest in two tries.

In the first game of the World Series between the Yanks and the Dodgers, Lyle made it three straight postseason wins. Replacing starter Don Gullett with one man down and two on in the ninth, and New York holding a 3–2 lead, Lyle allowed Lee Lacy to single and tie the score. He did not allow another hit as the game went into the twelfth before the Yanks could score.

Over the winter, New York spent $2,748,000 to sign free-agent fireman Rich Gossage to a six-year contract. Lyle, locked into a three-year pact for a comparatively trivial sum, was irked. He maintained that owner George Steinbrenner had agreed to reopen negotiations on his contract, a claim Steinbrenner denied.

Lyle embarked upon the 1978 campaign in a poor frame of mind, demanding every other day that he be traded to a team that would pay him what he was worth. As the season progressed and Gossage got most of the calls in gamesaving situations, Lyle became incensed. As teammate Graig Nettles aptly put it, Sparky had gone "from Cy Young to sayonara." Manager Billy Martin would bring Lyle in to relieve in the fifth or sixth inning, then pull him for Gossage in the seventh or eighth, thus depriving Sparky of any statistical benefit from a Yankee win. Martin's thinking was that, with Don Gullett sidelined for the season, the Yankees were left with only one left-handed starter, Ron Guidry; should one of the righties falter, by bringing in Lyle the Yankee manager might force his opposing number to pull his left-handed batters for right-handed ones; then, with the lineup predominantly right-handed, Gossage could come in and blow the ball past them.

Lyle didn't appreciate the strategy; all he knew was that he was no longer a gamesaver. On July 17, he came in against Kansas City in the fifth, replacing Jim Hunter with two out. After putting down the side in the sixth, he stormed into the dugout, threw his glove against the wall and said, "I'm no long-relief man," and took himself out of the game. This seeming act of insubordination was passed over, for that was the night Reggie Jackson refused to obey a sign to hit away, instead bunting his way into a strikeout, and bunting Billy Martin out of a job.

In 1978 Lyle and Gossage pitched in about the same number of games and innings, but the Goose outsaved Lyle 27 to 9. As the season progressed, it was clear that Gossage represented the Yankee future and Lyle the Yankee past. They could not continue to work in the same bullpen another year. Lyle had seen his career suddenly go into eclipse. At thirty-five, with an arm that has never given him any trouble, Sparky figured to provide several more years of top-flight relief work for some club, and approach or surpass the lifetime figures posted by Hoyt Wilhelm in saves, relief points, and even games pitched in relief. With a chance to go down in history as the greatest relief pitcher of all time, it would not have been fair for Lyle's outstanding career to dim in the shadow of a rising star. And much to Sparky's relief, that will not happen, not in New York at least. He opens the 1979 season as the top man in the Texas Ranger bullpen.

# 17

# The
# Ten Best:
# Fingers

Another pitcher in hailing distance of Wilhelm's career marks for saves and relief points is San Diego's Rollie Fingers. Although he also trails Sparky Lyle going into the 1979 campaign, Fingers is situated with a club that gives him plenty of work in the tight spots. Moreover, the 6-feet-4 right-hander with the handlebar moustache is two years younger than Lyle, and thus far has not fallen victim to the off years experienced by most firemen, Lyle included. A model of consistency, Rollie in 1978 had completed his eighth straight year with 20 or more relief points and his second straight 40-point year, the latter feat equaled in relief-pitching history only by Dick Radatz and Ron Perranoski.

Like Mike Marshall, as a boy Fingers had a hard time choosing between the mound and the field. He starred as both left fielder and pitcher for Upland High in the euphonious town of Cuca-monga, California, but failed to draw professional interest upon graduation. That changed the next year, as the then-skinny eighteen-year-old led Upland American Legion Post No. 73 to the championship and was named American Legion Player of the Year. Playing the outfield, he topped all batters in the Legion World Series with his .450 average and won the deciding game by hurling a two-hitter. Now the scouts were interested, though opinion was divided about how to use this new Babe Ruth. Fingers himself leaned

Rollie Fingers may be the best bet to replace Wilhelm as the game's greatest fireman.

toward pitching, as he hooked on with Kansas City despite a higher offer from Los Angeles. As Perranoski had reasoned earlier, the Dodgers' plethora of pitching prospects would provide an obstacle to reaching the majors, where the A's, chronic tailenders, offered no such impasse.

Rollie was assigned to Leesburg in the Florida State League for 1965, and with his sinking fastball pitched much better than his 8–15 record would seem to indicate. The next season he moved up to Modesto in the California League, and again pitched well as a starter (he was not made a fireman until he reached Oakland). Backed by such teammates as Reggie Jackson, Joe Rudi, and Dave Duncan, Rollie went 11–6 and fanned nearly a man an inning. The

A's elevated him to Birmingham in the Southern League for 1967, and he almost went no further.

On opening day, Fingers started against Evansville and pitched scoreless ball through three innings as his bride of nine days watched proudly from the stands. In the fourth, Fingers threw a change-up to batter Fred Kovner, who sent it back twice as fast as it had come. Fingers picked up the flight of the ball only three feet or so before it was upon him; he threw up his hands to protect himself, but the ball came through and shattered his jaw. He went down as if he had been shot, and lay motionless in the dirt, face down. His teammates rushed to the mound and rolled him over. Birmingham manager John McNamara, later to be his manager at both Oakland and San Diego, thought Fingers was dead. Blood was coming out of his right eye.

After a horrifying stillness, Fingers moved his leg and was semiconscious as he was taken off the field and to the hospital. There he proved allergic to a medication given him, and for three days vomited through his teeth, clamped together by the wiring of his jaw.

Incredibly, Rollie returned to active duty only six weeks later and managed to pitch 102 innings on the year. He seemed to lose something off his fastball, though, when he returned; his ratio of strikeouts to innings pitched declined 40 percent. He returned to Birmingham for 1968, but did get called up to Oakland in time to pitch one and a third forgettable innings of relief—as a result of that debut, his major-league ERA at the end of 1968 was 27.00.

In 1969, his first full season with the big club, Rollie appeared in 60 games, eight of them as a starter. He pitched creditably in both roles, but was outstanding in neither, and the jury was still out regarding how best to deploy his assets, a sinking fastball and good control. This situation was left unresolved through 1970 as Fingers started 19 games while relieving in 26 others. Sometimes he would look like a 20-game winner, other times he'd be pounded. Rollie became convinced he needed another pitch if he was to become a consistent starter. He went to the Dominican Republic to play winter ball and work on his slider, a pitch he'd been unable to throw to spots in previous experiments.

Plenty of work that winter gave Fingers mastery over the pitch, and when he returned Stateside, new Oakland manager Dick Williams installed him in the five-man rotation to open the 1971 season. In the early weeks, only he and rookie Vida Blue looked good, while the other starters—Hunter, Odom, and Chuck Dobson —were still trying to get in their rhythm. Once they found theirs, Fingers lost his. Pitching every fifth day in the majors for the first time, he'd prepare for the hitters to a maniacal degree, planning his pitches days in advance of his scheduled start, psyching himself up so that he couldn't sleep the night before his turn. When game time rolled around, Rollie had neither concentration nor conviction behind his pitches. On May 15, with a record of 1–4, he made the last of his eight starts that year; he was pointed in the direction of the pen, and assigned mopup duty.

When right-handed relief ace Bob Locker got blasted in early June, Fingers was taken off long relief and given a shot at putting out late-inning fires. And he warmed to the task immediately, pitching 29⅔ innings of scoreless ball into July. In the midst of the streak, on July 9, he took part in a sensational 20-inning 1–0 duel with the Angels. Blue, the Oakland starter, lasted 11 innings in which he allowed seven hits and struck out 17. The Angels' starter, Rudy May, was equally overpowering, allowing but three hits in 12 innings while whiffing 13. Rollie didn't get the decision in this game, but relieving Blue he hurled seven innings of two-hit ball while adding seven strikeouts. The two teams went on to set an all-time record of 43 strikeouts.

Shortly after this impressive showing, he was asked how he felt about becoming a gamesaver. "So far I don't mind it at all," he said. "I wouldn't mind remaining a relief man because they can make as much money as a starter." He was right: What Rollie didn't make from his salary and winners' shares of the World Series gate three years running, he is getting today.

Fingers finished 1971 with 17 saves, fourth in the American League. Next year, as he and his teammates became World Champions, the whole country was alerted to the rising star in the Oakland bullpen. During the regular season, Rollie led the A.L. with 11 wins in relief, saved 21, and fanned 113 in 111⅓ innings, a clip he had not approached since his minor-league days. The hard slider he had developed to make him a complete starter was now serving to make him a doubly deceptive relief pitcher.

In the American League Championship Series in Detroit, Fingers came into the first game in the ninth inning with the score 1–1 and Tigers on first and third. No one was out. Rollie and the A's had been a play-off bust the year before as Baltimore had breezed by them in three straight. This time the A's proved no patsies. Fingers retired Gates Brown on an infield pop and induced Jim Northrup to bounce into a double play; the A's went on to win in eleven. Although the Tigers gave them a tough battle, the A's won the play-off, and earned the right to be rolled over by the Big Red Machine, or so the outcome was predicted.

Oakland won the World Series against the Reds in seven

games, and Fingers pitched in six of them, winning one, losing one, and saving two. In Game One he combined with Vida Blue for four scoreless innings in relief of winner Ken Holtzman. In Game Two he came on for a weakening Jim Hunter with two on and two out in the ninth, with the A's clinging to a 2–1 margin; Rollie fanned Julian Javier for the final out. But Fingers's performance in the next contest is the one people still talk about.

In the eighth inning of Game Three, the Reds, leading 1–0, placed runners on first and third off starter Blue Moon Odom and reliever Vida Blue. With only one out, Blue had a count of 2–2 on Johnny Bench when Bobby Tolan broke for second. The pitch was a ball, and Tolan stole the base. With the count now full, the strategy seemed obvious: Now that first base was open, walk Bench to set up the double play. Manager Dick Williams replaced Blue with Fingers and, after much gesticulating and pointing in the direction of first base, Williams returned to the dugout.

Rollie took his eight allowed warm-up pitches, then readied to lob a wide one to catcher Gene Tenace, who extended his right hand to provide a target and poised to jump out of the catcher's box. But then Tenace dove into a crouch, and Fingers whizzed a slider over the outside corner. Bench, who had relaxed his bat on his shoulder, walked sheepishly to the dugout. "I guess they caught me with my pants down," Bench admitted after the game, but he could afford to smile about it: The Reds' 1–0 lead stood up through the final innings.

Rollie won Game Four as the A's rallied for two runs in the bottom of the ninth, and lost Game Five. His own fielding lapse figured in the defeat. On the sixth day he rested, and in Game Seven he came in with two Reds on base and no one out, and the A's holding a precarious 3–2 lead. Fingers protected it with two innings of hitless ball, and the A's were World Champs.

Fingers was equally brilliant in World Series play in each of the next two years. In 1973 against the Mets, he once more pitched in six of the seven contests, saving two. (The one earned run he allowed in his 12⅔ innings was the only score the Oakland bullpen allowed over 31 innings.) In 1974, pitted against L.A., he appeared in four games, winning one, saving two, and being named the Most Valuable Player of the five-game Series.

During the regular season those two years, Fingers continued to be one of the American League's finest firemen, recording 29 relief points in 1973 and 27 in 1974. In 1975 the A's failed to make it past the play-offs with Boston, and dreams of Yankee-type dynasty came to an end. But on a personal level, Rollie stepped up the pace, collecting 34 points, his best as an American Leaguer.

He also was one of four Oakland hurlers to take part in a weird no-hitter the last week of the season.

Rollie was getting better every year, it seemed, and he felt his salary was not advancing at a commensurate rate. When he and Charlie Finley reached a bargaining impasse in the early part of the 1976 season, Fingers let it be known that he, like Joe Rudi and Vida Blue, would play out his option—that is, not sign a contract and accept a 20 percent pay cut, the maximum allowable. As a free agent for 1977, he would sign with whatever team he pleased, and Charlie Finley would receive no compensation.

Attempting to circumvent this scenario Finley, one hour before the June 15 trading deadline, announced the sale of Fingers and Rudi to the Boston Red Sox for a million dollars apiece; Vida Blue was snatched up by the Yankees for $1.5 million. The next day, Fingers and Rudi donned the uniforms of their new club (Oakland was playing in Boston at the time, so the switch was easy), but were held out of action at Bowie Kuhn's request. On June 17, the commissioner voided all three sales for not being "in the best interest of baseball," and amid much wailing and threats, the three players were reassigned to Oakland.

Despite the turmoil surrounding the great sale that wasn't, Fingers pitched as well as ever, winning 13, saving 20, and posting a 2.53 ERA. He may have taken comfort in the fact that while he lost no money through his enforced return to Oakland—the pot of gold still awaited him at the conclusion of his contractual obligations for 1976—his adversary Charlie Finley lost a cool million for his refusal to come up with the extra thousands Fingers felt he deserved.

Thirteen clubs bid for Fingers's services in the historic reentry draft held on November 4, 1976. Six weeks later, Ray Kroc and the Padres announced that Rollie had decided to try his luck in the National League, and would be paid $1.6 million for his efforts over the next five years. A California native, Fingers was influenced by the opportunity to play not far from where he had grown up, and perhaps by the opportunity to link up once again with John McNamara, his manager at Birmingham and Oakland, and then the skipper of the Padres.

Fingers immediately changed the work habits of the San Diego pitching staff. Where in 1976 Padre starters completed 47 games, in 1977 they completed *six*, the all-time low team total. Where in 1976 Padre relievers had 18 saves, 16 of them by Butch Metzger, in 1977 they had 44, 35 of them by Fingers. While there was plenty of rescue duty to go around for Dave Tomlin and Dan Spillner (76 games apiece), when the game was on the line, it was

Fingers who got the call—at first from McNamara, and after he was released, from his replacement Alvin Dark, who had also managed Fingers at Oakland.

Rollie worked a career high 78 games and went 8–9 in addition to his 35 saves. While proving himself the most consistent fireman in the American League over the previous seven years, he had never once piled up enough relief points to take Fireman-of-the-Year honors. Now, in his first year in the National League, when you might expect a period of adjustment to the different hitters and the "lower strike zone," Fingers was the league's top relief hurler.

Going into 1978, Fingers had averaged 7.03 whiffs per nine innings, including his 37 starts; since 1971, when he was converted to a fireman by Dick Williams, his strikeout average was 8.60 per nine innings, one of the best ever. Yet in 1978 his strikeout figure declined to 6.06. Was Fingers losing his fastball? Probably. He insisted, "I've been sacrificing some of my velocity to get better control," yet his control has always been excellent—less than three passes per nine innings in every one of the last nine years.

Rollie appears to be in the midst of making the adjustment that all fastballers make between the ages of twenty-eight and thirty-two if they want to maintain their level of play. But as Rollie went more and more to the slider in 1978, N.L. hitters had no better luck than they did in 1977. Rollie recorded 37 saves, one short of the record, and repeated as National League Fireman of the Year. Rollie is a special breed of fireman, as his manager Roger Craig explains: "There have been relief pitchers with trick pitches who have lasted a number of years, but Rollie is the only power pitcher who has ever been consistently brilliant over a long period."

If 1978 is any indication, Fingers is the best current bet to overtake Wilhelm as the greatest relief pitcher of all time.

**18**

**The New Wave: 1974 -**

Until Mike Marshall's gargantuan accomplishment in 1974, the question had always been, What are a relief pitcher's limits? Then suddenly it seemed more relevant to ask, Are there limits at all? Since 1974, when the new, more restrictive save rule went into effect, saves in the National League have increased by over 60 percent, while complete games have decreased by 11 percent.* In the American League, use of the designated hitter tends to promote complete games and accordingly inhibit saves. Still, in the A.L. since 1974 the portion of games featuring a save has gone up by 27 percent, while complete games have fallen off by 15 percent. Only the five-year period 1904–1908 provides equally dramatic evidence of a revolution in relief pitching.

Marshall led the way, but many other firemen were in the vanguard in 1974. The American League's Fireman of the Year, Terry Forster, actually had more saves than Marshall. He was another in the line of fireballing relievers who starred in the major leagues before their twenty-first birthday. Terry had come to the White Sox at the age of nineteen, with only ten games of Class-A ball under his belt. He pitched creditably enough in limited action, but in 1972 he exploded for 29 saves, six wins, a 2.25 ERA, and

---

* The complete-game decline in the National League had been more pronounced—25 percent—from 1974 to 1977, but 1978 produced an aberrational jump in complete games in both leagues.

more strikeouts than innings pitched. He was joined that year by another twenty-year-old burner named Rich Gossage, who won seven games in relief without a loss (more on him later).

Nineteen seventy-three represented a retrenchment for Forster, who was tried as a starter 12 times with a resulting mark of 3–7. Restored to full-time fireman duty the next year (excepting one start), he responded with a performance that won him the A.L. Fireman-of-the-Year award. Still only twenty-two years old, Terry had worked in 172 games over the last three years, and the strain took its toll. A sore shoulder kept him on the disabled list through most of 1975, and there were fears that, like Billy McCool, he had burned out through overwork and overreliance on the high hard one.

Still beset by arm miseries, he came back in 1976 to post a dreadful mark of 2–12 in 29 outings, mostly as a starter. Gossage, coming off a Fireman-of-the-Year performance in 1975, was also made a starter in 1976. He went 9–17. The Chicago management, having perhaps wrecked two promising careers, disposed of the evidence. They packed off both Forster and Gossage to Pittsburgh, where Gossage excelled and Forster did not. His arm troubles were not yet behind him, and all he could manage for the Bucs was 33 appearances in which he won four, lost six, saved only one, and had a dismaying ERA of 4.45. At twenty, he had struck out better than nine men per game; at twenty-five, he could fan only six.

Like Gossage, Forster became a free agent at the end of the 1977 season, and despite his clouded future, the Dodgers gave him $850,000 to sign a five-year contract. It paid off. Although bone chips in his arm limited him to 65 innings, Terry bounced back to log 22 saves (eight of them in September), five wins, and a fine ERA of 1.94. In four postseason games, he did not permit a run. In fact, he did not give up a run after August 13! A star at twenty, seemingly washed up at twenty-four, he now looks to have a long and successful career.

The future does not look as rosy for the man who finished second to Forster, by only one point, in the 1974 Fireman-of-the-Year derby. Right-hander Tom Murphy joined the Milwaukee Brewers that year after six disappointing seasons as a starter in which he sometimes seemed on the verge of stardom but never demonstrated the necessary consistency. The Brewers shifted him to the bullpen, and there he found his home, winning 10, saving 20, and posting an ERA of 1.90. Although he saved 20 again the following year, his ERA soared to well over 4.00, a barrier he has not been able to penetrate as he has traveled from Milwaukee to Boston to Toronto.

Two other firemen who starred as sophomores in 1974 and are currently at crossroads in their career are Bill Campbell and Doug Bird. Campbell's injury-beset 1978 season was marked by only seven wins and four saves, quite a comedown from the lofty levels he'd attained the previous two seasons, in each of which he was the A.L. Fireman of the Year. The lanky right-hander with the varying motions and the devastating screwball and sinker had first attained notice in 1974, when with the Twins he saved 19 and won eight. Nineteen seventy-five was an off year, as the Twins toyed with using him as a starter, the role he'd filled exclusively in the minors. Though Bill showed some flashes, including a shutout, in 1976 new Twins' manager Gene Mauch took one look at the screwballing right-hander, instantly flashed back to a fellow named Marshall he'd once had at Montreal, and decided that the bullpen was the place for Bill.

Used only as a fireman in 1976, he topped A.L. relievers with 37 relief points, winning 17 to tie the league record held by John Hiller. And he accomplished this while under the strain of playing without a contract: Rather than up his preseason offer by $8,000, Twins' president Cal Griffith had let Campbell play out his option and allowed other teams to bid for his services at the conclusion of the 1976 season. Campbell gambled and won—had he gone 4–6 as he did in 1975, he would have commanded peanuts, but his 17–5 campaign drew an offer of $1 million from Boston for a five-year pact.

At the price, he proved a bargain as he kept the Boston pitching staff glued together throughout the 1977 season, saving 31 and winning 13. "We finished two games out with Bill Campbell," said manager Don Zimmer. "I don't know where we'd have finished without him." Unfortunately, Campbell's sore arm provided Zimmer the chance to find out. With an awesome attack, solid defense, and pitching that was just good enough, the Red Sox jumped out to a 14-game lead over the Yankees in July, only to see New York roar back to take the flag in a memorable play-off game. The Sox collapse involved the whole team, but might have been mitigated if their relief ace had been able to help Bob Stanley, the young right-hander who won 13 games coming out of the bullpen. Campbell must look to 1979 for evidence that he can return to form.

The same must be said of Doug Bird. The tall, slender right-hander had been the Kansas City Royals' top reliever in 1973–1975, but the advent of rookie reliever Mark Littell allowed Whitey Herzog to move Bird into the rotation in 1976. Bird's fine assortment of pitches enabled him to win as a starter, but he didn't really have the stamina to go nine. So in 1977 Herzog pulled the string of the yo-yo once again and brought Bird back to the pen, where he posted a career high of 25 relief points. Perhaps the alternating demands on his arm finally had an impact in 1978, or maybe it was just the arrival of The Mad Hungarian, Al Hrabosky, as top dog in the bullpen, but in 1978 Bird's ERA floated over the 5.00 mark, and he registered only a single save. At twenty-nine, he's young enough to have many good years left, but 1979 will likely provide the answer about his future.

Bird's teammate Hrabosky broke in at the other end of Missouri, with St. Louis in 1970. Unimpressive, he was sent down to Tulsa in 1971, and then down to Arkansas in the Double-A Texas League. Before Al left Tulsa, manager Warren Spahn told him, "The last time I saw you, you couldn't pitch in the big leagues. Now, you can't even pitch in Triple-A." It was hard to argue with a 12.86 ERA, but over the next few years, The Mad Hungarian would. A chunky 185-pound left-hander who looks shorter than his listed height of 5 feet 11, he throws one of the hardest fastballs in the big leagues; over his career he has struck out nearly eight men per nine innings. Yet not until 1974, when he was twenty-five, did he last a full season on a major-league roster. He started the season in comatose fashion, winning one, losing one, and posting no saves up to the All-Star break. Then he came alive, going 7–0 with eight saves in the second half. In one stretch of 26 games, covering 44⅓ frames, he allowed a total of one earned run.

The stage was set for Hrabosky to go to the head of the class in 1975, but again he started a little slowly—though he had 14 saves by the All-Star break, his won-lost record was only 3–2. Over the final months of the campaign, he went 10–1 with eight more saves, making for a total that led all N.L. relievers. His ERA on the season was 1.67.

Hrabosky affected a fierce manner with his Fu Manchu moustache and flowing hair, and infuriated hitters with his game-delaying psychological ploys. He would storm into the game looking as if he'd as soon kill the batter as get him out. Periodically he'd march behind the mound and, staring out past center field, commune with his demons for a seemingly interminable time; then he would bounce back to the rubber and, psychologically armed, proceed to dispose of the hitter.

In his attempts to be menacing Hrabosky would often succeed only in looking comical, but the St. Louis fans ate it up, as did the folks in Kansas City in 1978, when Hrabosky embellished his off-the-wall aura by wearing, as a deterrent to werewolves, a silver ring representing the "Gypsy Rose of Death." What it seems to come down to is that invoking the aid of spectral forces to get batters out is fine as long as it works; if the spell doesn't take, and you get blasted as Hrabosky did with the Cards in 1977, then get your clothes out of the cleaners, you're going on a trip.

Al's relief-point total in 1976 went from 35 to 21 and his ERA nearly doubled. In 1977 Vern Rapp took over as Cardinal manager and ruled that all facial hair must go. Like Samson, Hrabosky was left a pale shade of his hirsute self, and weakened horribly. Although his demands to be allowed to regain his source of strength were finally heeded at midseason, Al's performance did not pick up. He finished the season with 16 relief points and a 4.40 ERA, earning him a ticket to K.C. There he revived, to the tune of 20 saves and 8 wins.

The man for whom Hrabosky was traded, Mark Littell, had a hard-luck season with the Cards, going 4–8 with only 11 saves despite his respectable 2.80 ERA. To this point he is best known for a fatal home-run ball he threw to the Yankees' Chris Chambliss in the ninth inning of the final game of the 1976 play-offs. But he should be better known as one of the best strikeout artists ever to come out of the bullpen. Over the last three years, his only complete seasons in the majors, the big right-hander they call "Country" has struck out better than one batter for each inning he has pitched. In 1978, he fanned 130 in 106 frames—11 men per nine innings, the best ratio in baseball. In the minor leagues, 97 of his 100 appearances came as a starter, and he has seen sporadic use that way in the bigs. But with his fastball, relief seems the natural area in which to pursue stardom.

One of the better though less heralded relievers of the 1970s has been Cincinnati's Pedro Borbon, a right-hander with a snapping breaking ball. Since his first full season with the Reds in 1972, Pete has pitched no fewer than 60 games in any season, reaching a high of 80 in 1973. Trained as a fireman from his entry into pro ball with the Cardinal chain, he was long considered a workmanlike second or third arm in the pen behind such men as Clay Carroll or Rawly Eastwick. That perception changed when Borbon hit a career peak of 28 relief points in 1977. While his 8–2 won-lost record in 1978 was up to his previous standards, his ERA was a fat 5.00. Borbon has now had his first bad year, and it remains to be seen whether, at age thirty-three, he can rebound 100 percent.

Questions hover around the prospects of his one-time teammate Eastwick as well. A brilliant rookie season in 1975—a N.L.-high 22 saves, tying Hrabosky, plus three wins and two saves in postseason competition—seemed to hold out unlimited promise for the handsome fireballer. And 1976 bore fruit of that promise, as with 11 wins and 26 saves he copped the N.L. Fireman of the Year.

But 1977 was a nightmare for Eastwick. He failed to come to terms on his salary and announced his intention to play out his option. Them's fightin' words on the banks of the Ohio, where even a Cincinnati institution like Pete Rose can be made to appear a churlish ingrate for asking his due. Eastwick was in the doghouse for the first half of the season, picking up two wins and seven saves in only 23 games. On the trading deadline day, the pariah was sent to St. Louis, where he worked plenty and produced little. Still, in the reentry draft his lure was strong enough to merit a $1.1 million offer from the Yankees for five years' service.

Why the Yanks, with Lyle and Gossage, spent the money is a mystery, unless they were planning to dump Lyle before the season began. As it turned out, the Yankee staff was decimated by injuries in the early going of 1978, and the old adage that "you can never have too much pitching" proved its wisdom again. However, by this time the Yanks had packed Eastwick off to the Phils, who made sparing use of him. Two washout years in a row, yet most baseball people are betting on his return to productivity, in Philly or elsewhere.

The odds are longer against Rawly's left-handed colleague in the bullpen of the 1975 Reds, Will McEnaney. Also a freshman, Will collected 15 saves, five wins, a 2.47 ERA, and a satisfying save in the final game of the great World Series against the Red Sox. Next year was a comedown, as his ERA ballooned to 4.88 and he pitched a lot of mopup. But once again he recorded a final-game save in the 1976 Series, and the season ended on a high note. That was to be the last one for a while, as he was a dud with the 1977 Expos, and in 1978 the Pirates sent him down to the minors.

The Reds relief corps of 1975—Eastwick, McEnaney, Carroll, and Borbon—was one of the best, if not the best, of all time. It enabled the Reds to breeze to the pennant and take the World Series despite an exceedingly mediocre bunch of starters who, wisely, were permitted to complete only 22 games. Matched against this awesome foursome in the 1975 World Series was the Boston bullpen of Dick Drago, Jim Willoughby, Roger Moret, and Jim Burton—a less imposing collection of names, but one that matched pitches with the Reds' relievers until the final inning of the final game.

In the bottom of the eighth, Boston manager Darrell Johnson made a decision that will be debated forever on the banks of the Charles: to pinch-hit for his hot reliever, Jim Willoughby, who had only gone one and one third to that point and had given the Reds nothing to hit all Series long. The score was 3–3, and two Sox were down and none on; the hitter selected was Cecil Cooper, a 1-for-18

Series bust who promptly made his log 1-for-19. To pitch the ninth, Johnson chose Jim Burton, a twenty-five-year-old left-hander with half a season's experience in the major leagues and one third of an inning's experience in the Series. A walk, a sacrifice, an infield out, another walk, and Joe Morgan's single made losers of the Sox and Burton, who is still struggling to return to the majors.

The 1975 season saw two relievers, Dave LaRoche and Skip Lockwood, in similar situations. Both were coming off two execrable years that threatened their chances of continued employment. The left-handed LaRoche left too-cozy Wrigley Field for the more spacious grounds in Cleveland and relearned the trick of keeping the ball in the park. From 1975, when he gathered 17 saves and five wins, through 1978, when he collected 25 saves and 10 wins for the Angels, the National League flop was one of the very best firemen in either league.

Lockwood, a veteran starter shipped from the Angels to the A's, never wore the Oakland colors in earnest: He was dispatched to the minors, from which he was reprieved by the Mets in early August. Being sent down had been a tonic for Skip, who stripped his pitching repertoire to the basics—an excellent fastball and effective curve. His two-month blitz of the National League was breathtaking: in 48 innings, only 28 hits and 61 strikeouts. The bespectacled right-hander carried his momentum into 1976, when he finished third among N.L. relievers with 29 points, and 1977, when he notched 24. But in 1978 a propensity for experimenting with new pitches led to a number of late-inning long balls and placed him on manager Joe Torre's move list.

The N.Y. bullpen in 1978 also housed two once-promising firemen down on their luck. Butch Metzger had been co-winner of the Rookie-of-the-Year award in 1976 for his 11–4, 16-save performance with the Padres. "After spending five and a half years in the minor leagues," Metzger says, "I was determined to prove beyond a doubt that I was a major-league pitcher." And what better way to do it than to win his first ten decisions in 1976! A bad start in 1977 led the Padres, well-manned in the bullpen since their acquisition of Rollie Fingers, to ship Metzger to the Cards, with whom he pitched well: In one stretch of 11 games, he picked up four wins and six saves while not allowing a run. But in 1978 another poor start—this time in spring training—and Metzger was bound for the Mets. Pounded unmercifully for two months, he was finally sent to the Phils, who returned him to the minors.

The other rescue artist to join the last-place Mets with his career in a shambles was Dale Murray. In 1974, as a late-season addition to the Expos, he had saved 10 and won one in only 32 appearances, with a mind-boggling ERA of 1.03. The next year, the 6-feet-4, 205-pound right-hander with the sinking fastball led the N.L. in relief wins with 15. A mediocre 1976 led to his trade to Cincinnati, where the brain trust decided Dale could no longer get by throwing his sinker down the middle pitch after pitch (although over a three-year period covering 247⅓ innings, no batter had popped one of his sinkers over a fence). He experimented with the forkball, tried slowing his delivery and pitching to spots, and rapidly went from an effective "thrower" to an ineffective pitcher. With the Mets in the latter half of 1978, he was sometimes good, sometimes not; his career hangs in the balance as he heads into 1979.

As a rookie in 1976, Bruce Sutter was excellent, though not as spectacular as Murray had been. In his sophomore year, however,

Bruce Sutter. His forkball "starts out like a fastball and winds up like a dead fish."

the right-hander with the Shirley Temple hairdo was just about unhittable. His split-fingered fastball and curve kept a mediocre Cub outfit in first place all of June and July. By mid-July he had registered 24 saves, but then a knot behind his right shoulder put him on the shelf and the Cubs on the skids. For three weeks he was on the disabled list, and for a period of five weeks he failed to register a save.

There were fears that manager Herman Franks had permanently ruined Sutter through overuse, but Bruce came back in September to pitch as well as he had in the first half. On the eighth of that month, he fanned six Expos in succession, three of them with nine pitches. On the season, despite his five weeks of virtual uselessness, Sutter pitched in 62 games, saving 31, winning seven, and posting an ERA of 1.35.

What's more, he became quite a strikeout artist, despite possessing only ordinary speed. The forkball had long been a favorite with firemen—notably Roy Face and Lindy McDaniel—because its sudden drop would generally make the batter hit the ball top of center, producing a grounder. But the drop on Sutter's pitch was so sudden and steep—Houston's Terry Puhl says, "It starts out like a fastball and winds up like a dead fish"—that batters would swing over the ball entirely. In 1977 he fanned 129 men in only 107 frames.

Bruce pitched remarkably in the first half of 1978, as he had in the first half of 1977, again keeping the Cubs in contention. Just before the All-Star break, Bruce was named N.L. Player of the Week as he saved all five games the Cubs won. Then he was the winning pitcher in the All-Star Game, with one and two-thirds innings of hitless hurling.

At that point, his record in 34 outings was 5–3, with 14 saves and an ERA of 1.77. Yet he tailed off in the second half, managing to post 13 additional saves, but going 3–7 and seeing his second-half ERA balloon to 5.02. The problem in 1978 was not, thankfully, a sore arm but a flaw in his motion that Freddie Martin, the man who had taught the forkball to Bruce in 1974, was called in to correct. It looks as though Sutter will be one of the game's top firemen for years to come.

In 1977, three National League relief men tied for fifth in the running for Fireman of the Year behind Fingers, Sutter, Gossage, and Borbon. First of these is Charley Hough, the Dodgers' knuckleballing right-hander who today forms, with Terry Forster, one of the most effective righty-lefty duos in baseball; second is the Giants' fastballing left-hander Gary Lavelle, who teams with righty Randy Moffitt; and third is the Braves' Gene Garber, a bearded righty whose corkscrew motion first troubled N.L. batters when he was teamed with McGraw and Ron Reed in the Phillie bullpen of 1975.

When Mike Marshall departed for Atlanta midway through 1975, L.A.'s relief burden fell squarely on Charley Hough's shoulders. In 1976 he responded with a league-high 12 wins, 18 saves, and an ERA of 2.20. The following year, Charley had 19 saves by the All-Star break and was giving Sutter and Fingers a race for relief honors. But while Bruce was sidelined because of arm trouble, Hough was idled in the second half simply because his knuckler stopped knuckling. In 1978, used more sparingly than in the previous two campaigns, he turned in an effective though modest season in support of Forster.

When Gary Lavelle came up for his first full season in San Francisco in 1975, Randy Moffitt was in his third year as leader of the bullpen. Lavelle eased in gradually, cutting into Moffit's innings a bit by coming in to retire a lefty or two in key spots. In 1976, the duo worked beautifully together as Gary posted 22 relief points and Randy 20. But next year the Giant relief show became pretty much a one-man act as Lavelle was named to the All-Star squad, set a club record for saves with 20 and games with 73, and logged an ERA of 2.06 (on June 1 it had been 0.50!). In 1978 Gary's ERA slipped a bit, but he still posted 13 relief wins and 14 saves. And Randy got back on the beam, with 20 relief points. The pair helped keep the Giants in first place in the N.L. West through most of the season.

Gene Garber kicked around the major leagues for parts of five seasons before finding a home in Philadelphia midway through 1974, the season he adopted his Luis Tiant-style motion. Over the next three years he led the Phillie bullpen in relief points with 24, 20, and 27. Yet pitching for a team that was blessed with three other top relievers—McGraw, Reed, and Brusstar—Gene did not get the attention he might have with a team for whom he was indisputably top banana. Then in 1978 he got that chance, being traded to Atlanta, where he was terrific, recording a career-high 25 saves, notching an ERA of 2.15 while playing half his games in a hitter's park, and gaining national attention when he retired Pete Rose in his final attempt to prolong his hitting streak beyond 44 games.

In the American League, 1977 produced several new relief stars, all of whom found it difficult to repeat their success in 1978. One, Tom Johnson, surprised everyone by stepping in for the departed Bill Campbell and giving the Twins 16 relief wins and 15 saves. In 1978, however, injuries rendered him virtually useless and

Cal Griffith was forced to hire Mike Marshall to restock the bull-pen.

A similar surprise was provided by Lerrin LaGrow, a tall right-hander who had labored in the majors since 1970 with an abominable record of 16–41; indeed, his most memorable performance in that time came as a Tiger, when in Game Two of the 1972 play-offs with Oakland he had to dance a jig on the mound to avoid the bat Campy Campaneris threw at him. Nineteen seventy-seven afforded a reversal of fortunes for LaGrow as he collected 25 saves and seven wins coming out of the White Sox bullpen, but 1978 witnessed another reversal—a 4.40 ERA and only 16 saves.

Gary Lavelle. He led the National League with 13 relief wins in 1978.

Adrian Devine posted 25 relief points for Texas in 1977 after coming over in a trade from Atlanta. His good sinker kept the ball in the park, and this may have been the primary reason the Braves reacquired him for 1978: The Atlanta launching pad had just produced 25 percent more round-trippers than any other N.L. park. But injuries held Devine back, and forced the Braves to go out and get Garber.

Two other A.L. stars of 1977 fell back only marginally and contributed to what success their teams had in 1978. Jim Kern of the Indians continued to blow his fastball by most batters and came up with more than 20 relief points for the third straight time. But he also lost 10 games for the second straight time, and in the 1979 season he is hurling in tandem with Sparky Lyle in the uniform of the Texas Rangers.

Other teams have been trying, without success for some time, to acquire Enrique Romo from the Seattle Mariners ever since the midpoint of his great rookie season. Brother of former major-league reliever Vicente Romo, Enrique came to the Mariners' spring camp in 1977 as a nonroster player, invited on the strength of his outstanding 1976 with the Mexico City Reds. In his eleventh season of pro ball south of the border, Enrique went 20–4 with an ERA of 1.89; counting the play-offs and winter ball, he was 31–8. As a thirty-year-old rookie with Seattle, he saved 16 and won eight, and as a sophomore he was nearly as good. At thirty-one, Romo might never have fetched more in the open market than he would now, and in the off-season the Mariners dealt him to Pittsburgh in exchange for several young prospects.

In addition to Romo, the 1977 Seattle bullpen provided one of the top accomplishments in relief-pitching history. Journeyman John Montague, returning to the majors with the Mariners after banishment to Oklahoma City in 1976, retired 33 consecutive batters: the last 13 he faced against Oakland on July 22 and all 20 Angels he faced on July 24. This tied Steve Busby for the A.L. high and created a new mark for relievers, surpassing by one the old mark set by Lindy McDaniel. A long-relief man and spot starter, Montague was held back in 1978 by a hip-pointer injury.

The Toronto Blue Jays, like their expansion counterparts, may also have found a prize among their nonroster players. In the winter between the 1977 and 1978 seasons, the Blue Jays traded pitcher Pete Vuckovich and outfielder John Scott to the Cardinals for starter Tom Underwood and a minor-league throw-in, pitcher Victor Cruz. With Arkansas in the Cardinal chain, the twenty-year-old right-hander's 1977 record had been a sorry 3–8 with an ERA of 4.99. But what attracted Toronto's attention was his strikeout ratio—in three stops in the minors, he had struck out nearly 11 men per nine innings. He didn't make the Toronto squad in the spring, but was called up from Syracuse in early July despite a record of 2–3 and a bloated ERA of 5.67. The reason: He was striking out International League batters at a rate of 11½ a game, and management wanted to see how he did it.

In the American League Cruz proved nothing short of sensational. Pitching for a last-place club, in 32 games he went 7–3, saved nine, and had an ERA of 1.72; in 47 innings he struck out 51 and allowed 28 hits. This 5-feet-9, 175-pound youngster from the Dominican Republic is one to watch. He was much sought after by other clubs during the off-season, and was finally acquired in trade by Cleveland.

The 1978 Oakland bullpen was led by another Dominican right-hander, veteran Elias Sosa, playing with his sixth major-league club in six seasons. Dave Heaverlo and Bob Lacey also had fine years out of the bullpen, helping to keep Charlie Finley's cast of rejects and retreads in pennant contention through much of the year. Sosa, Heaverlo, and Lacey all appeared in 68 games or more, and combined for 19 wins and 29 saves. Lacey, the most flamboyant of the trio, did much to cement his nickname of Spacey with his actions on September 14. After being smacked for a homer by Kansas City's Amos Otis, Lacey waited at the plate for him to circle the bases. As Otis came in, Lacey extended his hand and said, "Nobody has ever hit my change-up like that before. That's the way it's supposed to be hit. I just want to shake your hand. Give me five."

A middling young pitcher whom the A's traded over to the Cincinnati Reds during the winter of 1977–1978 turned out to be a National League ace. Hard-throwing right-hander Doug Bair had come up in the Pittsburgh organization, graduating with a six-inning trial in 1976 before being traded to Oakland. In 1977 with the A's he was erratic, frequently seeing his control slip away from him. He won eight and saved four, not bad, but nothing compared to the season he would have with the Reds the next year. With Pedro Borbon failing to provide the quality relief that everyone had come to take for granted from him, Bair and Manny Sarmiento rushed into the breach. Though Manny cooled considerably in the second half of the season, Bair pressed on to post seven wins, 28 saves, and a fine ERA of 1.98.

One who made the league-switch in the other direction and also found himself a star was the Orioles' Don Stanhouse, an inferior starter for the better part of six years before the Expos converted him to relief for the second half of 1977. In that time he earned ten saves and six wins, and the Orioles, desperate for a righty reliever, went out after him. With six wins and 24 saves in 1978, he fulfilled expectations and then some.

A reliever who really caught hold of a comet in 1978, after years of virtual anonymity, was Pittsburgh's Kent Tekulve. A thirty-one-year-old toothpick of a man, he was the most effective relief pitcher in the National League in 1978, except for Rollie Fingers.

Tekulve had languished in the minors for six years while Dave Giusti was head man in the Pirate pen. Trained as a reliever almost from the outset, Kent had a sweeping sidearm motion that made him awfully difficult on right-handed batters but not so for lefties, for whom each pitch could be seen coming in all the way. The scouts' complaint, however, was not the motion; he needed more stuff.

He made progress in 1977, going 10–1, but with Gossage and Forster in Pittsburgh uniforms that year, the save situations weren't there for Kent. When those two took the free-agent route for 1978, the Pirates had no choice but to give him a chance at being the number-one reliever in all situations. They had to find out whether his 165 pounds, stretched out over a 6-feet-4 frame, could bear the strain of pitching day after day in a pennant race.

Tekulve showed them, though he ended the season weighing only 147 pounds. In August, when the Bucs made their big move from 14 games behind the Phils, Kent pitched 15 times, allowing only one earned run in 24 innings; he posted nine of his season-total 31 saves. On the year, by far his best to date, he appeared in 91 games, went 8–7, and had an ERA of 2.33.

The man Tekulve replaced as the Pirates' top fireman in 1978 was Rich "Goose" Gossage, a twenty-seven-year-old fastballing right-hander who had just arrived in Pittsburgh the previous year. Breaking in with the White Sox at the age of twenty, Goose combined with lefty Terry Forster to form the youngest relief pair ever seen in the majors. Gossage had pitched only three games for Sarasota and 25 more for Appleton before coming to the majors. His record (as a starter) in the Midwest League was 18–2, ERA 1.83.

After posting a 7–0 mark in relief in 1972, Gossage slipped back in 1973, all the way down to Iowa in the American Association. Before being sent down, the confused sophomore went 0–4, with an astounding ERA of 7.43; he walked more men than he fanned, and gave up more hits than innings pitched—in short, he was a mess. With Iowa he got his fastball back under control and returned to the big time for the 1974 campaign.

His 1972 bullpen mate Forster had also suffered in 1973 as the Sox fooled around with making him a starter. Back on relief call in 1974, he won the A.L. Fireman of the Year while Gossage was still trying to remember how he had got people out in 1972. Though Goose stayed in Chicago the whole year, his 4–6 record, augmented by only one save, left plenty of room for improvement.

Gossage had to learn how to stop worrying and enjoy himself out on the mound. He realized that if he was to become a successful reliever, he would have to adopt an I-don't-give-a-damn attitude, throwing his heat right in the hitter's alley and daring him to hit it. Hard-throwing firemen like Goose live by the fastball and die by the long ball, but that's the bargain that must be struck and accepted. Gossage had always had great physical equipment for relief work; all he needed was the aggressive, challenging on-field nature that most firemen, and all fastballers, must have to make it.

While arm miseries prevented Forster from defending his relief crown in 1975, Gossage kept the Fireman of the Year Award in the family. Saving 26 and winning one, Goose intimidated the batters

Rich Gossage, the American League's top fireman of 1978.

as they had intimidated him the year before. In 142 innings he struck out 130 and allowed only 99 hits. The curveball he'd sheepishly tried to slip by hitters the previous two years was put on the back burner, and the diet he now offered hitters was heat and more heat.

Then in 1976 Paul Richards replaced Chuck Tanner at the helm of the White Sox and commenced to transform both Forster and Gossage into starters. Terry finished 2–12, Goose 9–17, and next year all three—Forster, Gossage, and Richards—were gone. Reunited with Tanner at Pittsburgh, Gossage responded with a N.L.-high 11 relief wins and added 26 saves, his 37-point total placing him third in the N.L. behind Fingers and Sutter. His ERA was 1.62, and for every nine innings he pitched, he fanned better than ten men and allowed barely five hits. He accomplished all this without having signed a contract for 1977. Like Bill Campbell of the Twins the previous year, he refused to accept a contract offer based on an off year not entirely of his making, preferring to gamble that he would improve his showing and command attractive offers as a result of the reentry draft.

While playing out his option and compiling that tremendous 1977 record for the Bucs, Goose was being paid $46,800 per annum. Next year, with the Yankees, he earned nearly ten times that figure—a whopping $458,000 based on a proration of the $2,748,000 package he received for signing a six-year pact.

Sure, he was good, but why was he worth so much to George Steinbrenner, who already had Sparky Lyle and Dick Tidrow, and would have Rawly Eastwick too? Because his scouts tabbed the twenty-seven-year-old fastballer as the man most likely to become the dominant relief pitcher in the near future, and because it was thought Sparky had reached the apex of his career in 1977 and had nowhere to go but down. Besides, Steinbrenner couldn't take the chance that the Goose would fly to Boston or Baltimore or Milwaukee.

What George wants, George gets, and the Goose was got. But the way Gossage opened the season made Yankee fans suspect George had been had. In his Yankee debut, Gossage gave up a game-winning ninth-inning homer to Texas' Richie Zisk, and four games later he was touched for another late-inning long ball, which resulted in a Yankee loss. "I was trying to impress everybody," Gossage said later in the season, "but I was pressing instead." Trying to blow away every batter with his awesome fastball, which has been clocked at 98 miles per hour, Goose was overthrowing in the early season; he'd get behind on the count, aim the next pitch, taking something off it, and get clobbered.

Although he was selected for the All-Star squad for his dozen saves and 2.31 ERA, he did not pitch consistently well through the first half, as demonstrated by his 4–8 won-lost record; at that rate he would have established an all-time mark for relief losses. The Yankees were a troubled team at that point in the season, far behind the streaking Red Sox, and with Reggie Jackson insubordinate and Sparky Lyle grumbling, something had to be done to focus the Yankees' attention simply on playing ball, and that something was Billy Martin's resignation under fire. Bob Lemon came in and immediately calmed the troubled waters. The rest is now legend: The Yankees clawed their way from 14 games behind in July to finish first in a thrilling final-week conclusion that saw the Red Sox win their final six to tie for the title. The Yanks won the play-off game 5–4.

Gossage was instrumental in the late charge: 5–9 with 14 saves on July 24, the day Martin resigned, he went 5–2 in the remaining ten weeks, adding 13 saves. Over that span, Goose's ERA was 1.69. He saved the play-off game for Ron Guidry, and hurled ten frames of four-hit ball in postseason play, earning two wins and a save.

Winning his second American League Fireman-of-the-Year award, Gossage delivered the goods George Steinbrenner had paid for so dearly. Whether the next five years of his Yankee contract provide as fair a bargain remains to be seen, but a betting man would not obtain long odds against it.

Gossage represents the future of relief pitching, which rests in the hands of the power pitchers. This trend, slowly developing since the introduction of artificial turf a decade ago, repudiates the wisdom of the past 75 years, that in the pinch what was needed was a sinkerballer who could "throw those grounders" and get those double plays. Today, with so many clubs opting for the synthetic surface, the hard ground ball that was ideal for the double play on grass has become a very hazardous eventuality, scooting past infielders and, on the faster surfaces, rolling all the way to the outfield wall before any fielder can reach it. With men on base in the late innings, a ball hit in the air now represents a more satisfactory outcome to a pitch than does a grounder (a strikeout is perfect, of course). The parks that transformed lazy fly balls into four-baggers are almost all gone. Incredibly, one National League stadium was built before the 1960s, while in the American League only Fenway, Yankee Stadium, and Tiger Stadium afford much of a chance for the cheap home run.

The history of baseball has demonstrated an ever-greater specialization—from the days when substitution was not permitted at all through the advent of relief pitchers, pinch hitters, platoon play, percentage moves, and the designated hitter. John McGraw, when asked in the 1920s what he thought about the idea of having a designated hitter, replied that one might as well "go all the way and let a club play nine defensive players in the field and then have nine sluggers do all the hitting." This two-platoon system, unimaginable to the father of platoon play, may yet come to pass, as it has in football.

If one were to hazard a guess about the future of relief pitching in particular, it would be that we will see more narrow areas of specialization. Already we have long men and short men, and lefties and righties for percentage maneuverings; if major-league fields continue to be split between natural grass and synthetic, the better teams will have a four-man crew of short relievers: two power pitchers, a lefty and a righty; and two sinkerballers, also a lefty and a righty. And as synthetic surfaces slowly but surely eradicate the sod, the power pitchers will come to dominate the game—as they did in the nineteenth century, when fielders wore tiny gloves or no gloves at all, and the average game produced anywhere from six to 12 errors, most of these on hard ground balls.

This prediction comes with no guarantees and may appear foolish ten years from now. What *can* be said with assurance is that relief pitchers have become more important with every passing decade, almost every passing year. This trend may well continue toward the vanishing point: no complete games at all. And as that point nears, it will be meaningless to think of the starting pitcher as primary and the finishing pitcher as secondary; they will be equally important. We are not really far at all from that being the truth.

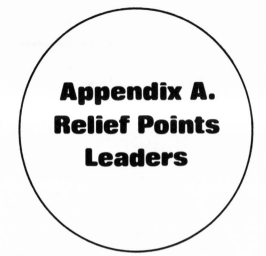

# Appendix A. Relief Points Leaders

## NATIONAL LEAGUE

1876  Jack Manning (*Bos.*), **9**

1877  Cal McVey (*Chi.*), **3**

1878  Tom Healey (*Pro.-Ind.*), Sam Weaver (*Mil.*), Harry Wheeler (*Pro.*), **1**

1879  Monte Ward (*Pro.*), **6**

1880  George Bradley (*Pro.*), Lee Richmond (*Wor.*), **3**

1881  Bobby Mathews (*Pro.-Bos.*), Monte Ward (*Pro.*), **2**

1882  Bobby Mathews (*Bos.*), Jim McCormick (*Cle.*), Hoss Radbourn (*Pro.*) Lee Richmond (*Wor.*), Monte Ward (*Pro.*), **1**

1883  Jim Whitney (*Bos.*), **5**

1884  John Morrill (*Bos.*), Hoss Radbourn (*Pro.*), **2**

1885  Fred Pfeffer (*Chi.*), **3**

1886  Ed Daily (*Phi.*), **3**

1887  Charlie Ferguson (*Phi.*), Al Maul (*Phi.*), Larry Twitchell (*Det.*), **2**

1888  Jimmy Ryan (*Chi.*), **3**

1889  Bill Sowders (*Bos.-Pitt.*), **4**

1890  Dave Foutz (*Bkn.*), Kid Gleason (*Phi.*), Bill Hutchison (*Chi.*), **3**

1891  Bill Hutchison (*Chi.*), **8**

1892  Gus Weyhing (*Phi.*), **7**

1893 Frank Killen (*Pitt.*), Tony Mullane (*Cin.-Bal.*), Cy Young (*Cle.*), 5

1894 Nig Cuppy (*Cle.*), **8**

1895 Cy Young (*Cle.*), **7**

1896 Chauncey Fisher (*Cin.*), Silver King (*Wash.*), **4**

1897 Kid Nichols (*Bos.*), Billy Rhines (*Cin.*), **5**

1898 Bill Damman (*Cin.*), Kid Nichols (*Bos.*), **6**

1899 Sam Leever (*Pitt.*), Joe McGinnity (*Bal.*), **5**

1900 Frank Kitson (*Bkn.*), **6**

1901 Bill Donovan (*Bkn.*), Jack Powell (*St. L.*), **5**

1902 Vic Willis (*Bos.*), **4**

1903 Clarence Currie (*St. L.-Chi.*), Carl Lundgren (*Chi.*), Joe McGinnitty (*N.Y.*), **4**

1904 Joe McGinnity (*N.Y.*), **7**

1905 Myke Lynch (*Pitt.*), **7**

1906 Hooks Wiltse (*N.Y.*), **9**

1907 Joe McGinnity (*N.Y.*), **7**

1908 Mordecai Brown (*Chi.*), **9**

1909 Howie Camnitz (*Pitt.*), **10**

1910 Doc Crandall (*N.Y.*), Deacon Phillippe (*Pitt.*), **11**

1911 Mordecai Brown (*Chi.*), **18**

1912 Slim Sallee (*St. L.*), **10**

1913 Larry Cheney (*Chi.*), **15**

1914 Larry Cheney (*Chi.*), Slim Sallee (*St. L.*), **8**

1915 Tom Hughes (*Bos.*), **15**

1916 Tom Hughes (*Bos.*), **14**

1917 Red Ames (*St. L.*), **11**

1918 Hod Eller (*Cin.*), **8**

1919 Jean Dubuc (*N.Y.*), **9**

1920 Bill Sherdel (*St. L.*), **14**

1921 Lou North (*St. L.*), **11**

1922 Claude Jonnard (*N.Y.*), **11**

1923 Rosy Ryan (*N.Y.*), **13**

1924 Rosy Ryan (*N.Y.*), **11**

1925 Johnny Morrison (*Pitt.*), **10**

1926 Jack Scott (*N.Y.*), **10**

1927 George Mogridge, (*Bos.*), **11**

1928 Jim Faulkner (*N.Y.*), **9**

1929 Johnny Morrison (*Bkn.*), **18**

1930 Joe Heving (*N.Y.*), **13**

1931 Jack Quinn (*Bkn.*), **20**

1932   Ben Cantwell (*Bos.*), **17**

1933   Dolf Luque (*N.Y.*), **12**

1934   Waite Hoyt (*Pitt.*), **12**

1935   Waite Hoyt (*Pitt.*), **11**

1936   Don Brennan (*Cin.*), Dick Coffman (*N.Y.*), **14**

1937   Mace Brown (*Pitt.*), Charlie Root (*Chi.*), **13**

1938   Mace Brown (*Pitt.*), **20**

1939   Bob Bowman (*St. L.*), **16**

1940   Joe Beggs (*Cin.*), **19**

1941   Hugh Casey (*Bkn.*), **15**

1942   Hugh Casey (*Bkn.*), **19**

1943   Clyde Shoun (*Cin.*), **20**

1944   Ace Adams (*N.Y.*), **19**

1945   Ace Adams (*N.Y.*), **26**

1946   Hugh Casey (*Bkn.*), **16**

1947   Hugh Casey (*Bkn.*), **28**

1948   Harry Gumbert (*Cin.*), **27**

1949   Ted Wilks (*St. L.*), **19**

1950   Jim Konstanty (*Phi.*), **38**

1951   Clyde King (*Bkn.*), **19**

1952   Joe Black (*Bkn.*), **29**

1953   Al Brazle (*St. L.*), **24**

1954   Jim Hughes (*Bkn.*), **32**

1955   Clem Labine (*Bkn.*), Jack Meyer (*Phi.*), **21**

1956   Hersh Freeman (*Cin.*), **32**

1957   Clem Labine (*Bkn.*), **22**

1958   Roy Face (*Pitt.*), **25**

1959   Roy Face (*Pitt.*), Lindy McDaniel (*St. L.*), **28**

1960   Lindy McDaniel (*St. L.*), **38**

1961   Stu Miller (*S.F.*), **31**

1962   Roy Face (*Pitt.*), **36**

1963   Ron Perranoski (*L.A.*), **37**

1964   Al McBean (*Pitt.*), **30**

1965   Ted Abernathy (*Chi.*), **35**

1966   Phil Regan (*L.A.*), **35**

1967   Ted Abernathy (*Cin.*), **34**

1968   Phil Regan (*L.A.-Chi.*), **37**

1969   Wayne Granger (*Cin.*), **36**

1970   Wayne Granger (*Cin.*), **41**

1971   Dave Giusti (*Pitt.*), **35**

1972    Clay Carroll (*Cin.*), **43**
1973    Mike Marshall (*Mon.*), **45**
1974    Mike Marshall (*L.A.*), **36**
1975    Al Hrabosky (*St. L.*), **35**
1976    Rawly Eastwick (*Cin.*), **37**
1977    Rollie Fingers (*S.D.*), **43**
1978    Rollie Fingers (*S.D.*), **43**

## AMERICAN LEAGUE

1901    Clark Griffith (*Chi.*), **4**
1902    Rube Waddell (*Phi.*), **6**
1903    Cy Young (*Bos.*), **4**
1904    Jack Chesbro (*N.Y.*), Casey Patten (*Wash.*), Ed Walsh (*Chi.*), **3**
1905    Rube Waddell (*Phi.*), **8**
1906    Nick Altrock (*Chi.*), **7**
1907    Ed Killian (*Det.*), Doc White (*Chi.*), **5**
1908    Ed Walsh (*Chi.*), **11**
1909    Frank Arellanes (*Bos.*), **11**
1910    Charley Hall (*Bos.*), **9**
1911    Ed Walsh (*Chi.*), **10**
1912    Ed Walsh (*Chi.*), **13**
1913    Chief Bender (*Phi.*), **18**
1914    George Baumgardner (*St. L.*), **8**
1915    Carl Mays (*Bos.*), Carl Weilman (*St. L.*), **10**
1916    Bob Shawkey (*N.Y.*), **17**
1917    Dave Danforth (*Chi.*), **16**
1918    George Mogridge (*N.Y.*), **11**
1919    Allan Russell (*N.Y.-Bos.*), **9**
1920    Bill Burwell (*St. L.*), **10**
1921    Jim Middleton (*Det.*), **11**
1922    Hub Pruett (*St. L.*), **11**
1923    Allan Russell (*Wash.*), **18**
1924    Fred Marberry (*Wash.*), **21**
1925    Fred Marberry (*Wash.*), **23**
1926    Fred Marberry (*Wash.*), **31**
1927    Wilcy Moore (*N.Y.*), **26**
1928    Willis Hudlin (*Cle.*), **13**
1929    Fred Marberry (*Wash.*), Wilcy Moore (*N.Y.*), **14**
1930    Lefty Grove (*Phi.*), Jack Quinn (*Phi.*), **14**

1931   Wilcy Moore (*Bos.*), **17**

1932   Fred Marberry (*Wash.*), **14**

1933   Jack Russell (*Wash.*), **24**

1934   Jack Knott (*St. L.*), **11**

1935   Jack Knott (*St. L.*), **12**

1936   Pat Malone (*N.Y.*), **17**

1937   Clint Brown (*Chi.*), **25**

1938   Johnny Murphy (*N.Y.*), **19**

1939   Clint Brown (*Chi.*), **29**

1940   Al Benton (*Det.*), **23**

1941   Johnny Murphy (*N.Y.*), **23**

1942   Mace Brown (*Bos.*), Johnny Murphy (*N.Y.*), **15**

1943   Gordon Maltzberger (*Chi.*), **21**

1944   Gordon Maltzberger (*Chi.*), **22**

1945   Joe Berry (*Phi.*), Jim Turner (*N.Y.*), **13**

1946   Earl Caldwell (*Chi.*), **21**

1947   Joe Page (*N.Y.*), **31**

1948   Joe Page (*N.Y.*), **23**

1949   Joe Page (*N.Y.*), **40**

1950   Tom Ferrick (*St. L.-N.Y.*), Mickey Harris (*Wash.*), **20**

1951   Ellis Kinder (*Bos.*), **24**

1952   Harry Dorish (*Chi.*), Satchel Paige (*St. L.*), **18**

1953   Ellis Kinder (*Bos.*), **37**

1954   Johnny Sain (*N.Y.*), **28**

1955   Ray Narleski (*Cle.*), **27**

1956   George Zuverink (*Bal.*), **23**

1957   Bob Grim (*K.C.*), **31**

1958   Dick Hyde (*Wash.*), **28**

1959   Turk Lown (*Chi.*), **24**

1960   Mike Fornieles (*Bos.*), **24**

1961   Luis Arroyo (*N.Y.*), **44**

1962   Dick Radatz (*Bos.*), **33**

1963   Dick Radatz (*Bos.*), **40**

1964   Dick Radatz (*Bos.*), **45**

1965   Eddie Fisher (*Chi.*), **39**

1966   Jack Aker (*K.C.*), **40**

1967   Minnie Rojas (*Cal.*), **39**

1968   Wilbur Wood (*Chi.*), **28**

1969   Ron Perranoski (*Minn.*), **40**

1970   Ron Perranoski (*Minn.*), **41**

1971    Ken Sanders (*Mil.*), **38**
1972    Sparky Lyle (*N.Y.*), **44**
1973    John Hiller (*Det.*), **48**
1974    Terry Forster (*Chi.*), **31**
1975    Rich Gossage (*Chi.*), **35**
1976    Bill Campbell (*Minn.*), **37**
1977    Bill Campbell (*Bos.*), **44**
1978    Rich Gossage (*N.Y.*), **37**

## AMERICAN ASSOCIATION

1882    Eddie Fusselbach (*St. L.*), **2**
1883    Tony Mullane (*St. L.*), **2**
1884    Bob Caruthers (*St. L.*), **3**
1885    Oyster Burns (*Bal.*), **3**
1886    Tony Mullane (*Cin.*), **4**
1887    Adonis Terry (*Bkn.*), **3**
1888    Tony Mullane (*Cin.*), **2**
1889    Tony Mullane (*Cin.*), **6**
1890    Herb Goodall (*Lou.*), **4**
1891    Clark Griffith (*St. L.-Bos.*), **7**

## UNION ASSOCIATION

1884    Billy Taylor (*St. L.*), **4**

## PLAYERS LEAGUE

1890    Bill Daley (*Bos.*), **4**

## FEDERAL LEAGUE

1914    George Mullin (*Ind.*), **10**
1915    Hugh Bedient (*Buf.*), **13**

# Appendix B.
# Saves Leaders

## NATIONAL LEAGUE

1876   Jack Manning (*Bos.*), **5**

1877   Cal McVey (*Chi.*), **2**

1878   Tom Healey (*Pro.-Ind.*), **1**

1879   Curry Foley (*Bos.*), Bobby Mathews (*Pro.*), Monte Ward (*Pro.*), **1**

1880   Lee Richmond (*Wor.*), **3**

1881   Bobby Mathews (*Pro.-Bos.*), **2**

1882   Monte Ward (*Pro.*), **1**

1883   Stump Weidman (*Det.*), Jim Whitney (*Bos.*), **2**

1884   John Morrill (*Bos.*), **2**

1885   Fred Pfeffer (*Chi.*), Ned Williamson (*Chi.*), **2**

1886   Charlie Ferguson (*Phi.*), **2**

1887   Larry Twitchell (*Det.*), Charlie Ferguson (*Phi.*), Mark Baldwin (*Chi.*), George Van Haltren (*Chi.*), Bob Pettit (*Chi.*), Mike Tiernan (*N.Y.*), Bill Stemmyer (*Bos.*), [*Unknown*] Fast (*Ind.*), **1**

1888   George Wood (*Phi.*), **2**

1889   Bill Bishop (*Chi.*), Bill Sowders (*Bos.-Pitt.*), Mickey Welch (*N.Y.*), **2**

1890   Dave Foutz (*Bkn.*), Kid Gleason (*Phi.*), Bill Hutchison (*Chi.*), **2**

1891   Kid Nichols (*Bos.*), John Clarkson (*Bos.*), **3**

1892  Gus Weyhing (*Phi.*), **3**

1893  Mark Baldwin (*Pitt.-N.Y.*), Frank Donnelly (*Chi.*), Frank Dwyer (*Cin.*), Tony Mullane (*Cin.-Bal.*), **2**

1894  Tony Mullane (*Bal.-Cle.*), **4**

1895  Ernie Beam (*Phi.*), Kid Nichols (*Bos.*), Tom Parrott (*Cin.*), **3**

1896  Cy Young (*Cle.*), **3**

1897  Kid Nichols (*Bos.*), **3**

1898  Kid Nichols (*Bos.*), **3**

1899  Sam Leever (*Pitt.*), **3**

1900  Frank Kitson (*Bkn.*), **4**

1901  Jack Powell (*St. L.*), **3**

1902  Vic Willis (*Bos.*), **3**

1903  Carl Lundgren (*Chi.*), Roscoe Miller (*N.Y.*), **3**

1904  Joe McGinnity (*N.Y.*), **5**

1905  Claude Elliott (*N.Y.*), **6**

1906  Cecil Ferguson (*N.Y.*), **6**

1907  Joe McGinnity (*N.Y.*), **4**

1908  Mordecai Brown (*Chi.*), Christy Mathewson (*N.Y.*), **5**

1909  Mordecai Brown (*Chi.*), **7**

1910  Mordecai Brown (*Chi.*), **7**

1911  Mordecai Brown (*Chi.*), **13**

1912  Slim Sallee (*St. L.*), **6**

1913  Larry Cheney (*Chi.*), **11**

1914  Red Ames (*Cin.*), Slim Sallee (*St. L.*), **6**

1915  Rube Benton (*Cin.-Pitt.*), Tom Hughes (*Bos.*), **5**

1916  Red Ames (*St. L.*), **7**

1917  Slim Sallee (*N.Y.*), **4**

1918  Fred Anderson (*N.Y.*), Wilbur Cooper (*Pitt.*), Joe Oeschger (*Phi.*), Fred Toney (*Cin.-N.Y.*), **3**

1919  Oscar Tuero (*St. L.*), **4**

1920  Bill Sherdel (*St. L.*), **6**

1921  Lou North (*St. L.*), **7**

1922  Claude Jonnard (*N.Y.*), **5**

1923  Claude Jonnard (*N.Y.*), **5**

1924  Jakie May (*Cin.*), **6**

1925  Guy Bush (*Chi.*), Johnny Morrison (*Pitt.*), **5**

1926  Chick Davies (*N.Y.*), **6**

1927  Bill Sherdel (*St. L.*), **6**

1928  Bill Sherdel (*St. L.*), Hal Haid (*St. L.*), **5**

1929  Guy Bush (*Chi.*), Johnny Morrison (*Bkn.*), **8**

1930  Hi Bell (*St. L.*), **8**

1931    Jack Quinn (*Bkn.*), **15**

1932    Jack Quinn (*Bkn.*), **8**

1933    Phil Collins (*Phi.*), **6**

1934    Carl Hubbell (*N.Y.*), **8**

1935    Dutch Leonard (*Bkn.*), **8**

1936    Dizzy Dean (*St. L.*), **11**

1937    Mace Brown (*Pitt.*), Cliff Melton (*N.Y.*), **7**

1938    Dick Coffman (*N.Y.*), **12**

1939    Bob Bowman (*St. L.*), Clyde Shoun (*St. L.*), **9**

1940    Jumbo Brown (*N.Y.*), Mace Brown (*Pitt.*), Joe Beggs (*Cin.*), **7**

1941    Jumbo Brown (*N.Y.*), **8**

1942    Hugh Casey (*Bkn.*), **13**

1943    Les Webber (*Bkn.*), **10**

1944    Ace Adams (*N.Y.*), **13**

1945    Ace Adams (*N.Y.*), Andy Karl (*Phi.*), **15**

1946    Ken Raffensberger (*Phi.*), **6**

1947    Hugh Casey (*Bkn.*), **18**

1948    Harry Gumbert (*Cin.*), **17**

1949    Ted Wilks (*St. L.*), **9**

1950    Jim Konstanty (*Phi.*), **22**

1951    Ted Wilks (*St. L.-Pitt.*), **13**

1952    Al Brazle (*St. L.*), **16**

1953    Al Brazle (*St. L.*), **18**

1954    Jim Hughes (*Bkn.*), **24**

1955    Jack Meyer (*Phi.*), **16**

1956    Clem Labine (*Bkn.*), **19**

1957    Clem Labine (*Bkn.*), **17**

1958    Roy Face (*Pitt.*), **20**

1959    Lindy McDaniel (*St. L.*), Don McMahon (*Mil.*), **15**

1960    Lindy McDaniel (*St. L.*), **26**

1961    Roy Face (*Pitt.*), Stu Miller (*S.F.*), **17**

1962    Roy Face (*Pitt.*), **28**

1963    Lindy McDaniel (*Chi.*), **22**

1964    Hal Woodeschick (*Hou.*), **23**

1965    Ted Abernathy (*Chi.*), **31**

1966    Phil Regan (*L.A.*), **21**

1967    Ted Abernathy (*Cin.*), **28**

1968    Phil Regan (*L.A.-Chi*), **25**

1969    Fred Gladding (*Hou.*), **29**

1970    Wayne Granger (*Cin.*), **35**

1971   Dave Giusti (*Pitt.*), **30**
1972   Clay Carroll (*Cin.*), **37**
1973   Mike Marshall (*Mon.*), **31**
1974   Mike Marshall (*L.A.*), **21**
1975   Rawly Eastwick (*Cin.*), Al Hrabosky (*St. L.*), **22**
1976   Rawly Eastwick (*Cin.*), **26**
1977   Rollie Fingers (*S.D.*), **35**
1978   Rollie Fingers (*S.D.*), **37**

## AMERICAN LEAGUE

1901   Bill Hoffer (*Cle.*), Joe McGinnity (*Bal.*), **3**
1902   Jack Powell (*St. L.*), **3**
1903   George Mullin (*Det.*), **3**
1904   Casey Patten (*Wash.*), **2**
1905   Rube Waddell (*Phi.*), **4**
1906   Chief Bender (*Phi.*), **3**
1907   Bill Dinneen (*Bos.-St. L.*), **4**
1908   Ed Walsh (*Chi.*), **7**
1909   Frank Arellanes (*Bos.*), **7**
1910   Ed Walsh (*Chi.*), **6**
1911   Ed Walsh (*Chi.*), **7**
1912   Ed Walsh (*Chi.*), **10**
1913   Chief Bender (*Phi.*), **12**
1914   Jack Bentley (*Wash.*), Red Faber (*Chi.*), Hub Leonard (*Bos.*), Roy Mitchell (*St. L.*), **4**
1915   Carl Mays (*Bos.*), **5**
1916   Bob Shawkey (*N.Y.*), **9**
1917   Dave Danforth (*Chi.*), **7**
1918   Jim Bagby (*Cle.*), **6**
1919   Allan Russell (*N.Y.-Bos.*), **5**
1920   Dickie Kerr (*Chi.*), Urban Shocker (*St. L.*), **5**
1921   Carl Mays (*N.Y.*), Jim Middleton (*Det.*), **7**
1922   Sam Jones (*N.Y.*), **8**
1923   Allan Russell (*Wash.*), **9**
1924   Fred Marberry (*Wash.*), **15**
1925   Fred Marberry (*Wash.*), **15**
1926   Fred Marberry (*Wash.*), **22**
1927   Garland Braxton (*Wash.*), Wilcy Moore (*N.Y.*), **13**
1928   Waite Hoyt (*N.Y.*), **8**

1929   Fred Marberry (*Wash.*), **11**
1930   Lefty Grove (*Phi.*), **9**
1931   Wilcy Moore (*Bos.*), **10**
1932   Fred Marberry (*Wash.*), **13**
1933   Jack Russell (*Wash.*), **13**
1934   Jack Russell (*Wash.*), **7**
1935   Jack Knott (*St. L.*), **7**
1936   Pat Malone (*N.Y.*), **9**
1937   Clint Brown (*Chi.*), **18**
1938   Johnny Murphy (*N.Y.*), **11**
1939   Johnny Murphy (*N.Y.*), **19**
1940   Al Benton (*Det.*), **17**
1941   Johnny Murphy (*N.Y.*), **15**
1942   Johnny Murphy (*N.Y.*), **11**
1943   Gordon Maltzberger (*Chi.*), **14**
1944   Joe Berry (*Phi.*), George Caster (*St. L.*), Gordon Maltzberger (*Chi.*), **12**
1945   Jim Turner (*N.Y.*), **10**
1946   Bob Klinger (*Bos.*), **9**
1947   Eddie Klieman (*Cle.*), Joe Page (*N.Y.*), **17**
1948   Russ Christopher (*Cle.*), **17**
1949   Joe Page (*N.Y.*), **27**
1950   Mickey Harris (*Wash.*), **15**
1951   Ellis Kinder (*Bos.*), **14**
1952   Harry Dorish (*Chi.*), **11**
1953   Ellis Kinder (*Bos.*), **27**
1954   Johnny Sain (*N.Y.*), **22**
1955   Ray Narleski (*Cle.*), **19**
1956   George Zuverink (*Bal.*), **16**
1957   Bob Grim (*K.C.*), **19**
1958   Ryne Duren (*N.Y.*), **20**
1959   Turk Lown (*Chi.*), **15**
1960   Mike Fornieles (*Bos.*), Johnny Klippstein (*Cle.*), **14**
1961   Luis Arroyo (*N.Y.*), **29**
1962   Dick Radatz (*Bos.*), **24**
1963   Stu Miller (*Bal.*), **27**
1964   Dick Radatz (*Bos.*), **29**
1965   Ron Kline (*Wash.*), **29**
1966   Jack Aker (*K.C.*), **32**
1967   Minnie Rojas (*Cal.*), **27**
1968   Al Worthington (*Minn.*), **18**

1969  Ron Perranoski (*Minn.*), **31**

1970  Ron Perranoski (*Minn.*), **34**

1971  Ken Sanders (*Mil.*), **31**

1972  Sparky Lyle (*N.Y.*), **35**

1973  John Hiller (*Det.*), **38**

1974  Terry Forster (*Chi.*), **24**

1975  Rich Gossage (*Chi.*), **26**

1976  Sparky Lyle (*N.Y.*), **23**

1977  Bill Campbell (*Bos.*), **31**

1978  Rich Gossage (*N.Y.*), **27**


## AMERICAN ASSOCIATION

1882  Eddie Fusselbach (*St. L.*), **1**

1883  Bob Barr (*Pitt.*), Tony Mullane (*St. L.*), **1**

1884  Oyster Burns (*Bal.*), Hank O'Day (*Tol.*), Frank Mountain (*Col.*), **1**

1885  Oyster Burns (*Bal.*), **3**

1886  Bones Ely (*Lou.*), Dave Foutz (*St. L.*), Nat Hudson (*St. L.*), Ed Morris (*Pitt.*), Joe Strauss (*Bkn.*), **1**

1887  Adonis Terry (*Bkn.*), **3**

1888  Pop Corkhill (*Bkn.*), Bob Gilks (*Cle.*), Tony Mullane (*Cin.*), **1**

1889  Tony Mullane (*Cin.*), **5**

1890  Herb Goodall (*Lou.*), **4**

1891  Charlie Buffinton (*Bos.*), **3**


## UNION ASSOCIATION

1884  Billy Taylor (*St. L.*), **4**


## PLAYERS LEAGUE

1890  George Hemming (*Cle.-Bkn.*), Hank O'Day (*N.Y.*), **3**


## FEDERAL LEAGUE

1914  Russ Ford (*Buf.*), **6**

1915  Hugh Bedient (*Buf.*), **10**

# Appendix C.
# Relief Wins
# Leaders

## NATIONAL LEAGUE

1876    Jack Manning (*Bos.*), **4**

1877    Tricky Nichols (*St. L.*), **2**

1878    Sam Weaver (*Mil.*), Harry Wheeler (*Pro.*), **1**

1879    Monte Ward (*Pro.*), **5**

1880    George Bradley (*Pro.*), **3**

1881    Hoss Radbourn (*Pro.*), Monte Ward (*Pro.*), Curry Foley (*Buf.*), **1**

1882    Bobby Mathews (*Bos.*), Jim McCormick (*Cle.*), Hoss Radbourn (*Pro.*), Lee Richmond (*Wor.*), **1**

1883    Monte Ward (*N.Y.*), **4**

1884    Hoss Radbourn (*Pro.*), John Coleman (*Phi.*), **1**

1885    Henry Boyle (*St. L.*), Danny Richardson (*N.Y.*), Charlie Ferguson (*Phi.*), Fred Pfeffer (*Chi.*), **1**

1886    Ed Daily (*Phi.*), **3**

1887    Al Maul (*Phi.*), **2**

1888    Jimmy Ryan (*Chi.*), **3**

1889    Charlie Buffinton (*Phi.*), **3**

1890    Jesse Burkett (*N.Y.*), Lee Viau (*Cin.-Cle.*), **2**

1891    Bill Hutchison (*Chi.*), **7**

1892    Gus Weyhing (*Phi.*), **4**

1893 Frank Killen (*Pitt.*), 5

1894 Nig Cuppy (*Cle.*), 8

1895 Cy Young (*Cle.*), 7

1896 Pink Hawley (*Pitt.*), Silver King (*Wash.*), Mike Sullivan (*N.Y.*), 3

1897 Billy Rhines (*Cin.*), 5

1898 Pink Hawley (*Cin.*), Bill Damman (*Cin.*), 4

1899 Joe McGinnity (*Bal.*), Jesse Tannehill (*Pitt.*), Deacon Phillippe (*Lou.*), Al Orth (*Phi.*), Ted Lewis (*Bos.*), 3

1900 Ted Lewis (*Bos.*), 4

1901 Bill Donovan (*Bkn.*), 4

1902 Leroy Evans (*N.Y.-Bkn.*), Chick Fraser (*Phi.*), Mike O'Neill (*St. L.*), Togie Pittinger (*Bos.*), 2

1903 Clarence Currie (*St. L.-Chi.*), Joe McGinnity (*N.Y.*), Togie Pittinger (*Bos.*), 2

1904 Mordecai Brown (*Chi.*), Win Kellum (*Cin.*), Christy Mathewson (*N.Y.*), Joe McGinnity (*N.Y.*), Jack Suthoff (*Cin.-Phi.*), 2

1905 Mike Lynch (*Pitt.*), 5

1906 Hooks Wiltse (*N.Y.*), 4

1907 Andy Coakley (*Cin.*), Chick Fraser (*Phi.*), Lefty Leifield (*Pitt.*), 4

1908 Mordecai Brown (*Chi.*), Joe McGinnity (*N.Y.*), 4

1909 Howie Camnitz (*Pitt.*), 7

1910 Doc Crandall (*N.Y.*), Deacon Phillippe (*Pitt.*), 7

1911 Doc Crandall (*N.Y.*), 7

1912 Doc Crandall (*N.Y.*), Charlie Smith (*Chi.*), 6

1913 Art Fromme (*Cin.-N.Y.*), 6

1914 Paul Strand (*Bos.*), 5

1915 Tom Hughes (*Bos.*), 10

1916 Tom Hughes (*Bos.*), 9

1917 Red Ames (*St. L.*), 8

1918 Hod Eller (*Cin.*), 8

1919 Jean Dubuc (*N.Y.*), 6

1920 Bill Sherdel (*St. L.*), 8

1921 Slim Sallee (*N.Y.*), 6

1922 Rosy Ryan (*N.Y.*), 7

1923 Rosy Ryan (*N.Y.*), 9

1924 Art Decatur (*Bkn.*), 7

1925 Johnny Morrison (*Pitt.*), 6

1926 Guy Bush (*Chi.*), 6

1927 Dutch Henry (*N.Y.*), George Mogridge (*Bos.*), 6

1928    Jim Faulkner (N.Y.), **7**

1929    Johnny Morrison (Bkn.), **10**

1930    Joe Heving (N.Y.), **7**

1931    Bob Osborn (Pitt.), **6**

1932    Ben Cantwell (Bos.), **12**

1933    Dolf Luque (N.Y.), **8**

1934    Waite Hoyt (Pitt.), **7**

1935    Guy Bush (Pitt.), Waite Hoyt (Pitt.), Charlie Root (Chi.), Al Smith (N.Y.), **5**

1936    Dick Coffman (N.Y.), **7**

1937    Dick Coffman (N.Y.), Charlie Root (Chi.), **8**

1938    Mace Brown (Pitt.), **15**

1939    Junior Thompson (Cin.), **8**

1940    Joe Beggs (Cin.), **12**

1941    Hugh Casey (Bkn.), **8**

1942    Howie Krist (St. L.), **8**

1943    Clyde Shoun (Cin.), **13**

1944    Xavier Rescigno (Pitt.), **8**

1945    Ace Adams (N.Y.), **11**

1946    Hugh Casey (Bkn.), **11**

1947    Hugh Casey (Bkn.), Harry Gumbert (Cin.), **10**

1948    Harry Gumbert (Cin.), **10**

1949    Ted Wilks (St. L.), **10**

1950    Jim Konstanty (Phi.), **16**

1951    Clyde King (Bkn.), **13**

1952    Hoyt Wilhelm (N.Y.), **15**

1953    Clem Labine (Bkn.), **10**

1954    Hoyt Wilhelm (N.Y.), **12**

1955    Clem Labine (Bkn.), **10**

1956    Hersh Freeman (Cin.), **14**

1957    Dick Farrell (Phi.), **10**

1958    Don Elston (Chi.), **9**

1959    Roy Face (Pitt.), **18**

1960    Larry Sherry (L.A.), **13**

1961    Stu Miller (S.F.), **14**

1962    Jack Baldschun (Phi.), **12**

1963    Ron Perranoski (L.A.), **16**

1964    Al McBean (Pitt.), Billy O'Dell (S.F.), Ron Taylor (St. L.), **8**

1965    Billy O'Dell (S.F.), **10**

1966    Phil Regan (L.A.), **14**

1967 Dick Farrell (*Hou.-Phi.*), 10
1968 Ron Kline (*Pitt.*), Phil Regan (*L.A.-Chi.*), 12
1969 Frank Linzy (*S.F.*), 14
1970 Dave Giusti (*Pitt.*), Ron Herbel (*S.D.-N.Y.*), Joe Hoerner (*Phi.*), Clay Carroll (*Cin.*), Don McMahon (*S.F.*), 9
1971 Jerry Johnson (*S.F.*), 12
1972 Mike Marshall (*Mon.*), 14
1973 Mike Marshall (*Mon.*), 14
1974 Mike Marshall (*L.A.*), 15
1975 Dale Murray (*Mon.*), 15
1976 Charlie Hough (*L.A.*), 12
1977 Rich Gossage (*Pitt.*), 11
1978 Gary Lavelle (*S.F.*), 13

## AMERICAN LEAGUE

1901 Clark Griffith (*Chi.*), 3
1902 Rube Waddell (*Phi.*), 6
1903 Patsy Flaherty (*Chi.*), 3
1904 Jack Chesbro (*N.Y.*), 3
1905 Clark Griffith (*N.Y.*), Bill Hogg (*N.Y.*), Rube Waddell (*Phi.*), George Winter (*Bos.*), Cy Young (*Bos.*), 4
1906 Nick Altrock (*Chi.*), 7
1907 Ed Killian (*Det.*), 5
1908 Rube Vickers (*Phi.*), 8
1909 Frank Arellanes (*Bos.*), Eddie Cicotte (*Bos.*), George Mullin (*Det.*), 4
1910 Joe Wood (*Bos.*), 6
1911 Fred Blanding (*Cle.*), Vean Gregg (*Cle.*), 5
1912 Charley Hall (*Bos.*), 6
1913 Byron Houck (*Phi.*), 8
1914 Walter Johnson (*Wash.*), 6
1915 Doc Ayers (*Wash.*), Carl Weilman (*St. L.*), 6
1916 Bob Shawkey (*N.Y.*), 8
1917 Dave Danforth (*Chi.*), 9
1918 Dave Danforth (*Chi.*), George Mogridge (*N.Y.*), 6
1919 Dickie Kerr (*Chi.*), Allen Sothoron (*St. L.*), 5
1920 Jim Bagby (*Cle.*), Bill Burwell (*St. L.*), 6
1921 Benn Karr (*Bos.*), Guy Morton (*Cle.*), 5
1922 Ed Rommel (*Phi.*), 8

1923 Allan Russell (*Wash.*), 9
1924 Ken Holloway (*Det.*), 9
1925 Elam Vangilder (*St. L.*), 11
1926 Hooks Dauss (*Det.*), 11
1927 Wilcy Moore (*N.Y.*), 13
1928 Ed Rommel (*Phi.*), 8
1929 Ed Rommel (*Phi.*), 8
1930 Hank Johnson (*N.Y.*), 9
1931 Bump Hadley (*Wash.*), 8
1932 Chief Hogsett (*Det.*), 6
1933 Jack Russell (*Wash.*), 11
1934 Joe Cascarella (*Phi.*), Jack Knott (*St. L.*), 7
1935 Chief Hogsett (*Det.*), Johnny Murphy (*N.Y.*), Leon Pettit (*Wash.*), Russ Van Atta (*St. L.*), 6
1936 Pat Malone (*N.Y.*), 8
1937 Johnny Murphy (*N.Y.*), 12
1938 Johnny Murphy (*N.Y.*), 8
1939 Clint Brown (*Chi.*), Joe Heving (*Bos.*), 11
1940 Johnny Murphy (*N.Y.*), 8
1941 Johnny Murphy (*N.Y.*), 8
1942 Mace Brown (*Bos.*), 9
1943 Johnny Murphy (*N.Y.*), 12
1944 Joe Berry (*Phi.*), Gordon Maltzberger (*Chi.*), 10
1945 Joe Berry (*Phi.*), 8
1946 Earl Caldwell (*Chi.*), 13
1947 Joe Page (*N.Y.*), 14
1948 Earl Johnson (*Bos.*), 9
1949 Joe Page (*N.Y.*), 13
1950 Tom Ferrick (*St. L.-N.Y.*), 9
1951 Ellis Kinder (*Bos.*), 10
1952 Satchel Paige (*St. L.*), 8
1953 Ellis Kinder (*Bos.*), 10
1954 Sandy Consuegra (*Chi.*), 8
1955 Dixie Howell (*Chi.*), Tom Hurd (*Bos.*), Ray Narleski (*Cle.*), 8
1956 Ike Delock (*Bos.*), 11
1957 Bob Grim (*K.C.*), 12
1958 Dick Hyde (*Wash.*), 10
1959 Turk Lown (*Chi.*), 9
1960 Gerry Staley (*Chi.*), 13

1961   Luis Arroyo (*N.Y.*), **15**

1962   Gary Bell (*Cle.*), Dick Radatz (*Bos.*), **9**

1963   Dick Radatz (*Bos.*), **15**

1964   Dick Radatz (*Bos.*), **16**

1965   Eddie Fisher (*Chi.*), **15**

1966   Jack Sanford (*Cal.*), **12**

1967   Minnie Rojas (*Cal.*), 12

1968   Wilbur Wood (*Chi.*), **12**

1969   Moe Drabowsky (*K.C.*), **11**

1970   Dick Hall (*Bal.*), Stan Williams (*Minn.*), **10**

1971   Fred Scherman (*Det.*), **10**

1972   Rollie Fingers (*Oak.*), **11**

1973   Lindy McDaniel (*N.Y.*), **12**

1974   John Hiller (*Det.*), **17**

1975   Rollie Fingers (*Oak.*), **10**

1976   Bill Campbell (*Minn.*), **17**

1977   Tom Johnson (*Minn.*), **16**

1978   Bob Stanley (*Bos.*), **13**

## AMERICAN ASSOCIATION

1882   Eddie Fusselbach (*St. L.*), Guy Hecker (*Lou.*), Cub Stricker (*Phi.*), Harry Wheeler (*Cin.*), **1**

1883   Tony Mullane (*St. L.*), Billy Taylor (*Pitt.*), **1**

1884   Bob Caruthers (*St. L.*), **3**

1885   Norm Baker (*Lou.*), John Coleman (*Phi.*), Charlie Eden (*Pitt.*), Dave Foutz (*St. L.*), Jack Lynch (*N.Y.*), Gus Shallix (*Cin.*), **1**

1886   Tony Mullane (*Cin.*), **4**

1887   Hardie Henderson (*Bkn.*), Silver King (*St. L.*), Toad Ramsey (*Lou.*), **1**

1888   Bob Caruthers (*Bkn.*), Nat Hudson (*St. L.*), Silver King (*St. L.*), Henry Porter (*K.C.*), Tony Mullane (*Cin.*), Steve Toole (*K.C.*), Phenomenal Smith (*Bal.-Phi.*), Billy Serad (*Cin.*), **1**

1889   Bob Caruthers (*Bkn.*), **4**

1890   Jack Stivetts (*St. L.*), Hank Gastright (*Col.*), **3**

1891   Clark Griffith (*St. L.-Bos.*), **7**

## UNION ASSOCIATION

1884   Yank Robinson (*Bal.*), **2**

## PLAYERS LEAGUE

1890    Bill Daley (*Bos.*), **4**


## FEDERAL LEAGUE

1914    George Mullin (*Ind.*), **8**
1915    Doc Crandall (*St. L.*), **6**

# Appendix D.
# Complete-Game
# and
# Save Records

| | GAMES | COMPLETE GAMES | PERCENT-AGE OF COMPLETE GAMES | SAVES | PERCENT-AGE OF SAVES |
|---|---|---|---|---|---|
| 1876 | 514 | 472 | 91.8 | 13 | 2.5 |
| 1877 | 354 | 326 | 92.1 | 4 | 1.1 |
| 1878 | 360 | 352 | 97.8 | 1 | 0.3 |
| 1879 | 632 | 609 | 96.4 | 3 | 0.5 |
| 1880 | 664 | 608 | 91.6 | 12 | 1.8 |
| 1881 | 668 | 631 | 94.5 | 3 | 0.4 |
| 1882 | 668 | 642 | 96.1 | 1 | 0.1 |
| 1883 | 780 | 717 | 91.9 | 11 | 1.4 |
| 1884 | 894 | 863 | 96.5 | 6 | 0.7 |
| 1885 | 884 | 863 | 97.6 | 7 | 0.8 |
| 1886 | 960 | 934 | 97.3 | 6 | 0.6 |
| 1887 | 984 | 970 | 98.6 | 8 | 0.8 |
| 1888 | 1064 | 1048 | 98.5 | 6 | 0.6 |
| 1889 | 1036 | 947 | 91.4 | 15 | 1.4 |
| 1890 | 1062 | 982 | 92.5 | 10 | 0.9 |
| 1891 | 1090 | 948 | 87.0 | 26 | 2.4 |
| 1892 | 1806 | 1625 | 90.0 | 23 | 1.3 |
| 1893 | 1546 | 1296 | 83.8 | 31 | 2.0 |
| 1894 | 1566 | 1292 | 82.5 | 35 | 2.2 |
| 1895 | 1566 | 1281 | 81.8 | 45 | 2.9 |

| | GAMES | COMPLETE GAMES | PERCENT-AGE OF COMPLETE GAMES | SAVES | PERCENT-AGE OF SAVES |
|---|---|---|---|---|---|
| 1896 | 1556 | 1306 | 83.9 | 28 | 1.8 |
| 1897 | 1576 | 1361 | 86.4 | 25 | 1.6 |
| 1898 | 1794 | 1609 | 89.7 | 16 | 0.9 |
| 1899 | 1806 | 1590 | 88.0 | 32 | 1.8 |
| 1900 | 1108 | 936 | 84.5 | 12 | 1.1 |
| 1901 | 1108 | 976 | 88.1 | 13 | 1.2 |
| 1902 | 1098 | 996 | 90.7 | 16 | 1.5 |
| 1903 | 1102 | 955 | 86.7 | 28 | 2.5 |
| 1904 | 1224 | 1089 | 89.0 | 28 | 2.3 |
| 1905 | 1224 | 1000 | 81.7 | 31 | 2.5 |
| 1906 | 1214 | 954 | 78.6 | 48 | 4.0 |
| 1907 | 1208 | 933 | 77.2 | 32 | 2.6 |
| 1908 | 1232 | 836 | 67.9 | 54 | 4.4 |
| 1909 | 1222 | 795 | 65.1 | 55 | 4.5 |
| 1910 | 1226 | 698 | 56.9 | 69 | 5.6 |
| 1911 | 1216 | 680 | 55.9 | 81 | 6.7 |
| 1912 | 1216 | 660 | 54.3 | 66 | 5.4 |
| 1913 | 1208 | 641 | 53.1 | 77 | 6.4 |
| 1914 | 1230 | 670 | 54.5 | 73 | 5.9 |
| 1915 | 1222 | 679 | 55.6 | 69 | 5.6 |
| 1916 | 1224 | 682 | 55.7 | 76 | 6.2 |
| 1917 | 1224 | 722 | 59.0 | 59 | 4.8 |
| 1918 | 1008 | 666 | 66.1 | 39 | 3.9 |
| 1919 | 1112 | 658 | 59.2 | 46 | 4.1 |
| 1920 | 1228 | 694 | 56.5 | 76 | 6.2 |
| 1921 | 1224 | 624 | 51.0 | 92 | 7.5 |
| 1922 | 1230 | 600 | 48.8 | 68 | 5.5 |
| 1923 | 1230 | 616 | 50.1 | 74 | 6.0 |
| 1924 | 1224 | 620 | 50.7 | 66 | 5.4 |
| 1925 | 1224 | 634 | 51.8 | 67 | 5.5 |
| 1926 | 1222 | 610 | 49.9 | 84 | 6.9 |
| 1927 | 1228 | 613 | 49.9 | 81 | 6.6 |
| 1928 | 1224 | 558 | 45.6 | 105 | 8.6 |
| 1929 | 1222 | 566 | 46.3 | 115 | 9.4 |
| 1930 | 1232 | 534 | 43.7 | 109 | 8.8 |
| 1931 | 1228 | 611 | 49.8 | 94 | 7.7 |
| 1932 | 1232 | 553 | 44.9 | 91 | 7.4 |
| 1933 | 1224 | 595 | 48.6 | 99 | 8.1 |
| 1934 | 1210 | 509 | 42.1 | 129 | 10.7 |
| 1935 | 1226 | 534 | 43.6 | 106 | 8.6 |
| 1936 | 1232 | 487 | 39.5 | 136 | 11.0 |
| 1937 | 1226 | 559 | 45.6 | 102 | 8.3 |

| | GAMES | COMPLETE GAMES | PERCENT-AGE OF COMPLETE GAMES | SAVES | PERCENT-AGE OF SAVES |
|---|---|---|---|---|---|
| 1938 | 1204 | 520 | 43.2 | 115 | 9.6 |
| 1939 | 1220 | 515 | 42.2 | 129 | 10.6 |
| 1940 | 1224 | 544 | 44.4 | 115 | 9.4 |
| 1941 | 1230 | 516 | 42.0 | 109 | 8.9 |
| 1942 | 1212 | 541 | 44.6 | 99 | 8.2 |
| 1943 | 1228 | 551 | 44.9 | 117 | 9.5 |
| 1944 | 1230 | 562 | 45.7 | 108 | 8.8 |
| 1945 | 1228 | 515 | 41.9 | 123 | 10.0 |
| 1946 | 1234 | 493 | 40.0 | 119 | 9.6 |
| 1947 | 1232 | 458 | 37.2 | 136 | 11.0 |
| 1948 | 1230 | 453 | 36.8 | 142 | 11.5 |
| 1949 | 1232 | 472 | 38.3 | 109 | 8.8 |
| 1950 | 1228 | 498 | 40.6 | 135 | 11.0 |
| 1951 | 1238 | 459 | 37.1 | 136 | 11.0 |
| 1952 | 1230 | 444 | 36.1 | 146 | 11.9 |
| 1953 | 1232 | 430 | 34.9 | 162 | 13.1 |
| 1954 | 1232 | 377 | 30.6 | 181 | 14.7 |
| 1955 | 1230 | 385 | 31.3 | 160 | 13.0 |
| 1956 | 1232 | 360 | 29.2 | 200 | 16.2 |
| 1957 | 1232 | 356 | 28.9 | 195 | 15.8 |
| 1958 | 1232 | 356 | 28.9 | 198 | 16.1 |
| 1959 | 1236 | 376 | 30.4 | 171 | 13.8 |
| 1960 | 1232 | 354 | 28.7 | 213 | 17.3 |
| 1961 | 1232 | 328 | 26.6 | 212 | 17.2 |
| 1962 | 1620 | 458 | 28.3 | 289 | 17.8 |
| 1963 | 1620 | 459 | 28.3 | 276 | 17.0 |
| 1964 | 1620 | 448 | 27.7 | 304 | 18.8 |
| 1965 | 1618 | 416 | 25.7 | 306 | 18.9 |
| 1966 | 1616 | 402 | 24.9 | 303 | 18.8 |
| 1967 | 1618 | 417 | 25.8 | 291 | 18.0 |
| 1968 | 1620 | 471 | 29.1 | 293 | 18.1 |
| 1969 | 1944 | 531 | 27.3 | 356 | 18.3 |
| 1970 | 1942 | 470 | 24.2 | 411 | 21.2 |
| 1971 | 1942 | 546 | 28.1 | 329 | 16.9 |
| 1972 | 1858 | 507 | 27.3 | 361 | 19.4 |
| 1973 | 1940 | 447 | 23.0 | 429 | 22.1 |
| 1974 | 1942 | 439 | 22.6 | 257 | 13.2 * |
| 1975 | 1940 | 427 | 22.0 | 351 | 18.1 |
| 1976 | 1944 | 449 | 23.1 | 362 | 18.6 |
| 1977 | 1944 | 321 | 16.5 | 429 | 22.1 |
| 1978 | 1942 | 389 | 20.0 | 414 | 21.3 |

* *New, more restrictive save rule in effect.*

# AMERICAN LEAGUE

| | GAMES | COMPLETE GAMES | PERCENT-AGE OF COMPLETE GAMES | SAVES | PERCENT-AGE OF SAVES |
|---|---|---|---|---|---|
| 1901 | 1084 | 937 | 86.4 | 19 | 1.8 |
| 1902 | 1088 | 954 | 87.7 | 14 | 1.3 |
| 1903 | 1096 | 954 | 87.0 | 17 | 1.6 |
| 1904 | 1216 | 1098 | 90.3 | 9 | 0.7 |
| 1905 | 1212 | 975 | 80.4 | 25 | 2.1 |
| 1906 | 1202 | 956 | 79.5 | 33 | 2.7 |
| 1907 | 1198 | 893 | 74.5 | 42 | 3.5 |
| 1908 | 1224 | 842 | 68.8 | 50 | 4.1 |
| 1909 | 1214 | 823 | 67.8 | 55 | 4.5 |
| 1910 | 1218 | 855 | 70.2 | 53 | 4.4 |
| 1911 | 1220 | 760 | 62.3 | 68 | 5.6 |
| 1912 | 1222 | 791 | 64.7 | 57 | 4.7 |
| 1913 | 1218 | 686 | 56.3 | 77 | 6.3 |
| 1914 | 1226 | 652 | 53.2 | 72 | 5.9 |
| 1915 | 1222 | 663 | 54.3 | 70 | 5.7 |
| 1916 | 1230 | 627 | 51.0 | 93 | 7.6 |
| 1917 | 1226 | 662 | 54.0 | 86 | 7.0 |
| 1918 | 1004 | 616 | 61.4 | 57 | 5.7 |
| 1919 | 1114 | 640 | 57.5 | 40 | 3.6 |
| 1920 | 1216 | 705 | 58.0 | 67 | 5.5 |

| | GAMES | COMPLETE GAMES | PERCENT-AGE OF COMPLETE GAMES | SAVES | PERCENT-AGE OF SAVES |
|---|---|---|---|---|---|
| 1921 | 1228 | 654 | 53.3 | 86 | 7.0 |
| 1922 | 1232 | 634 | 51.5 | 88 | 7.1 |
| 1923 | 1222 | 609 | 49.8 | 93 | 7.6 |
| 1924 | 1224 | 580 | 47.4 | 109 | 8.9 |
| 1925 | 1224 | 575 | 47.0 | 108 | 8.8 |
| 1926 | 1222 | 546 | 44.7 | 110 | 9.0 |
| 1927 | 1228 | 585 | 47.6 | 115 | 9.4 |
| 1928 | 1230 | 615 | 50.0 | 113 | 9.2 |
| 1929 | 1220 | 604 | 49.5 | 100 | 8.2 |
| 1930 | 1232 | 565 | 45.9 | 106 | 8.6 |
| 1931 | 1226 | 584 | 47.6 | 102 | 8.3 |
| 1932 | 1224 | 572 | 46.7 | 102 | 8.3 |
| 1933 | 1208 | 518 | 42.9 | 123 | 10.2 |
| 1934 | 1220 | 548 | 44.9 | 100 | 8.2 |
| 1935 | 1212 | 559 | 46.1 | 101 | 8.3 |
| 1936 | 1224 | 591 | 48.3 | 102 | 8.3 |
| 1937 | 1226 | 555 | 45.3 | 113 | 9.2 |
| 1938 | 1210 | 570 | 47.1 | 95 | 7.9 |
| 1939 | 1222 | 512 | 41.9 | 121 | 9.9 |
| 1940 | 1232 | 551 | 44.7 | 121 | 9.8 |
| 1941 | 1232 | 569 | 46.2 | 111 | 9.0 |
| 1942 | 1218 | 587 | 48.2 | 100 | 8.2 |
| 1943 | 1226 | 544 | 44.4 | 136 | 11.1 |
| 1944 | 1232 | 561 | 45.5 | 115 | 9.3 |
| 1945 | 1208 | 625 | 51.7 | 95 | 7.9 |
| 1946 | 1232 | 561 | 45.5 | 108 | 8.8 |
| 1947 | 1232 | 503 | 40.8 | 154 | 12.5 |
| 1948 | 1230 | 444 | 36.1 | 172 | 14.0 |
| 1949 | 1232 | 507 | 41.2 | 136 | 11.0 |
| 1950 | 1232 | 500 | 40.6 | 154 | 12.5 |
| 1951 | 1232 | 479 | 38.9 | 140 | 11.4 |
| 1952 | 1232 | 505 | 41.0 | 160 | 13.0 |
| 1953 | 1226 | 434 | 35.4 | 185 | 15.1 |
| 1954 | 1232 | 463 | 37.6 | 169 | 13.7 |
| 1955 | 1232 | 363 | 29.5 | 199 | 16.2 |
| 1956 | 1232 | 398 | 32.3 | 167 | 13.6 |
| 1957 | 1228 | 354 | 28.8 | 196 | 16.0 |
| 1958 | 1230 | 387 | 31.5 | 206 | 16.7 |
| 1959 | 1232 | 366 | 29.7 | 208 | 16.9 |
| 1960 | 1232 | 312 | 25.3 | 217 | 17.6 |
| 1961 | 1614 | 417 | 25.8 | 289 | 17.9 |
| 1962 | 1616 | 386 | 23.9 | 329 | 20.4 |

| | GAMES | COMPLETE GAMES | PERCENT- AGE OF COMPLETE GAMES | SAVES | PERCENT- AGE OF SAVES |
|---|---|---|---|---|---|
| 1963 | 1616 | 406 | 25.1 | 313 | 19.4 |
| 1964 | 1620 | 349 | 21.5 | 364 | 22.5 |
| 1965 | 1620 | 323 | 19.9 | 372 | 23.0 |
| 1966 | 1610 | 334 | 20.7 | 364 | 22.6 |
| 1967 | 1616 | 365 | 22.6 | 356 | 22.0 |
| 1968 | 1618 | 426 | 26.3 | 307 | 19.0 |
| 1969 | 1942 | 451 | 23.2 | 389 | 20.0 |
| 1970 | 1944 | 382 | 19.7 | 467 | 24.0 |
| 1971 | 1932 | 537 | 27.8 | 360 | 18.6 |
| 1972 | 1858 | 502 | 27.0 | 372 | 20.0 |
| 1973 | 1944 | 614 | 31.6 | 390 | 20.1 |
| 1974 | 1940 | 650 | 33.5 | 260 | 13.4 ° |
| 1975 | 1926 | 625 | 32.5 | 318 | 16.5 |
| 1976 | 1934 | 590 | 30.5 | 321 | 16.6 |
| 1977 | 2262 | 586 | 25.9 | 416 | 18.4 |
| 1978 | 2262 | 645 | 28.5 | 390 | 17.2 |

° *New, more restrictive save rule in effect; also reflects introduction of designated hitter in previous year.*

## AMERICAN ASSOCIATION

| | GAMES | COMPLETE GAMES | PERCENT- AGE OF COMPLETE GAMES | SAVES | PERCENT- AGE OF SAVES |
|---|---|---|---|---|---|
| 1882 | 466 | 438 | 94.0 | 1 | 0.2 |
| 1883 | 778 | 732 | 94.1 | 2 | 0.3 |
| 1884 | 1280 | 1264 | 98.8 | 3 | 0.2 |
| 1885 | 888 | 848 | 95.5 | 7 | 0.8 |
| 1886 | 1088 | 1071 | 98.4 | 5 | 0.5 |
| 1887 | 1072 | 1048 | 97.8 | 6 | 0.6 |
| 1888 | 1078 | 1057 | 98.1 | 3 | 0.3 |
| 1889 | 1092 | 982 | 89.9 | 21 | 1.9 |
| 1890 | 1052 | 962 | 91.4 | 17 | 1.6 |
| 1891 | 1094 | 954 | 86.7 | 19 | 1.7 |

## UNION ASSOCIATION

|      | GAMES | COMPLETE GAMES | PERCENT-AGE OF COMPLETE GAMES | SAVES | PERCENT-AGE OF SAVES |
|------|-------|----------------|------------------------------|-------|----------------------|
| 1884 | 844   | 759            | 89.9                         | 8     | 0.9                  |

## PLAYERS LEAGUE

|      | GAMES | COMPLETE GAMES | PERCENT-AGE OF COMPLETE GAMES | SAVES | PERCENT-AGE OF SAVES |
|------|-------|----------------|------------------------------|-------|----------------------|
| 1890 | 1050  | 930            | 88.6                         | 20    | 1.9                  |

## FEDERAL LEAGUE

|      | GAMES | COMPLETE GAMES | PERCENT-AGE OF COMPLETE GAMES | SAVES | PERCENT-AGE OF SAVES |
|------|-------|----------------|------------------------------|-------|----------------------|
| 1914 | 1218  | 741            | 60.8                         | 66    | 5.4                  |
| 1915 | 1222  | 716            | 58.6                         | 70    | 5.7                  |

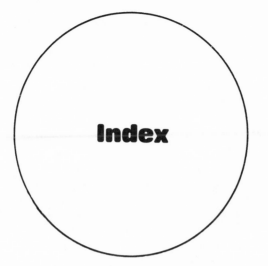

# Index

## ABOUT THE AUTHOR

John Thorn went to college in Beloit, Wisconsin, home of the illustrious Zip Zabel. In less distant times, he worked as an editor in
New York City. Today he lives in Saugerties, New York, with his
wife and son. *The Relief Pitcher* is his second book about baseball.